A UNION FOR APPALACHIAN

HEALTHCARE WORKERS

WEST VIRGINIA AND APPALACHIA
Edited by Ronald L. Lewis, Ken Fones-Wolf, and Kevin Barksdale

Wheeling's Polonia: Reconstructing Polish Community in a West Virginia Steel Town
William Hal Gorby

Never Justice, Never Peace: Mother Jones and the Miner Rebellion at Paint and Cabin Creeks
Lon Kelly Savage and Ginny Savage Ayers

The Industrialist and the Mountaineer: The Eastham-Thompson Feud and the Struggle for West Virginia's Timber Frontier
Ronald L. Lewis

Memorializing Motherhood: Anna Jarvis and the Struggle for Control of Mother's Day
Katharine Lane Antolini

Working Class Radicals: The Socialist Party in West Virginia, 1898–1920
Frederick A. Barkey

"They'll Cut Off Your Project": A Mingo County Chronicle
Huey Perry

An Appalachian Reawakening: West Virginia and the Perils of the New Machine Age, 1945–1972
Jerry Bruce Thomas

An Appalachian New Deal: West Virginia in the Great Depression
Jerry Bruce Thomas

Culture, Class, and Politics in Modern Appalachia
Edited by Jennifer Egolf, Ken Fones-Wolf, and Louis C. Martin

Governor William E. Glasscock and Progressive Politics in West Virginia
Gary Jackson Tucker

Matewan before the Massacre: Politics, Coal, and the Roots of Conflict in a West Virginia Mining Community
Rebecca J. Bailey

Sectionalism in Virginia from 1776 to 1861
Charles H. Ambler

A UNION

FOR APPALACHIAN HEALTHCARE WORKERS

THE RADICAL ROOTS AND HARD FIGHTS OF

LOCAL 1199

JOHN HENNEN

WEST VIRGINIA UNIVERSITY PRESS / MORGANTOWN

ISBN 978-1-952271-23-6 (cloth) / 978-1-952271-24-3 (paperback) /
978-1-952271-25-0 (ebook)

Library of Congress Cataloging-in-Publication Data

Names: Hennen, John, 1951– author.

Title: A union for Appalachian healthcare workers : the radical roots and hard fights of
    Local 1199 / John Hennen.

Other titles: West Virginia and Appalachia.

Description: Morgantown : West Virginia University Press, 2021. | Series: West Virginia
    and Appalachia | Includes bibliographical references and index.

Identifiers: LCCN 2021015318 | ISBN 9781952271236 (cloth) | ISBN 9781952271243
    (paperback) | ISBN 9781952271250 (ebook)

Subjects: LCSH: Service Employees International Union. Local 1199 (New York, N.Y.)—
    History—20th century. | Hospitals—Employees—Labor unions—Appalachian
    Region—History—20th century. | Medical personnel—Labor unions—
    Appalachian Region—History—20th century. | Allied health personnel—Labor
    unions—Appalachian Region—History—20th century. | Labor movement—
    Appalachian Region—History—20th century.

Classification: LCC RA971.35 .H456 2021 | DDC 331.88/1136211097568—dc23

LC record available at https://lccn.loc.gov/2021015318

Book and cover design by Than Saffel / WVU Press

Background cover image by Lee Bernard (Courtesy of the Huntington *Herald-Dispatch*)

Contents

Acknowledgments

My great thanks go to the following narrators who kindly shared their memories and insights in interviews: Roger Adkins, Teresa Ball, Terry Beam, Richard Bowyer, Penny Burchett, Phil Carter, David Cormier, Grant Crandall, Larry Daniels, David Evans, Joyce Gibson, Ira Gruper, Carol Haught, Frank Helvey, Wayne Horman, Anna May Jenkins, Gabe Kramer, David McGee, David Mott, Keith Peters, Jo Anna Martin Risner, Mary Schafer, Judy Siders, Seymour (Sy) Slavin, Kay Tillow, Kay Tillow (interview by David Cline), Walter Tillow (interview by David Cline), Maxine Toney, Bob Wages, Don West (interview by Tom Woodruff and Michael Kipnick), Heather Whitman, and Tom Woodruff.

The following people contributed to this book through informal, unrecorded discussions, comments at presentations, or by sharing documents. I have probably forgotten someone, and for that I apologize: Clay Adkins, Dennis Arthur, Al Bacon, Fred Barkey, Jeff Biggers, Kay Bishop, Faith Bowyer, Pamela Booth, Joe Brennan, George Brosi, Jeanine Caywood, Andrea Copley-Smith, Damon Core, Emily Crabtree, Mark Dudzic, Anita Dunkle, Claire Drucker, John Ernst, Kate Fosl, Peter Fosl, David Freeland, Patty Freeland, Sandy Gordon, Jerry Dine Harris, Lisa Hetrick, Tom Jeffire, Eugene Jordan, Donald Kersey, Tom Kremer, Kathy McCormick, Sally Maggard, Jack Nuckols, the late Paul Nyden, Simon Perry, Dave Peyton, Alec Plymale, Jordan Pomerantz, Dave Regan, Clint Salmons, Paul Salstrom, Harold Schlechtweg, Gordon Simmons, Les Smith, Paul E. Smith, Jim Smythers, Tom Stough, Dave Suetholtz, Ken Ward, Ann Werboff, Kathy Wynn, Carter Zerbe.

My friends and colleagues from the West Virginia University history department, the Institute for Labor Studies at WVU, Morehead State University, and Virginia Tech University have been a constant source of support to me, not only during this long project but in every facet of my academic and daily life. My students' engagement in class and overall goodwill have always been an inspiration. I also appreciate support from several summer research fellowships and a sabbatical leave for the spring semester of 2008 from Morehead State.

My mentors and coworkers in Appalachian studies and activism, labor history, and labor studies awakened my interest in these fields and provided constant support, valuable critiques, and years of friendship. They include Ronald L. Lewis, Elizabeth Fones-Wolf, Ken Fones-Wolf, Sarah Etherton, John Remington, Alan Banks, Kevin Barksdale, Sandra Barney, Dwight Billings, Kris Durocher, Ron Eller, Steve Fisher, the late Jake Gibbs, the late Greg Goldey, John Inscoe, Tom Kiffmeyer, Helen Lewis, Steve Parkansky, Lou Martin, Anita Puckett, Paul Rakes, Emily Satterwhite, Shaun Slifer, and the late Owen Tapper. I am beholden to Gabe Kramer, who is now an officer with SEIU Healthcare Pennsylvania. Gabe was with SEIU District 1199/WV/KY/OH in Columbus when I was doing research on sabbatical, and he welcomed me to rummage through several file cabinets and photograph collections from the 1970s and 1980s. Gabe secured the relevant permission for me to use material from these files. I am deeply indebted to Derek Krissoff, Sara Georgi, Lee Motteler, and Charlotte Vester at the West Virginia University Press for their cheerful patience and skillful editing throughout the writing and editing process. My niece, Andrea Van Hook, is my webmaster and mentor in social media—a thankless task given my Luddite proclivities. Thanks to Mary Jo Ivan, Nick Steelman, and Becky Williams at the SEIU District 1199 WV/KY/OH office in Columbus for their help in securing permission to use images from union publications and collections.

I am grateful for the generous and patient assistance from the following folks: Richard Strassberg, Barbara Morley, and the staff at the Kheel Center for Labor-Management Documentation and Archives at Cornell University; Chrystal Venham and the staff at the West Virginia Regional and History Collection at WVU; the staffs at the Ohio Historical Society in Columbus; the West Virginia Department of Arts, Culture and History in Charleston; the Drinko Library at Marshall University in Huntington; and the Kentucky State Archives in Frankfort.

I was fortunate to meet many wonderful public servants at the Wetzel County Courthouse in New Martinsville, West Virginia; the Marion County Courthouse in Fairmont, West Virginia; the Public Library in Prestonsburg, Kentucky; the Public Library in Paintsville, Kentucky; the Public Library in Welch, West Virginia; the Cabell County Courthouse and the Municipal Hall in Huntington, West Virginia; and the Tazewell County Courthouse in Tazewell, Virginia.

I reserve my greatest thanks to my wife and friend, Sue Creasap. She has sustained me with her love and support for over two decades now and has made me a better and happier person. Now we can walk the dogs.

Abbreviations

ACF	American Car and Foundry
ACP	American Communist Party (also CP)
AFL	American Federation of Labor
AFL-CIO	American Federation of Labor-Congress of Industrial Organizations
AFSCME	American Federation of State, County, and Municipal Employees
AFT	American Federation of Teachers
AMP	Appalachian Movement Press
ARMCO	American Rolling Mill Company
BCOA	Bituminous Coal Operators Association
BUS	Black United Students
CHH	Cabell Huntington Hospital
CIA	Central Intelligence Agency
CIO	Congress of Industrial Organizations
CIP	Civic Interest Progressives
CORE	Congress of Racial Equality
CP	Communist Party, America
CTW	Change to Win
EFCA	Employee Free Choice Act
EIPs	Employee Involvement Programs
ERPs	Employee Representation Plans
FE	United Farm Equipment Workers
FGH	Fairmont General Hospital
FMCS	Federal Mediation and Conciliation Service
FREE	Freedom and Equality for Everyone
HRMC	Highlands Regional Medical Center
IBEW	International Brotherhood of Electrical Workers
IBT	International Brotherhood of Teamsters
ILWGU	International Ladies Garment Workers Union
IUE	International Union of Electrical Workers

KDH	King's Daughters Hospital
KWA	Kentucky Workers Alliance
LID	League for Industrial Democracy
LMRA	Labor Management Relations Act
LPN	Licensed Practical Nurse
MAPS	Marshall Action for Peaceful Solutions
MFDP	Mississippi Freedom Democratic Party
MTR	mountaintop removal mining
NAACP	National Association for the Advancement of Colored People
NAM	National Association of Manufacturers
NLRA	National Labor Relations Act
NUHHCE	National Union of Hospital and Health Care Employees
OPEC	Organization of Petroleum Exporting Countries
PATCO	Professional Air Traffic Controllers Association
PIAR	People's Institute for Applied Religion
RN	Registered Nurse
ROTC	Reserve Officer Training Corps
RWDSU	Retail, Wholesale Department Store Union
SCEF	Southern Conference Education Fund
SCHW	Southern Conference on Human Welfare
SCLC	Southern Christian Leadership Conference
SDS	Students for a Democratic Society
SEIU	Service Employees International Union
SERB	State Employee Relations Board (Ohio)
SESCO	Southeastern Employers Service Corporation
SMCRA	Surface Mine Control and Reclamation Act
SNCC	Student Nonviolent Coordinating Committee
TAA	Teaching Assistants Association
UAW	United Autoworkers
UE	United Electrical, Radio, and Machine Workers of America
UHW	United Health Care Workers
UMWA	United Mine Workers of America
UNITE-HERE	Union of Needletrades, Industrial, and Textile Employees-Hotel Employees and Restaurant Employees
UPWA	United Packinghouse Workers of America
USSC	United States Supreme Court
USWA	United Steelworkers of America
WPA	Works Progress Administration
YAF	Young Americans for Freedom

Introduction

The West Virginia teachers' strike in 2018 briefly focused attention on the history of labor-management conflict in the state. A cross-section of mainstream and progressive media drew a crooked line to the teachers' rebellion from earlier battles between coal operators and miners, especially the Mine Wars of 1913–1921. This attention to a significant part of the state's working-class history was welcome and a long time coming. Some academic and independent historians have studied and written that history for decades, but the contributions of regular working people are still too often airbrushed out of the standard narratives of American history. As I write these words, the world is grappling with how to survive the shocks of the coronavirus pandemic. The curious phrase "essential workers," although it has been around for a while, has now become part of our daily vocabulary. It reflects an awareness, finally, that the workers who feed us, protect us, clean up after us, drive us around, deliver our stuff, teach our children, and care for the old, the sick, and the injured are not just assistant people. They are "essential." Will our appreciation for essential workers inspire a structural realignment in America's distribution of wealth? Or is it just a transitory thing, which soon enough will fade back into the old reality, that the more essential the work, the less the pay?

This book tells the story of how some essential workers in Appalachia built a healthcare workers' union, usually referred to as "1199," between 1969 and 1989. That union had a history dating back to the early 1930s, where the original New York City Local 1199 was founded by a Russian immigrant with radical ideas. His name was Leon Davis. His radicalism was defined in part because of his political affiliation. In the early 1930s, when he began organizing pharmacists and drugstore workers, he was a Communist, active in the Trade Union Unity League. But he was also radical in the greater sense, in that he believed that marginalized workers in the hospital industry—Blacks, Puerto Ricans, poor Whites, women—were human beings who should be recognized, respected, and paid a decent wage. They were pharmacists, nurses, nurse assistants, janitors, housekeepers, laundry workers, maintenance workers, cooks, and dishwashers. Davis believed these workers were entitled to a dignified and comfortable life as much as anyone else. That was a radical notion. No other unions in the 1950s, when 1199 began organizing hospital workers, wanted much to do with them.

Over time, 1199's immersion in the civil rights movement (the union adopted the slogan "Union Power, Soul Power") and its highly visible mobilizing tactics began to earn this small union a reputation among voiceless workers outside of New York City. It also caught the attention of activists who believed the labor movement could be a powerful force for social and economic justice but were disappointed by the Cold War conservatism and sluggishness of many unions. When Local 1199 in New York publicly announced its opposition to the war in Vietnam, it piqued the interest of critics of the war, especially young campus activists. Many of them concluded that 1199 embodied the progressive, democratic values that could reinvigorate a dormant labor movement. In 1969, at the urging of Coretta Scott King, Leon Davis and his allies began to expand 1199 beyond the borders of New York, with a dream to unify all healthcare workers into a single force for racial, social, and economic justice. That was when 1199 came to Appalachia.

Today SEIU 1199WV/KY/OH includes about thirty-one thousand members within its jurisdiction, divided into two regions. Region I locals are in West Virginia, eastern Kentucky, and eleven counties in southern Ohio. Most of Region I's membership is now part of an entity called WV/KY Healthcare, with nine thousand members. Region II includes the rest of Ohio, including the state's major metropolitan areas. This study, with some variation, focuses on what is now defined as Region I, although in the early days of 1199 that designation was not used. In addition to the focus on Region I, there are also overviews of 1199's pioneering work in the current Region II, in western Pennsylvania (1199P), and in southwestern Virginia (1199V).

This story of Local 1199 in Appalachia draws from two recognized "schools" of labor history, which may be identified as the "institutional" approach and the "new labor history." Pioneering institutional labor historians from the University of Wisconsin, John R. Commons, Selig Perlman, and Philip Taft, created the field of labor history. They focused on the bureaucratic framework of established unions within the existing labor federations, the American Federation of Labor and the Congress of Industrial Organizations, which merged to form the AFL-CIO in the mid-1950s. Briefly stated, the emphasis was on the institutions of labor such as union leadership and the machinery of collective bargaining, and this institutional emphasis dominated labor history for half a century.

The "new labor history" has transformed the study of working-class life over the last half century. The democratization of higher education after World War II engendered a cohort of academic historians who themselves came from working-class backgrounds. Encouraged by the availability of GI Bill education benefits, they revised the institutional emphasis on labor history. Influenced by the social and cultural dynamism of the postwar decades, the new labor (or new social history) historians abandoned the old institutional/bureaucratic model in favor of research about historically marginalized groups and communities. The women's studies, African American studies, Native American studies, gender studies, and Appalachian studies movements emerged along with the new labor history to create new narratives of American and global history.

The new labor history was a necessary corrective to the traditional school's exclusionary description of high-level bargaining between what historian Brian Kelly referred to as the "lieutenants of labor and their counterparts in the boardrooms of organized capital." My own interest in 1199 was propelled by the union's multicultural history of militant protest and direct action. That is a central part of the 1199 story and one in which its veterans take a great deal of pride. It remains my favorite feature of 1199, past and present. But by chance, in the early 1990s I had the good luck to work for a year as a labor educator. For this work I had to acquire a general knowledge of contract administration, collective bargaining, and labor law in order to facilitate classes for union members. This allowed me to integrate my interest in the inspirational drama of labor history and movement activism with a greater awareness of how unions work. I became more aware of how workers can maximize their leverage for social and economic justice through the (admittedly sometimes mundane) institutional mechanism of a union. Therefore, this book depends on an appreciation of both schools. To me, there is no contradiction in that. A good union should provide the bureaucratic machinery and education that allows workers to improve their lives and promote social justice through democratic means—and must never lose sight of the power of direct action. All institutions are imperfect, and unions are no exception. But a vital, progressive organized labor movement has the potential to be the most powerful and effective counterforce to the organized power of capital. Realizing that potential has always been the aspirational heart of 1199.[1]

I have debated about how to identify the union throughout the book. The merging of union locals can open up a maddening mix of letters, slashes, and numbers. I thought briefly of creating my own name for the union, like 1119AP (for Appalachia) but quickly jettisoned that idea. This list hopefully will be a useful guide to the union's changing nomenclature:

Local 1199 or **Local 1199NY** designates the original New York City district of the union. The union began expanding outside of New York in 1969. The original New York local formed and became the anchor district of the National Union of Hospital and Health Care Employees (NUHHCE). It was officially founded at a convention in 1973, although it had been organizing as the National Union since 1969. In this book it is referred to as "the national" or the "National Union."

Local 1199P in Pennsylvania was founded in 1969.

Local 1199WV in West Virginia began in 1970 as an "area" of the expanding union.

Local 1199OH in Ohio was founded as an area in 1971.

Local 1199V in Virginia was founded as an area in 1972.

Local 1199KY in Kentucky was founded as an area in 1975.

In 1980, 1199WV and 1199KY merged to form a new district within the National Union, called **1199WV/KY.**

In 1982, 1199OH merged with 1199WV/KY to expand the district to become **1199WV/KY/OH.**

In 1989, the National Union merged with the Service Employees International Union (SEIU). By vote of the membership, 1199WV/KY/OH approved its inclusion in the merger and became **SEIU District 1199/WV/KY/OH.**

Chapter 1 summarizes the early development of Local 1199's founding chapter in New York City and the context for radical political expression in Depression-era Appalachia. These stories are told through biographical sketches of Leon Davis and Don West, which trace their growing commitment to radical thought and action. It also introduces the ideological and philosophical overlap between these two "radical elders" and two student activists who became central figures in the expansion of 1199 into West Virginia, Kentucky, and Ohio. Tom Woodruff and Danie (pronounced "Danny") Joe Stewart and many other future 1199ers respected the leftist thought and theories of workers' organization practiced by these radical elders.

Leon Davis, as noted earlier, was a Russian immigrant and the founder of the original Local 1199 in New York in the early 1930s. Don West was a progressive educator and radical activist, much of whose early writing was republished by Woodruff and Stewart's Appalachian Movement Press in the 1970s. These radical elders played significant roles in the political education and early work in the labor movement of the two campus radicals and, in the case of Davis, had a continuing direct effect on their work with 1199 in Appalachia. A union official of my acquaintance refers to the persistence of the elders' principles as a "Red Thread" woven between generations.

Chapter 2 analyzes the political and social environment of Marshall University and Huntington, West Virginia, in the context of the local civil rights movement, the student antiwar movement, and the radicalization of a core of Marshall activists between 1962 and 1969. In this environment Stewart and Woodruff began to develop their analysis of social justice and political power. They were both active in the Marshall antiwar movement and the struggle to establish a campus chapter of the Students for a Democratic Society. Their growing interest in the history of Appalachian labor struggles brought them into contact with West. This analysis includes the era's often overlooked coalitions between some campus radicals and some left-leaning unions. It addresses the eventual decision of Stewart and Woodruff to confront economic and social injustice through the instrument of the labor movement. They were attracted to 1199 because of its demonstrated leadership in organizing marginalized workers and its involvement in the civil rights and antiwar movements. They were almost certainly aware that Martin Luther King Jr. repeatedly called 1199 his favorite union.

Chapter 3 opens with a brief summary of the first steps taken by Local 1199 to build a national movement for healthcare workers, that being involvement in a hospital employees' strike in Charleston, South Carolina. The striking workers, almost all of whom were African American, failed to get union recognition but did make some important breakthroughs in terms of basic benefits. The Charleston strike drew national attention to the union and confirmed its reputation as a militant voice for historically ignored minority and low-wage workers in a vital industry. This chapter also summarizes the early campaigns of Local 1199 in western Pennsylvania, where the union was called 1199P. Here the union began to address the question of whether a "civil rights" union would be able to mobilize and organize White workers. The chapter documents successful and unsuccessful organizing campaigns and, relying in part on the narrative of organizer Kay Tillow, recounts the efforts by 1199P to overcome obstacles to interracial unionism within a predominantly White workforce. Chapter 3 then turns to the pioneering work of 1199 in southern West Virginia (1199WV), led by West Virginia native and veteran organizer Larry Harless. The chapter closes with a brief introduction to the crucial role of member involvement and self-direction in sustaining a viable local. This was and is a fundamental structural and educational element in a small and struggling "social justice" union (and a recurring theme throughout the book).

Chapter 4 analyzes the campaigns to organize two small hospitals in south-central Appalachian cities, Beckley, West Virginia, and Richlands, Virginia. In Beckley, the mostly women workers at the hospital conducted a spirited strike for union recognition and came up against the most powerful political forces in their community. Their campaign failed but contributed to the growing appreciation of hospital workers for 1199WV in the region. Their stand ensured that the West Virginia efforts would get continuing support from the new national 1199, which was establishing its organizational status as a union closely allied with but distinct from the original Local 1199 in New York. The recognition strike at the Clinch Valley Clinic Hospital in Richlands, Virginia, transpired in a right-to-work state. Against long odds, the workers at Clinch Valley displayed a willingness to take significant risks, including civil disobedience and arrest. They won, but the success was short lived. Immediately the hospital's management set in motion a strategy to "decertify" (get rid of) the union.

Chapter 5 documents a pivotal effort by 1199WV to build the union at Cabell Huntington Hospital in 1974–1975. The Cabell Huntington drive benefited from a commitment to a "West Virginia" campaign by the now formally established national union (National Union of Hospital and Health Care Employees). The Cabell Huntington campaign operated within a national context of legislative changes that expanded organizing rights for hospital employees. Those changes precipitated, however, increasingly sophisticated antiunion tactics by employers. They relied on practices that had evolved over decades, culminating in the growth of a powerful "union avoidance" industry. The Cabell Huntington campaign therefore reflects the entanglement of local, state, and national political forces that the Huntington workers had to reckon with. The victory at Cabell Huntington was 1199WV's most visible to date and marked the beginning of a crucial phase in the union's Appalachian presence. The contract was not a strong one, however, with weaknesses the hospital administration endeavored to exploit during its two-year tenure.

Chapter 6 analyzes the struggle by workers at a major eastern Kentucky hospital, the Highlands Regional Medical Center (HRMC). These workers sought job security, basic economic benefits, and respect in a region beset by the fluctuations in coal markets and employment. The HRMC workers ran an imaginative campaign at the hospital and in the community and created 1199's first local in Kentucky (1199K or 1199KY). The union activists at HRMC faced significant efforts by union avoidance specialists but devised innovative worker-to-worker outreach and education tactics to inoculate fellow workers from the familiar patterns of behavior used by antiunion employers. And, they later worked closely with striking Cabell Huntington workers who faced determined management resistance to negotiating a meaningful second contract in 1977, convincing them that the hospital was committed to ridding itself of the union. The union survived and got an improved contract, one which ensured 1199ers that they had the capacity to win a more equitable voice in the operation of the hospital and make their union a permanent force at their workplace.

Chapter 7 focuses on several critical battles for 1199WV. In 1976 the workers at Martins Ferry Hospital (in northern Ohio) lost their union election following what Leon Davis described as "an extraordinary campaign of fear and coercion" by the management's professional "union-busters." In 1978, 1199WV won its first big victory among registered nurses at Fairmont General Hospital, which became another of the foundational locals in the union's survival during difficult times. The Fairmont activists' mobilization of support from the public and other unions in the region was a determining factor in a hard-fought win at the hospital. Also important was the local leadership's sustained pressure on the City Council, which appointed the hospital's Board of Directors. This major achievement was soon followed by a major loss in a long and bitter struggle in the small northern West Virginia river town of New Martinsville. This was a disturbingly divisive conflict that revealed fault lines of class and economic differences in the town and at the hospital.

After a brief recitation of the union's trajectory in the 1980s, chapter 8 turns to a monumental three-and-a-half-month strike at Highlands Regional in 1981. Here the union probably could not have survived management's expensive campaign to "bust" the union without extensive support from other local unions and the National Union. Tension, intimidation, and violence permeated this strike, which was the first staged by the newly formed District 1199WV/KY. Management's rigorous determination to weaken or abolish the union at HRMC was also the first major employer resistance faced by 1199WV/KY in the Reagan era. The strike at Highlands Regional ended just before the Professional Air Traffic Controller's strike, when President Reagan's firing of the PATCO strikers set the tone for a concerted and presidentially authorized corporate assault against the labor movement. The chapter closes with an analysis of how the consolidation of the healthcare industry, along with the muscular union avoidance strategies that management practiced during the Reagan years, shaped labor relations at several 1199WV/KY locals. At the national and district levels of 1199, sentiment emerged that maybe the proud, militant, but small hospital workers' union might have to combine forces with a larger union to survive.

In 1982, the Ohio locals of 1199 (1199OH) joined with 1199WV/KY to form an expanded district, 1199WV/KY/OH. The first part of chapter 9 focuses on the relationship of the union to state and public employees, a subject that has been touched upon in previous chapters. When public employees in Ohio secured expanded collective bargaining rights through legislation in 1983, 1199WV/KY/OH jumped into a competitive fray with other healthcare unions to win the loyalty of the expanded pool of potential members. The Ohio campaign resulted in a partial victory but also highlighted the National Union's competitive disadvantage against larger, more heavily capitalized unions. This chapter also looks at the early 1980s' uphill battles fought by 1199WV/KY/OH to organize West Virginia state hospital workers and summarizes the strong success rate from 1986 to 1988, primarily in private nursing homes and community health centers. The latter half of chapter 9 revisits Fairmont General Hospital, where the registered nurses and other professional employees struck to protect their union in the face of a concerted union-busting assault. This fight is placed in the context of the corporate consolidation of the healthcare industry in the 1980s, and it led to a judicial intervention to finally resolve the strike, with both sides claiming victory but also accepting tactical retreats.

Chapter 10, the concluding chapter, ties together three distinct but interdependent developments in the history of 1199 at national and local levels. First, there is a summary of a bewildering turn of events that ended up with the original New York 1199 seceding from the National Union. Then, the chapter turns to the internal debate roiling the National Union as powerful leadership factions clashed over whether to merge with the Service Employees International Union or with the American Federation of State, County, and Municipal Employees (AFSCME). There is a brief summary of the concerns 1199WV/KY/OH members (and the other sixteen districts) expressed about the 1989 merger. There is also an analysis of the controversial growth strategy of the SEIU during the mid-1990s to 2010, including the tumultuous presidency of Andy Stern from 1996 to 2010. During these years, Tom Woodruff became an important figure in the SEIU at the national level. The chapter ends with a personal case study highlighting the legacy inherited by a current SEIU District 1199WV/KY/OH leader, Joyce Gibson, whose mother was a key figure in the founding and flourishing of the union at Cabell Huntington. The chapter includes an update on the recent history and possible future of the district.

I should note that the expression "hard fights," used at several points throughout the book, has a broad meaning. It does not only refer to arrests, tension in the streets, or fighting on the picket line. Those are here, but the hard fights were not limited to these. The hard fights to get and keep a union included marching, leafleting, endless phone calls and meetings, court appearances, negotiations with intransigent bosses, confronting powerful legal, economic, and political forces, and educating coworkers and the public. Those fights are commonly not spectacular or visible, but they are essential—and continuous.

I first became aware of 1199 (in conversation that was the usual way of identifying 1199WV/KY/OH) in 1985, when I was a "nontraditional" (i.e., "older") graduate student at Marshall University. During a bitter UMWA strike against Massey Energy in the spring of 1985, I and a few other students joined an 1199 protest against an appearance by CEO E. Morgan Massey at a local country club. Following this episode, the staff at the union's building on Eighth Avenue in Huntington invited our all-purpose antiwar and social justice organization to print up our flyers on their copier. In exchange they gave us union buttons to wear and urged us to come out for future union rallies and protests. The union also cosponsored many of our events, such as protests and teach-ins about Reagan's Central American policy, lobbying trips to Washington for annual April Actions, protests to cuts in veterans' benefits, rallies for laid-off workers, Nuclear Freeze panel discussions, and the like. Those experiences catalyzed my growing interest in the history, structure, and place in American society of organized labor. I even managed to get myself hired as an organizer for 1199 in 1986 but almost immediately realized I had neither the discipline nor the drive that a labor organizer needs. I retreated to a PhD program, and it worked out okay.

That background should be sufficient to establish that I am not neutral in my opinions about the old 1199, or the labor movement in general, then or now. Objectivity demands fairness, not neutrality, so throughout this book, I have done my best to be fair. Readers may question my interpretation of things, but they are based on critical and logical consideration of a range of evidence. Any factual errors or unsupported conclusions are on me, of course, and no one else.

Professor Phil Carter, director of the social work program at Marshall University for many years, suggested a long time ago that I work on a book about Dan Stewart. Stewart, as documented here, was one of the key individuals in the history of 1199/WV/KY/OH. When Stewart died in 1997, Phil's students, who sponsored an annual conference on community organizing, began calling it the Dan Stewart Tri-State Organizing Conference. I was invited to speak in 1998, and I met two of Stewart's longtime friends, Frank Helvey and

Roger Adkins, both of whom later helped me in my research. It was at that 1998 meeting that Phil, who was an ally of Stewart in the Huntington civil rights movement and who later did trainings for 1199WV/KY/OH, prodded me to do a biography of Dan. That isn't quite what this book turned out to be, but that meeting got me started, and I am happy that it did.

Chapter 1

Radical Elders, or a Multigenerational Red Thread

Leon J. Davis was seventy-four years of age, a bearded, flowing-haired Russian immigrant from New York City with a history in radical trade unionism when he met with fourteen Appalachian healthcare workers in late July 1980. The assembled were members of the West Virginia and Kentucky chapters of Local 1199, the National Union of Hospital and Health Care Employees AFL-CIO. They were meeting with Davis in Charleston, West Virginia, to be sworn in as the executive board for their newly recognized joint district to be known as District 1199 WV/KY.[1]

As one of seven autonomous regional districts of the National Union, 1199/WV/KY would be authorized to operate under its own bylaws and its own financial and administrative structure, provided it did so consistent with its status as "an inseparable part or segment of the National Union." Some fifty delegates from six hospitals and one nursing home had met at the Uptowner Inn in Huntington to form the district and draft those bylaws in March of 1980, and the fifteen hundred members of the two state chapters had approved their work in April elections. The National Union of which District 1199 WV/KY was chartered by the AFL-CIO was the Hospital Division of the Retail, Wholesale, and Department Store Union (RWDSU).

The National Union began as a pharmacist and drugstore employees union in Depression-era New York City. When he visited West Virginia in 1980, Davis was the president of both the National Union and of New York's Local 1199. Davis began organizing drugstore workers in 1929, joining a group of mostly Jewish pharmacists and clerks who formed the union that became 1199 in 1932. Davis's history in the labor movement included involvement in the American Communist Party's Trade Union Unity League (TUUL) in the 1930s.[2]

The fourteen 1199WV/KY members sworn in by Davis were seven men and seven women, all White save for one African American, Alberta Easley from the Heartland Nursing Home in Charleston. They were licensed practical nurses, nurses' aides, medical technicians, housekeepers, food service workers, and maintenance workers. All were in their late twenties and thirties. Two, Ermel Cook of Cabell Huntington Hospital and Tanya Boggess of Fairmont General Hospital (both in West Virginia), had been elected district vice presidents by their peers. Two others, Danie Joe Stewart and Tom Woodruff, were organizers who had been employed by the National Union since the mid-seventies. The two West Virginia natives were well known and respected by the membership and had been elected president (Woodruff) and secretary-treasurer (Stewart) of the new district. Stewart and Woodruff were graduates of Marshall University in Huntington. Each had been deeply involved in campus civil rights and antiwar mobilizations and organizations, and each had gravitated to Local 1199 for its activist history in the social justice, civil rights, and antiwar movements. Stewart was thirty-five in 1980, Woodruff a few years younger. Their paths had intersected at Marshall in part because Stewart had done a hitch in the marines before finishing college.[3]

Leon Davis had a reputation as a micromanager who could unleash withering chastisement of the National Union staff. But he was revered for his unfailing devotion to workers' rights and his respect and affection for the rank and file. Tom Woodruff once said that he believed Davis perceived a deep harmony of interest linking oppressed women, Blacks, and Puerto Ricans in New York with poor West Virginians struggling for dignity and economic survival. Regardless of cultural and racial differences, New York city dwellers and rural-industrial Appalachians alike were toiling in patient wards, in boiler rooms, in stifling laundries, and in chaotic hospital kitchens and dish rooms. They were, in the words of the early Populists, all in the same ditch. Any prejudices or differences had to be confronted and overcome to get out of that ditch. Local 1199 was rooted in that first principle of real working-class solidarity. Davis welcomed the new WV/KY district's executive board and summarized the union's organizing principle: "Your history in 1199 has been one of fighting effectively and with determination for your rights. Management, on the other hand, is stubbornly anti-union, so we have to renew our commitment to stay the course with 1199."[4]

As District 1199 WV/KY was forming, another septuagenarian was directing an eclectic agenda of community-based cultural and political education at the Appalachian South Folklife Center at Pipestem, in Summers County, West Virginia, about ninety miles southeast of Charleston. Don West, a native Georgian, farmer, progressive educator, Congregationalist minister, Communist fellow-traveler (he claimed to have cut party ties in 1940), and radical labor organizer and poet, had founded the center in 1966 with his wife Connie, an artist and teacher, and daughter Hedy, a folksinger. West, like Leon Davis, was seventy-four in 1980, with two years yet to go as director of the center. West and Connie, who married in 1928, had opened the center as a place for native Appalachians to discover some of their culture and history and learn how to apply their personal experiences to resolving the social and economic problems of the region, including structural poverty and underemployment, limited or deficient educational opportunities, and poor medical care.

A cofounder with Myles Horton of the Highlander Folk School (now the Highlander Research and Education Center) in Tennessee in 1932, West was influenced as a young man by the Danish folk school movement. He had visited schools in Elsinore and Copenhagen in 1931 to learn about the movement's emphasis on "cooperative community enterprises, collaborative education, and methods of cultural preservation." Horton was also a disciple of the Danish movement, and his vision of the value of experiential education and the revolutionary potential of an Appalachian people's school was compatible with West. But Horton's and West's commonalities could not overcome ideological and tactical differences. West left Highlander after a year.[5]

As we will see later, West attracted a measure of fame through the 1930s and 1940s due to his poetry. West's subjects included the "proud heritage of southern abolitionists, labor organizers, and civil rights activists."[6] His literary work, however, rooted as it was in West's take on the brutality of the capitalist system, fell out of favor and out of print during the post–World War II Red Scare. West's writing on working-class struggle and racial justice from the pre–Cold War period, however, enjoyed a renaissance in conjunction with the campus radicalism and emerging Appalachian consciousness movement of the late 1960s. The reprinting and distribution of West's early work became an important endeavor for a small publishing and printing collective located in Huntington, the Appalachian Movement Press. Founded in 1969, AMP's operators included Danie Stewart and Tom Woodruff.[7]

The intersection of the beliefs and work of intergenerational radical activists Davis, West, Stewart, and Woodruff exemplifies a logical continuity connecting struggles to achieve an equitable society. Davis and West refined an unwavering commitment to social justice and workers' rights in the context of the Great Depression. Their beliefs were based in part on the moral instruction inherited from their parents' generation—Davis's family struggled for survival in a persecuted Russian Jewish community, and West descended from poor Georgia sharecroppers and dirt farmers. Both families survived daunting circumstances only through a web of communal interrelationships and trust among their families and neighbors. As they matured, Davis and West applied such communitarian principles to an informed analysis of the unwillingness of a powerful ruling class to tolerate a society organized to meet the basic human needs of all. As a corollary to their skepticism about elite rule, they developed a countervailing faith in the potential for marginalized workers to build democratic institutions, restructure economic power, and assume control over their destinies. The struggles of the 1930s, led by the early CIO, the "alternative unions" of the TUUL, and unemployed workers' organizations, were founded upon the possibilities West and Davis envisioned. Sometimes that vision served as a model for a later generation.[8]

West's critique of capitalism had roots in the oppression he witnessed growing up, played out in the brutal poverty and powerlessness of people like his family and neighbors who labored in the sharecropping system and textile and timber industries in rural and small-town Georgia. By early adulthood, during the desperate crisis of the early Depression, he was developing an intellectual analysis of systemic economic injustice and learning ways to attack it. He was aided in these pursuits by mentors at Lincoln Memorial University and the Vanderbilt School of Religion.

Woodruff and Stewart's commitment to building a working-class counterforce to corporate power was likewise dependent on their educational environment in a time of national upheaval, a college campus in the 1960s and early 1970s. Their formal and informal learning in socially and culturally rebellious times steered them to oppositional rather than accommodationist responses to institutional authority. Stewart became immersed in the local civil rights movement during his freshman year at Marshall University, affiliating with the Civic Interest Progressives, an interracial student-led civil rights organization in Huntington. Woodruff and Stewart were instrumental in the formation of the Students for a Democratic Society chapter at Marshall in 1968–1969. Like many of their contemporaries, the Marshall radicals witnessed grinding poverty in parts of the Appalachian region, the consuming materialism of middle-class urban and suburban life, and the national nervous breakdown brought on by the U.S. war in Southeast Asia. Stewart and Woodruff concluded that the liberal consensus of post–World War II America was flawed. The deep inequalities—income, educational, racial, residential—in the country could *not* be remedied by existing institutions. What the country needed was a "radical reconstruction of values," as Martin Luther King Jr. declared.[9] Their pursuit of that reconstruction took form in interrelated stages: (1) the immediacy of the civil rights movement and student rebellion; (2) the channeling of social and cultural resistance through "people's education" at the AMP; (3) and the pursuit of justice and power through a militant labor union.

To many campus activists, organized labor represented an adversary, if not an enemy, complicit in the shallow materialism and corrosive militarism that afflicted American society. These were fair arguments, in many cases. But organized labor's complicity in maintaining the status quo was not monolithic.

There were exceptions among the nation's unions. Not all fit the supposedly universal New Left notions of organized labor as politically reactionary, hopelessly and helplessly complacent, corrupt, glacially bureaucratic, nationalistic, overpaid, and overfed. Some were different. Stewart and Woodruff, as we will see, learned that Local 1199 was different.

Leon Davis

Leon Davis was born in the Belarusian village of Pinsk in 1906. His Jewish family included nine children, headed by a devout mother and a storekeeping father.[10] In American parlance, his parents would probably be identified as lower middle class. In civil war Russia, as revolutionary Bolsheviks of the Red Army battled a Polish-Ukrainian alliance of White counterrevolutionaries for hegemony in Davis's village, they might have been known as bourgeoisie or, if they owned land, as kulaks. Kulaks were an officially despised segment of relatively well-off peasants, against whom the Bolsheviks inflamed class resentment from poorer neighbors and imposed various modes of coercion and intimidation to undermine their status and seize their property. From 1918 to 1920, Pinsk was in succession administered by a joint German-Ukrainian government, occupied by the Red Army, and seized by forces of the anti-Red Polish Army. One historian defined this period, for the citizens of Pinsk, as being a time "between the hammer and the anvil." If anything, it appears that Pinskers, among whom there was a fairly prominent pro-Bolshevik faction, may have fared marginally better under Red domination than under the Poles. This was of course merely a matter of degree, especially for the targeted classes such as the Davis clan, but the precarity of the village's population intensified with the supplanting of the Bolshevik forces by the encroaching Polish Army. According to one account, the Jewish population especially "suffered horribly at their hand: there were many cases of robbery and murder." Economic and political uncertainty, perhaps catalyzed by the summary execution of thirty-five of the leading Jewish men in the community in the spring of 1919, fed the determination of Davis's parents to get their children to greater safety. They fortunately still had sufficient resources to send Leon and his older brother to live with an aunt in Hartford, Connecticut, in 1921.[11]

Relocating to New York City in 1927, Davis began pharmacy training at Columbia University and worked part-time as a drugstore clerk, leaving school in 1929 to work full-time in that capacity. Through his work in drugstores he found his new calling as a labor organizer and discovered the Trade Union Unity League, the labor organizing vanguard of the American Communist movement. Davis and a few others formed the New York Drug Clerks Association in 1929, a largely Jewish organization with the objective of organizing all pharmaceutical workers into one industrial union rather than dividing or excluding any workers according to job, race, or sex. In 1932 the NYDCA merged with a separate small group of leftist drugstore workers to form New York's Retail Drug Employees Union, soon known as Local 1199. This was a period in Depression-era America when there were all sorts of radicals in every New York neighborhood. "To be a socialist was nothing," recalled Sy Slavin, whose political education began in the Brownsville section in Brooklyn just as Davis was mobilizing drugstore workers. "There were all sorts of varieties of socialists around. There was a Jewish socialist group, there were communists, there was the Socialist Party of Norman Thomas." On every street corner in his neighborhood, said Slavin, someone would prop up an American flag and conduct lively seminars on radical economics. People saw themselves not only as individuals but as part of a working class. "If you wanted to influence society," said Slavin, "you had to be close to the working class." The aura of revolutionary class solidarity "was in the air that you breathed."[12]

Davis was immersed in this environment, earning $16 a week as Local 1199's first full-time organizer in 1936. The union incrementally expanded into New York's independent and chain drugstores. Also in 1936, Local 1199 became a division of the international Retail, Wholesale Department Store Union, an affiliation that lasted until 1984. Davis became active in Communist Party affairs, and his involvement was for decades invoked by conservative unionists and antiunionists as justification for Red-baiting 1199—we see this legacy at work later.

Leon Fink and Brian Greenberg, historians of New York City's Local 1199, point out that historically Communist-led unions, like 1199, faced "political assault" from inside and outside the labor movement during the post–WWII Red Scare. The eclipsing of the Roosevelt era's atmosphere of safe spaces for both the Communist and non-Communist left, accelerated by the hardening battle lines of the Cold War, signaled harsh times for radicals and former Popular Front sympathizers. Hostile government-led investigations and a web of public and private self-described patriotic groups, as well as divisions within labor among prior allies, forced the expulsion of eleven "Red" unions (not including Local 1199) from the CIO in 1949 and 1950. "That 1199 emerged with nearly 4,000 members and over half the independent drugstores in New York City under contract," say Fink and Greenberg, "was no small achievement."[13]

The survival of Local 1199 during the Red Scare could possibly be attributed to its relatively small size, making for close contact between staff and the rank and file, and hence the likelihood of mutual trust and cohesion was more likely than in larger organizations. The union was partly insulated as well by its international "parent," the RWDSU.[14] When Davis was ordered to testify before the Congressional Committee on Labor and Education (the Hartley Committee) in 1948, he managed through facile answers to deflect any definitive conclusions about his personal political affiliations. He claimed that as a working person he had little familiarity with "economics or social philosophy" and was too unschooled in theory to know "whether Lenin was right or somebody else was." He claimed, however, that the Communist Party had done "more good than harm in the labor movement." Years later, after keeping publicly silent about his politics, he revealed that shortly before his 1948 testimony he had resigned from the party "for the good of the union." Fink and Greenberg conclude that "union ties to the Communist party grew increasingly irrelevant and largely disintegrated in the 1950s." Davis's public actions, writing, and rhetoric supported his claim to nonaffiliation with the party. He insisted that all union staffers be independent "from all outside political directives," and he apparently took his own advice.[15]

By 1957, 80 percent (about six thousand) of the city's drugstore workers were members of the union. At the urging of organizing director Elliott Godoff, himself a Ukrainian immigrant, Local 1199 began to organize hospital workers. For a number of legal reasons and cultural biases, the established unions had little or no interest in trying to organize hospital workers in the 1950s and 1960s. Longtime 1199 cultural director Moe Foner summarized the main reasons for this in his 2002 memoir, *Not for Bread Alone*. A major reason was that many hospital workers toiled in a decentralized web of "voluntary"—or private not-for-profit—facilities. These were excluded from collective bargaining rights as designated by the National Labor Relations Act. They had originally been covered but lost that status under provisions of the 1947 Labor Management Relations Act (better known as Taft-Hartley.) Workers in public hospitals were likewise not covered by federal collective bargaining guarantees, and few states had legislated such protection. Workers in private for-profit hospitals, however, were covered by federal labor laws.

Another major reason for the labor movement's indifference to hospital workers, says Foner, was that in urban areas, most such workers were "extremely low-paid minority women. Most unions weren't interested in organizing such workers." Foner clearly implies that to most unions, hospital workers represented a type of underclass, a lumpen proletariat, if you will, lacking either the capacities or discipline to sustain a union. The racial and gender subtexts of this perception are unavoidable—as Foner puts it, hospital workers would mean "a low return in dues and a new kind of membership that most unions were unaccustomed—or even unwilling—to deal with." Foner and other 1199 staffers referred to them as "forgotten workers."[16] As reported in an *1199 News* retrospective,

> In New York City in the late 1950s thousands of full-time hospital workers had to seek supplementary assistance from welfare agencies in order to support themselves and their families. In effect, they were full-time workers at part-time pay.
>
> Hospital workers in 1959 were paid as little as $26 for a six day, 48-hour week. Laboratory technicians with Ph.D's made $60 a week. There was no job security and little chance for advancement. Split shifts were common with unpaid time in between. Overtime with no extra pay and working every weekend were just part of the job. Job classification systems were unheard of. It was a bitter joke that people who worked in hospitals couldn't afford to get sick. Hospitalization benefits for hospital workers did not exist.
>
> Aggravating these conditions was the fact that by the late 1950s, the racial and ethnic composition of the work force had changed dramatically. The majority of the lowest-paid workers in major urban hospitals were blacks. Many were women recently arrived from the rural south whose only previous job experience was in domestic and service work. It was natural for such people to seek work in hospitals.
>
> Many hospitals took this opportunity to strengthen their already paternalistic attitude toward employees. Racism made it even easier to treat hospital workers like children or domestic servants. . . . Demeaning and harsh treatment robbed hospital workers of pride and dignity on the job.[17]

By 1960, these same marginalized workers were finding their voice. Local 1199 became a major force in New York City's healthcare industry, by virtue of militant working-class rhetoric and mobilization combined with a comprehensive educational model for members that trained them in the arts of collective bargaining and shop-floor contract administration. Soon, 1199ers were realizing steadily increasing wages and benefits previously unheard of for rank-and-file healthcare workers. Technical skills were complemented by the interweaving of cultural programming within 1199's educational agenda. Patterned after the cultural model practiced by District 65, a New York wholesale and warehouse workers union, Local 1199 evolved a system in which the union became the center of social life for its members. Dances, dramatic performances, family dinners, children's programs and summer camps (long a staple of New York's radical labor movement), and reminders to "Sing While

You Fight" were integrated into the union's "broad social justice commitment." The cultural program was directed by Moe Foner, member of a noteworthy family of academics and labor activists, whom Davis hired away from District 65 in 1952. Foner's work for the next thirty-plus years helped sustain the union's commitment, from its inception, to "an organizing crusade to win a measure of self-respect and dignity for these overwhelmingly African American and Hispanic hospital workers. . . . Interracial and interethnic solidarity," say Fink and Greenberg," was "an abiding theme of 1199 agitation." The union staff built by Davis was expected—required—to honor and strengthen Davis's personal commitment to expose, attack, and destroy Jim Crowism in northern cities. "In 1199," he announced, "we mix and live as one." As actor Ossie Davis said when Davis stepped down as union president in 1982, "Leon Davis always understood that the struggle for a piece of bread is important, but you have to fight for social and spiritual things, too."[18]

As Local 1199 embarked on its ambitious hospital campaigns, conservative unionists' suspicion of its leadership's prior Communist involvement (Davis, Godoff, and Foner all had Communist histories) threatened to undermine the union's credibility. District 65, which Foner described as "the center of left-unionism in New York," was a faithful ally but had a similar radical history. General acceptance by New York's trade unions was assured, though, when Harry Van Arsdale, the influential president of New York's Central Labor Council (CLC), lent his support to Local 1199's crucial (and victorious) 1958 effort to win recognition at the city's Montefiore Hospital. Van Arsdale realized that CLC advocacy for minority workers at Montefiore could help the council's standing with civil rights groups who had chastised the CLC for indifference to the movement. Van Arsdale also leveraged his influence with Mayor Robert F. Wagner Jr. to recognize bargaining rights for public employee unions in the city. Within a few months after the major win at Monterfiore, Local 1199 won a simultaneous forty-six-day strike at three city hospitals. A fifty-six-day strike in 1962, which featured Davis serving thirty days in jail, was settled when Governor Nelson Rockefeller intervened. The governor committed his office to extending collective bargaining rights for employees in nonprofit public hospitals. Rockefeller introduced his bill in February 1963, and in April it took effect, with a major caveat: hospitals outside New York City had lobbied hard, and successfully, to be exempt. Only public workers in nonprofit hospitals in New York City, therefore, were covered by the state's labor relations act.

The Rockefeller agreement was therefore an incomplete victory, but it was significant. Martin Luther King Jr. labeled the settlement "historic," and Rockefeller announced that poorly paid hospital workers would now have "collective bargaining rights which workers in most other industries have had for more than a quarter-century." By 1968, 1199 had organized twenty-one thousand members with a minimum weekly pay of $100 for the lowest-paid job. Organizing money generated from membership dues allowed Davis to take steps toward building a national union for all healthcare workers. Encouraged by Coretta Scott King, whose late husband often called 1199 his favorite union, Davis's organizers began in 1969 to move 1199 into new territory beyond New York City.[19]

Don West

West, born in 1906, was the eldest son in a large hard-scrabble farm family in Gilmer County in northern Georgia. Raised among the rural poor, West absorbed the values of hard work, communitarian Christianity, and racial equality from his parents and his influential maternal grandfather, Kim Mulkey. The family moved from their homogeneous, close-knit community near Cartecay, Georgia, to Cobb County in 1918. West later claimed that not until he was fifteen years old did he ever see a Black person, at the Ellijay, Georgia, railroad yards. By that time he had so internalized his familial principle of the God-given dignity of all people—especially the poor—that West was well insulated from the nearly universal tenets of White supremacy that surrounded him. Historian John Inscoe notes that the West family ignored the "racial mores" of their new lowland South home, shocking local Whites by inviting Black families into their home. Throughout his long and often tumultuous life as a farmer, educator, labor organizer, proletarian writer, and Congregationalist minister (ordained in 1932), West seems never to have given up on his conviction that the inherent nobility of his White neighbors would bloom with the radical transformation of social and economic relations. In spite of many instances in which he and his wife Connie were themselves threatened and victimized by racist Whites, West held on to his vision of interracial working-class solidarity, of Black and White workers toiling, organizing, and living in harmony.[20]

At sixteen, West entered the Berry School in Rome, Georgia, a Christian industrial training school. He was expelled in his second year for leading a protest against the showing of *Birth of a Nation* on campus. He later, at age twenty-one, enrolled in Lincoln Memorial University (LMU) in Harrogate, Tennessee, where he was mentored by English professor Harry Harrison Kroll. Kroll, a former sharecropper, had become a respected and successful writer of more than twenty novels. "He wrote from hard personal experience and sketched vivid portraits of class conflict and interracial unity in the modernizing south," says West biographer James Lorence. Kroll encouraged West and his other students, including Jesse Stuart, to write from their own experience in the vernacular of their culture. He showed students "the legitimacy of Appalachian culture as source material for successful literary work, a lesson Don West was primed to embrace." Kroll was fired from LMU in 1929, allegedly for the sexual content of his 1928 novel *The Mountain Singer*.[21]

Kroll's dismissal undoubtedly stoked West's already smoldering anti-authoritarianism. At both Berry and LMU, West had rebelled at the paternalism with which most faculty and administrators treated the southern Appalachian poor and intellectually accepted the racism that permeated southern life. West led a student strike at LMU, pushed by his conviction that the administration treated students as "uncultured hillbillies." For this act he was promptly expelled from the school in 1928, but he returned to the campus and was re-admitted for the fall semester in 1929. As he matured, West more seriously questioned the structural inequities of capitalism, merging his analysis of class conflict with the principles of the social gospel he had absorbed as a youth. Kroll had influenced this thinking as well, introducing West to the workers' struggles in local industries.

West's development in these areas was catalyzed by his matriculation at the Vanderbilt School of Religion between 1929 and 1932, where he learned of the "revolutionary Jesus" from the liberal theologian Alva Taylor. Taylor involved his students directly with striking miners at the Fentress Coal Company in Wilder, Tennessee, and with striking textile workers in Gastonia, North Carolina. At Wilder in 1932, West worked alongside local organizer Barney Graham, who was murdered by company gunmen. West officiated at Graham's funeral, his first such assignment, because "there wasn't a preacher nor a church who would take his funeral." West also developed an interest in the Danish folk school movement, which was modeled on democratic education and social organization. He witnessed the Danish system firsthand when he traveled to Denmark in 1931, studying at the International People's College at Elsinore. During West's time at Vanderbilt, where he studied along with other social justice advocates such as Claude Williams and Howard Kester, he "took a sharp turn toward the political Left on the road to an ideological utopia that offered a solution to the problem of poverty in a land of plenty." West became deeply involved with the Communist Party USA.[22]

West's social radicalism, but not his commitment to the doctrines of the Communist Party, complemented the perspective of Tennessee native Myles Horton, whose upbringing and values of Christian socialism paralleled West's. Both envisioned a school for the Southern mountain poor, Black and White. West and Horton courted a benefactor who donated property in Monteagle, Tennessee, for the founding of the Highlander Folk School (now the Highlander

Research and Education Center) in 1932. After a brief (and unsuccessful) homage to a classic professor-student structure, the school's mission evolved into one of providing a safe place for mountain adults, many with little or no formal education, to apply their own lived experiences to an analysis of social and economic injustice in their communities. As Horton told interviewer Bill Moyers in 1982, oppressed people's awareness of the value of their "experiential knowledge" can be a "powerful dynamic force." The people "in these hollows, and these factories and these mines, you know, can take much more control of their lives" than they had realized. As one observer noted, Highlander was a place for adults, an environment for the elevation of people's education above hierarchical learning. The formal education of participants in Highlander's "learning circles" was "irrelevant. There is no fixed curriculum, no set classes, no grades, no certificates. There is, however . . . time for individual reflection, for singing and dancing. Each group of students sets its curriculum and learning goals democratically, students are in charge."[23] Highlander has been a touchstone for the labor, civil rights, Appalachian identity, and global justice movements now for almost ninety years.

Highlander's philosophy of small "d" democracy and people's education reflected the thinking of Don West, but he and Myles Horton did not exist harmoniously. Both were strong willed and assertive, but West thought of Horton as insufficiently radical politically. Consequently, West stayed as a staff member for only a year. He left to dedicate himself more completely to the Communist Party, including work at the party's National Training School in New York. Here his life intersected with the Black Alabama Communist Hosea Hudson, who later credited West with teaching him to read.[24] The Communist Party assigned West to work with the Angelo Herndon Defense Committee in Atlanta in 1934. Herndon, a nineteen-year-old Black Communist, was arrested in 1932 for organizing an interracial hunger march, convicted of "attempting to incite insurrection," and sentenced to twenty years in prison. After four years of appeals filed by the International Labor Defense, the Communist Party's legal defense arm, and with the support of Black civic groups, religious organizations, and some labor unions as well as the Communist Party, the U.S. Supreme Court ruled Georgia's insurrection law unconstitutional and ordered that Herndon be released in 1937.[25]

By that time West, wanted for insurrection in Georgia for his connection to the Herndon case, had left his home state to organize coal miners and poor people struggling with Depression conditions in eastern Kentucky. It was familiar turf for West. As a student he had witnessed the 1931–1932 Harlan and Bell County strike headed by the National Miners Union (NMU), the Communist alternative to the United Mine Workers. The NMU was formed during the Communist Party's "dual unionism" period, when the party founded revolutionary industrial unions to displace conservative American Federation of Labor organizations. West was ostensibly in eastern Kentucky to try to revive the NMU, but it was in a state of collapse and at any rate the Communist Party was on the verge of abandoning dual unionism in favor of its Popular Front strategy. The revolutionary industrial unions of the dual union period, comprising the Trade Union Unity League, disbanded by late 1935, with many of its organizers eventually moving into leadership roles in the nascent Congress of Industrial Organizations.[26]

West, as an Appalachian Marxist, was a prime target for Red-baiting and during his career endured many beatings, jailings, and death threats. Lorence suspects that West's persistent public preaching of the Social Gospel, "which typically featured a forceful argument that 'American citizens had a right to join any organization they wanted to,' " was more alarming to coal associations and their law enforcement allies than West's rhetoric on Marxist theory. Such dangerous subversion landed both West and his wife Connie in a Pineville (Bell County) jail when they joined in strike agitation by Kayjay miners in October 1935. Connie was released after a week, but Don lingered in the tank for six weeks, charged with criminal syndicalism. Local allies collected the money for his release, on the condition that he and Connie leave Kentucky. For good measure, local thugs loosened their car's lug nuts, and they barely escaped death when all four wheels fell off. A few weeks later, West sneaked back into Kentucky from Tennessee via Black Mountain in Harlan County, in order to take up new duties as a district organizer for the Communist Party. Recognized by unfriendly locals, West was beaten nearly to death by a gang of attackers.[27]

Undeterred, soon after these harrowing experiences West was again organizing in Kentucky, under the alias of "George Brown." He dedicated himself to the work of the Kentucky Workers Alliance (KWA), one of eighteen state alliances in a national network of unemployed workers dedicated to direct collective action. Such action had several purposes. The KWA worked to destroy the stigma attached to systemic unemployment and to pressure government at all levels to confront immediate emergencies while restructuring industrial capitalism itself. In 1935 the state alliances merged with other jobless groups including the Communist Party's Unemployed Councils, the Socialist Workers Alliance of America, the National Unemployment League, and a loose confederation of A. J. Muste's Unemployed Leagues, which were most active in rural areas and small towns in West Virginia, Pennsylvania, North Carolina, and Kentucky. The new national organization was named the Workers Alliance of America and claimed sixteen hundred locals in forty-three states by 1936.[28]

West (as Brown) traveled throughout the state for the KWA, helping to build locals comprised of Works Progress Administration (WPA) workers and the unemployed, stressing the importance of interracial and farmer-labor cooperation, protesting regional disparities and racial discrimination in federal WPA wages and farm relief, agitating for guaranteed jobs, and educating workers about the power of class solidarity. He was, says Lorence, "fiery in his advocacy of human rights," preaching about a "class conscious Jesus, a mountaineer's Jesus, a worker's Jesus." He also organized fund-raising events to support the Abraham Lincoln Battalion, a major priority for the Communist Party. The Lincoln Battalion was comprised of idealistic volunteers—Socialists, Communists, nonaligned Reds, anarchists, adventurers—who pledged to fight for the loyalist government in Spain, which was under assault from Spanish Fascists in the Spanish Civil War. Connie's brother Jack Adams, one of West's comrades in the KWA, was killed in Spain.[29]

West's radical journey was not remarkable for dedicated American leftists. But his literary achievement was. While still a student at Vanderbilt in 1931, he published his first book of poetry, a celebration of mountain life and culture called *Crab-Grass*. The "unanticipated notoriety" following this publication began to establish West's literary reputation.[30] Poetry was his preferred genre, and after *Crab*-Grass he was frequently published in the pages of leftist newspapers and journals such as the *Liberator*, *New Masses*, *Partisan Review*, and the Communist Party's paper, *The Daily Worker (DW)*. The day in 1934 when he left the Communist Party Workers' Training School for his job with the Herndon committee in Atlanta, the *DW* carried his poem "Angelo Herndon Dreams," which predicted a future of "black kids and white/Singing songs together."[31]

West's writing was infused with the stuff of his life: the fierce pride in mountain culture and working-class struggles, dedication to interracial workers' solidarity and racial justice, and disdain for industrial capitalism and imperialism. West's poetry reflected the Southern mountains' religious, agrarian, and oral traditions, in accord with, as Jeff Biggers has written, "his Scottish exemplar Robert Burns, another poet who understood how to plow a furrow." West the writer benefited from his place in time, a period when the cultural programs of the New Deal were expanding awareness of and a taste for "common man" art and literature. Depression-era proletarian literature carved out, according to critic Cary Nelson, "a brief moment in American literary history [when] writing poetry became a credible form of revolutionary action." Following *Crab-Grass* in 1931, West published *Between the Plow Handles*, published by Highlander in 1932, and *Toil and Hunger* by the Haaglund Press in 1940. A Communist Party anthology entitled *Proletarian Literature* included some of West's poetry. West and a few other writers traversed a speaking circuit of libraries and bookstores throughout the Appalachian South, broadening the popular appreciation of working-class poetry and literature.[32]

West periodically returned to his role as an educator, pioneering in what later was called "student-centered" teaching, a cooperative style that he had observed at Elsinore and practiced at Highlander. He earned wide praise as superintendent of the Lula-Belton schools in Hall County, Georgia, in the early 1940s, where public support from students and their parents contained and rolled back a local anticommunist flareup directed at West. He left Hall County in 1945, however, supported by a research grant from the Rosenwald Foundation to promote innovative rural education. Briefly based in New York, West produced a book of poetry entitled *Clods of Southern Earth,* issued by Boni and Gaer in New York in 1946. Remarkably for any poet, this collection sold thousands of copies. The Peoples Institute for Applied Religion (PIAR), directed by Claude Williams, distributed fourteen thousand copies to CIO unions shortly after the book was published.[33]

West later parlayed his eclectic credentials into a job at Oglethorpe University in Atlanta, teaching creative writing, sacred literature, and applied democracy. With West at Oglethorpe, Connie teaching school, and *Clods of Southern Earth* selling, for a while the West family (Connie and Don had two daughters, Ann and Hedy) enjoyed some unfamiliar financial stability. West began an affiliation with the Southern Conference on Human Welfare (SCHW), a White liberal organization devoted to working for racial and economic justice in the South. Its director was James Dombrowski, another former Highlander educator.[34] Although West claimed until the end of his life that he had no connection to Communist Party work after 1940, his association with alleged "pink" organizations like SCHW and PIAR fueled Southern White suspicions of fellow traveling. West's engagement with the Communist-supported Progressive presidential campaign of Henry Wallace in 1948 and his refusal to disavow his commitment to radicalism made him and Connie constant targets of Georgia's anticommunist forces.[35] Eventually, anticommunist pressure compelled the Oglethorpe trustees to fire West from the faculty. When not employed, West periodically returned to his north Georgia homestead at Douglasville to raise and market vegetables and work on his writing. Even this refuge was denied him when the Georgia Klan, following years of periodic vigilante harassment of the Wests, burned down his home, including his ten-thousand-volume library, lovingly collected over decades. Also lost was the family's coveted collection of mountain crafts, his grandfather's tools, and Don's original manuscripts. West, who was doing research at the Library of Congress at the time, was almost broken by this "blow that shook his faith in human nature to the core." He later published a poem called "For these sad ashes" to lament the personal and cultural losses from the fire.[36]

Given the many ordeals of their "hard journey," it must have been a joyful time when West and Connie, along with their folksinging daughter Hedy, fulfilled their dream of building a people's educational center by opening the Appalachian South Folklife Center. Here the Wests gradually earned the affectionate respect of local citizens who overcame their initial wariness of the old Reds in their midst. West also mentored a new generation of Appalachian activists who arrived to study his particular take on Appalachian dignity and radical history, admire and learn from Connie's art, and enjoy the regular music festivals coordinated by Hedy. Many of these visitors were acolytes from the antiwar and emerging Appalachian identity movements of the mid-to-late 1960s.

Among these pilgrims were some established radical activists from Marshall University in Huntington who were determined to build a revolutionary politics in the mountains. They regarded West's memory and writing as foundational texts and sought to make his writing, old and new, accessible to Appalachian activists. They were particularly interested in West's unshakable faith in working people and radical alternatives to the "business unionism" of the conventional labor organizations. In 1969 they established a publishing collective called the Appalachian Movement Press (AMP) to introduce West's writing to a new wave of activists. West had some initial misgivings about the "hippie printers," but he soon embraced the radical publishing project.[37]

Two of the hippie printers were Marshall graduates who prefaced their publishing project by playing principal roles in a dramatic town-gown battle in 1968–1969. The conflict was rooted in local manifestations of the civil rights movement, student antiwar mobilization, opposition to corporate influence in academic departments, and resistance to the survival of in loco parentis at Marshall. All of these issues on the Marshall campus derived from the multiple forces of local and national upheaval, inflamed by racial injustice and the American war in Southeast Asia. The cultural and political crises that fractured and transformed the nation erupted at Marshall in the context of a struggle for official recognition of the campus chapter of the Students for a Democratic Society. The founders of the AMP and the future 1199 organizers referred to at the beginning of this chapter were deeply engaged in these struggles. Danie Joe Stewart was a Salt Rock, West Virginia, native and U.S. Marine Corps veteran, and Charleston native Tom Woodruff was a member of Workers Education Union Local 189 of the American Federation of Teachers.[38] "Yeah, yeah, I was running something called the Appalachian Movement Press, we did printing for unions and progressive organizations but we also published a series of pamphlets about labor history in Appalachia. We did Don West, published a book of his poetry that was probably the last book of his that was published." [39]

The year 1969 marked the beginning of the Appalachian Movement Press, and it was also the year that Leon Davis heeded the urging of Coretta Scott King and carried Local 1199 into the American South with a convulsive organizing campaign in Charleston, South Carolina. Also in 1969 a former Student Nonviolent Coordinating Committee (SNCC) activist, veteran of the Mississippi voting rights movement, and progressive labor organizer named Kay Tillow joined the 1199P (Pennsylvania) campaign in Pittsburgh. Hospital workers in Baltimore, including those at Johns Hopkins Hospital, signed on with 1199. One of the Baltimore organizers was a Pineville, West Virginia, native named Larry Harless, who in 1970 returned to his home state, bringing Local 1199 with him. By 1974, Harless had brought Stewart and Woodruff into the West Virginia campaign.

Chapter 2

Busting Loose at Marshall

Danie Joe Stewart, seventeen years old, a graduate of Salt Rock Junior High and Barboursville High schools, arrived on campus for freshman classes at Marshall University, a regional university in Huntington, West Virginia, in the fall of 1962. Founded in 1837 as Marshall Academy by education-minded citizens of Guyandotte, Virginia, and named for the recently deceased chief justice John Marshall, the college had gained university status from the State of West Virginia in 1961.[1] Situated on the Ohio River near where the Tri-State region of West Virginia, Ohio, and Kentucky converge, Huntington in the early 1960s was a vibrant manufacturing, transportation, and commercial center. The town was founded in 1871 and had fulfilled the vision of railroad builder Collis P. Huntington when he had selected the location then called Holderby's Landing as the western terminus for the Chesapeake and Ohio Railroad (C & O). West Virginia's coal fields shipped much of their product through Huntington by the C & O and by barge on the Ohio, and the city became a vital river port and manufacturing center. The industries begun in Huntington's environs in the late nineteenth and early twentieth century were still prospering in the early 1960s: bottle and decorative glassmaking, railroad car production, steel fabrication, lumber and brick production, banking, and ancillary industries and businesses supported a population of about eighty-five thousand in 1960.[2]

Marshall was an important employer and cultural touchstone in Huntington. Its location on the eastern edge of the city's central business district made the downtown easily accessible to the school's approximately six thousand students when Stewart arrived. Marshall mainly served southern West Virginia and southeastern Ohio students, but a significant portion of students migrated from Pennsylvania, New Jersey, and New York, drawn by Marshall's good reputation for teacher preparation and its affordable tuition, even for out-of-state students.[3] The reasonable costs, at a time when state legislatures were generously subsidizing postsecondary education, were attractive to rural and small-town families in the region, many of whose children represented the first generation to attend college. Stewart, the son of a plumber, was from a large family of modest means, and from accounts by some who knew him he intended to "make a name for himself" at Marshall.[4]

A close high school friend of Stewart remembers that his winning personality had helped him earn a prominent social and political profile in high school, including leadership in class offices and student organizations. Stewart continued on this track during his early Marshall career, becoming active in student government.[5] Roger Adkins recalled that Stewart was deeply impressed by Robert Kennedy (RFK) during his visit to Barboursville High School in the fall of the 1959–1960 school year, when RFK was running interference for his older brother John's 1960 West Virginia Democratic primary run. By the beginning of his freshman year at Marshall, Danie had become a "huge fan of [John F.] Kennedy," says Adkins, who was also attracted by the Kennedy mystique. Although Stewart commuted to campus with Adkins from Barboursville (about ten miles east of Marshall), he often ended up hitchhiking home at night after student senate meetings or caucuses. Adkins, as well as Stewart friends Frank Helvey and Phil Carter, agreed that had Stewart followed the road of conventional politics, he might have been governor someday. Stewart once confided to Adkins that his ultimate ambition was to be elected president, like JFK. Bob Wages, who years later hired Stewart as organizing director for the Oil, Chemical and Atomic Workers, emphasized that Stewart was dogged and driven, a "type A" personality, agreeing that he would have been a force to be reckoned with if he had gone into electoral politics.[6]

Within weeks after beginning at Marshall, Stewart began to campaign for the office of freshman class president. He mobilized support from commuter students and independents (non-Greeks), few of whom had displayed much interest in campus politics previously. He recruited them into a newly formed "Campus Party" and won the election. By the next year, the Campus Party had morphed into the Independent Party, and he was elected president of the sophomore class. Stewart's campaign style was face-to-face; he "really worked the crowd," according to Roger Adkins, greeting students at the gates in front of Old Main on Sixteenth Street (now Hal Greer Boulevard) as they entered campus for morning classes. Stewart talked with them about campus-centered issues, including the need for students to directly lobby state legislators for academic and facilities support for Marshall.

Stewart positioned the Independent Party as the voice for students who were both outside of and critical of the Greek system. Stewart was one of only two independents in student government. In an interview published only two days before the murder of his political hero, John F. Kennedy, Stewart told the *Parthenon*, Marshall's student paper, "Considering that our whole Student Government is nothing but a Greek machine, I have a pretty tough time of it.

. . . It bugs me," he said, that fraternities, representing a minority of students, had "massive control" over student representation and "henceforth, the entire campus." This observation, as Stewart would no doubt later concur, overstated the influence of students on university policy, but it nonetheless reflected an expanding sense of democratic governance that would be refined as he matured. Greek overrepresentation, Stewart claimed, "is a pretty bad thing to say about our democracy." He was determined that the Independent Party would be "a force to be reckoned with" and "elevate Marshall campus elections from a popularity poll to a campaign of real issues." [7]

Stewart carried out the routine duties of his office as sophomore class president, but he was also having his mind stretched by professors such as Simon Perry in his major field of political science and William Cook in economics. Both emphasized that education should be used actively in the service of creating a just political economy; it was the clear responsibility of students to stand up for racial and economic fairness. Democracy could work only if people "acted out" democratic principles, or as civil rights activist Anne Braden put it, "make democracy work on a new level." Roger Adkins said that Simon Perry inspired him and Stewart with insights into the subtexts of American political economy that were "totally different" from what they had been taught before. Perry introduced them to how power worked, to the "informalities" of "deep politics." Perry and Cook's tutelage was the equivalent of permitting "the blind suddenly being able to see." [8]

The Civil Rights Movement

Every American, hopefully, knows something about the lunch counter sit-ins carried out by African American college students in the early 1960s. On February 1, 1960, four Black students from North Carolina Agricultural and Technical College in Greensboro, North Carolina, refused to vacate their seats at a Woolworth's lunch counter when they were refused service. They followed the principles of nonviolent protest practiced by forerunners such as Mohandas Gandhi, Congress of Racial Equality (CORE) "freedom rides" in the late 1940s, and Montgomery, Alabama's, 1955–1956 bus boycotters. Their action dramatized the willingness of growing numbers of Black Americans to confront the written and unwritten rules of Jim Crowism throughout the country. "By the time Greensboro's students had finished the first week of demonstrating," says historian William Chafe, "the new tactic they had discovered had already begun to transform student consciousness elsewhere." Within a few days, the sit-in movement had spread to Nashville, led by Fisk University students. Within two months, "demonstrations had broken out in fifty-four cities in nine states. It was as if an entire generation was ready to act, waiting for a catalyst."[9]

Sit-ins were potentially dangerous. Enraged White customers, often contemporaries of the Black demonstrators, sometimes lashed out violently. The demonstrators were trained in nonviolent civil disobedience by civil rights veterans, learning not to initiate or respond to any violent provocation, either from angry customers or from police. The attacks came, but over the next year more than fifty thousand protesters, some White but mostly Black, led sit-ins in a hundred cities. The sit-ins prompted the northern-based Congress of Racial Equality to again organize Blacks and Whites to travel on buses together through the South as a challenge to segregation in interstate travel. They were known as Freedom Riders, and they faced violent mobs, beatings with fists and iron bars, and indifferent or hostile law enforcement officers. From the crucible of the sit-ins and the Freedom Rides emerged a new, dynamic student-led civil rights organization, dedicated to "militant non-violence," called the Student Nonviolent Coordinating Committee, or SNCC.

The history of this stage of the modern civil rights movement, from 1960 to 1966, has been well documented and cannot be retold here. But it should be noted that one of the most significant lessons from the era is that although there were charismatic leaders whose names are well known, there were hundreds of thousands of foot soldiers, men and women, educated and illiterate, middle class and poor, some courageous Whites joining with courageous Blacks, who drove this insurgency. The sit-ins sparked an upheaval that Martin Luther King Jr. described as "an electrifying movement of Negro students [that] shattered the placid surface of campuses and communities across the South." One of those campuses was Marshall, and one of those cities was Huntington.[10]

The March 8, 1963, *Parthenon* announced the formation of an organization called the Civic Interest Progressives, or CIP. A small interracial group of Marshall students founded the CIP for the purpose of "eliminating discriminatory practices" on the campus and in the city. Within a few months, the CIP had pulled Marshall and Huntington into the main currents of the civil rights movement. The CIP exerted a profound influence on Dan Stewart, serving as the organizational catalyst for his radicalization. Soon any vestige of a career in electoral politics was fading, supplanted by a growing commitment to the civil rights movement, student rebellion, and, later, progressive unionism. Stewart's involvement with the CIP led seamlessly to his role in the formation of a chapter of the Students for a Democratic Society (SDS) at Marshall in 1968. By that time, the campus and the nation were undergoing a seismic "cultural shift," and Danie Joe Stewart had served two years in the U.S. Marine Corps.[11]

According to historian Cicero Fain, the African American population of Huntington was rooted in the construction of the Chesapeake and Ohio Railroad between 1869 and 1872. Thousands of Black workers from the South joined with native White and immigrant workers recruited by Collis P. Huntington's road, which promised steady work and good wages in exchange for backbreaking and dangerous work cutting trees, carving out roads, driving spikes, laying track, and blasting tunnels.[12] At the completion of the railroad, many of these Black migrants settled in the towns and villages that had grown up near the tracks or joined others in the central Appalachian coalfields. The Black population of West Virginia, emerging from this new Black proletariat, grew from 5,781 in 1880 to 21,584 in 1900 and to 41,945 in 1910. These figures help explain why West Virginia was the only Southern state to increase in population between 1890 and 1910.[13] Huntington's African American population stood at 4,630 in 1930, or 6.1 percent of the total. Historian Ancella Bickley estimates that the Black population of Huntington in 1960 was about 4,500, or 5.3 percent of the city's total.[14] These figures are comparable to other West Virginia African American centers such as Charleston, Beckley, Bluefield, and Welch. The numbers demonstrate why Fain concludes that the African American population in West Virginia "never reached a number or percentage that threatened the prevailing power structure."

Jim Crow was alive in Huntington. Schools were segregated and, although there were early racially mixed neighborhoods in the city, as it prospered investors and realtors built new housing developments with restrictive covenants. These were overturned by the West Virginia Supreme Court in 1929—a case pursued by Huntington's National Association for the Advancement of Colored People—but residential segregation endured through redlining and the restrictive mores of "genteel racism," which West Virginia's White power brokers called "benevolent segregation."[15]

As in other segregated cities, a Black commercial and professional class developed to provide needed services, cultural attractions, and "uplift" for the Black proletariat and sustain community cohesion. Black students were taught by dedicated Black teachers at Barnet Elementary and Douglass High School, the centers of the "colored district," a roughly thirty-five-square-block area south of Seventh Avenue, bisected by Sixteenth Street. Here citizens attended Black churches, shopped in Black-owned stores, socialized in Black-owned diners and saloons, were groomed by Black barbers and hairdressers, and sent their loved ones to Black undertakers. They visited neighbors from porches or stoops on modest houses or tumbledown shacks lining lively streets such as "Buffington Row" and Charleston and Artisan Avenues or along the alleys intersecting them.[16]

Clarksburg resident Phil Carter, a star basketball player who entered Marshall as a freshman in 1959, recalled the vibrant social life on the district's Eighth Avenue near the Sixteenth Street intersection, with its array of Black-owned nightclubs and restaurants. There were Black fraternal associations and "very nice social clubs [that] your aspiring and upper class or upper middle class owned," in which established African American Huntingtonians welcomed Marshall College's Black athletes and "socialized all of us to what appropriate behavior was in those kinds of social settings. You had to wear a tie, sometimes a sports coat. Couldn't come in there with any tennis shoes and the older men . . . that were members in these clubs, such as the Bisons' Club, they took care of you. You were somebody special." [17]

Carter summarized the aura of hope tempered by apprehension that surrounded Black communities in this immediate post–*Brown v. Board of Education* era, when exciting changes were in motion, but so was uncertainty. Access to previously restricted businesses might undermine the vitality of Black-owned businesses, and some shopkeepers and club owners urged Black wage earners to spend their money in a way that kept resources in historically Black neighborhoods. Aside from such commercial concerns, many Black Huntingtonians were unsettled about the potential loss of social cohesion that would accompany the imminent shutdown of their schools. Students sensed a threat to the "dignity and pride" that came with ownership of one's school, a threat to the "closeness" inherent in being with the familiar. Douglass High School did indeed close down in 1961, and the building's centrality as a community center receded. [18] Phil Carter explained the culture shock experienced by Black students when schools were integrated. He transferred from Clarksburg's all-Black Kelly Miller High to previously all-White Washington Irving in 1957: "I didn't realize the impact of this transformation from seeing all Black teachers, Black principals, Black assistant principals, Black janitors, Black woodshop teachers, Black band directors, Black majorettes, Black drum majors, Black captains of the football and basketball team. All of this to going into a White school where the Blacks in authority evaporated. They absolutely disappeared." [19]

In tune with young civil rights activists nationally, Carter and other Black Marshall activists such as Patricia Austin—whom Carter described as one of the most brilliant Black leaders in the country—and basketball player Bruce Moody, a New York native, felt the indignity of being "the other" in a White civic and academic environment. Moody was older than Carter and served as his mentor and role model for Black awareness and resistance to Jim Crow. Carter, like Moody, was especially insulted by Jim Crowism in Huntington's movie theaters and at a popular campus diner across Sixteenth Street from the college's main entrance, where Blacks could not sit inside but had to pick up their food at a window by the parking lot. Moody, deeply respected by Marshall's Black students, planted the seed that grew into the Civic Interest Progressives:

> Bruce Moody and some of the other guys were finishing up their under-graduate degrees or either working on their master's degrees and Bruce convened his cadre and we went on a mission and the mission was to desegregate the public theaters, beginning with the old Palace Theater first. . . . If Bruce told people he was from New York, they would let him go to the Keith-Albee and he would take some of us in with him.
>
> I think in '61, remember in February of '60, the sit-in movement began, so all across the country, I guess, every student everywhere was beginning to question, 'I have a responsibility not only in the class room and to obtain a degree, but I have a responsibility to leave things better off than the way I found them wherever I am' and there were a couple of us and it was, I never really counted up the numbers . . . Bruce pulled together about eight or nine of us. I know that I was there for those initial [meetings], Pat Austin was there. Sandy, Bruce's wife to be, was there. Thomasina, Sandy's sister, was there. I believe it was Mary Moore and there were a couple more people.
>
> There was no name to this. This was simply busting loose. This was a group of people who probably had been thinking about the same thing and I'm quite sure Bruce had been thinking about it [since] the moment he arrived in Huntington.[20]

The formation of the Civic Interest Progressives, says Carter, was an extension of the work done by Moody and these few others. When they graduated and left Marshall, "some of the rest of us picked up the responsibility" and took the organizing steps leading to the CIP. "We began to organize and identify the kind of people that we needed," people who showed the capacity to keep the faith when "people began to go to jail and legal cases were filed against the students." Carter became an activist. "By senior year (1963) I didn't even care about playing basketball anymore. I was somewhere else."[21]

By the spring of 1963, when the founding of the CIP was announced in the *Parthenon*, some Huntington businesses—including the theaters targeted by the Moody cadre in 1961—had quietly integrated. Almost immediately the CIP formed an alliance with the Huntington NAACP, working closely with attorneys Herbert Henderson and Jim Gipson, to accelerate the process. Asked for a comment about the new civil rights organization on campus, Marshall president Stewart H. Smith issued a statement condemning racial discrimination, but he also disavowed any "coercion *or public demonstrations*" in protest to such discrimination (italics added). Pat Austin later summarized the CIP's take on thinking like Dr. Smith's: "The road to freedom, to which I refer, is marked with guide posts saying 'Go Slow, Negro,' meaning 'Don't Go, Negro.' "[22]

Before long everyone in Huntington knew about the Civic Interest Progressives, as did much of the rest of the country, by means of their nonviolent protests against two holdout Huntington restaurants, Bailey's Cafeteria and the White Pantry. The White Pantry episode led to the courtroom of Cabell County Circuit Court Judge John Hereford, who wrote an opinion highly regarded for its logic and clarity of expression.

The management of Bailey's initially resisted integration with court action before giving in to public pressure brought on by an innovative protest tactic used by the CIP. The management of the White Pantry responded with assault and reckless endangerment of Black students sitting in. The appropriately named White Pantry was a midtown diner with a few booths and a counter with a row of stools. It may have been the violence with which the owner, a man named Roba Quesenberry, responded to peaceful protesters that forced some Huntingtonians—and Marshall students—to face just how ugly the "benign segregation" in town really was. The White Pantry was well known to Black students as an unwelcoming place; Phil Carter said no Black students really ever wanted to eat there.[23] But the White Pantry offered a fortuitous locale where clear lines between right and wrong could be drawn.

Bailey's was a popular family cafeteria on Ninth Street between Fourth and Fifth Avenues in the center of Huntington's busy downtown. It enjoyed a brisk lunch and supper trade peopled by employees of the midtown stores, banks, and law offices. Those workers often met their spouses and children for supper at Bailey's at the end of the workday. Bailey's employees made a point to remember children's names and, as the family finished their desserts, brought around a basket of toys or treats from which the kids could pick one to take home. Bailey's projected an aura of geniality, neighborliness, and the stable nuclear family, right down to the country steak, green beans, and cherry pie. But it served only White people.

In addition to picketing, at Bailey's the CIPs adopted a variation of the by now familiar sit-in tactics in order to make a point in front of the customers. Tom Stafford was one of the White activists in the CIP, a respected leader, and a confirmed pacifist. He suggested a tactic he called the "share-in" for handling Bailey's. As reported by William Calderwood in the May 1, 1963, *Parthenon*, under the title, "Ten Students Stage 'Share-In' ":

Five Negro students, aided by five white students of the Civic Interest Progressives, staged a 'share-in' at Bailey's Cafeteria last Thursday between 3 and 6 p.m. after being refused service.

The Negroes, Phil Carter, Gus Cleckley, George Hicks, Willie Tucker, and Pat Austin were refused service after the group attempted to go through the serving line. Five white students, Aubrey King, Tom Stafford, William 'Chip' Caldwell, Robert Wooten, and a girl who didn't want her name used, then invited the Negro students to share their table and food.

"The share-in concept," said Stafford, "is derived from principles of ideals of justice, brotherhood, and love. The share-in experience is the attempt to apply to social practice these ideals." [24] Judge Hereford denied the restaurant's plea for an injunction to halt further pickets or share-ins at Bailey's. Bailey's manager, Floyd E. Walker, then negotiated an agreement with the Huntington Commission on civil rights, delegates from the CIP, and CIP attorneys Herbert Henderson and Jim Gipson. Bailey's would immediately begin a two-week "phase-in of service to Negro customers." "I am glad," said Herb Henderson, "that Mr. Walker has apparently changed his ideas and feels that Negroes are a part of the public." [25]

The CIP began picketing and sit-ins at the White Pantry in early August 1963. Sporadically throughout the rest of the summer, groups of Black and White students and supporters would show up on the sidewalk outside the diner to march and carry picket signs proclaiming "No More Jim Crow," "We Want Freedom Now," and "Job Freedom for All," perhaps alluding to the impending August 28, 1963, "March for Jobs and Freedom" in Washington. Quesenberry insisted he would not serve Blacks because they would drive away his White customers and stated that he would never "serve Negroes until a law compelled him to do so." On one occasion when demonstrators entered the White Pantry and took seats, White customers slipped out while Quesenberry scurried around, turned off the air-conditioning, lit sulphur cake insecticides, and quickly left, leaving some protesters locked inside. Another day he reportedly "sprayed insecticide, mopped the floor with an ammonia solution, and turned on the heat." Frequent sidewalk demonstrations dispersed at the request of police, who declined to make arrests either of Quesenberry, the picketers, or crowds of White hecklers milling around outside. Ultimately Quesenberry filed trespassing and assault charges against Carter and five other protesters and petitioned in Circuit Court for an injunction against any further picketing. [26]

On September 7, 1963, Judge John Hereford denied the White Pantry's petition and took the opportunity to make a statement on civil and human rights. It was his opinion that "the denial of service to Negroes at the restaurant is contrary to state law." Tom Miller reported as follows:

> Judge Hereford said Quesenberry "has no right to come into a court of law and ask me to protect him in doing something that the Supreme Court of the United States says is improper when done by a governmental body. I am going to go further," the judge continued. "When a man such as the plaintiff gets a license from the city of Huntington, . . . and when the business he is operating has to be inspected by the health department or the fire department of that city . . . and when the Negroes help pay with their taxes for inspection of a restaurant open only to whites, it is not good Americanism and contrary, to my way of thinking, to the laws of West Virginia."
>
> Judge Hereford expressed surprise that the resistance of the demonstrators had been so "passive." He commented that they apparently had been well-trained to remain silent in the face of the great indignities that have been heaped upon them.[27]

Phil Carter confirmed, in responding to questions from the Judge and Herbert Henderson, that it was indeed part of CIP training not to offer resistance or to use profanity. "It's not the suffering we consider, but our objective of eradicating injustice. Nothing stands in our way of achieving this goal. Suffering is something we must accept and will accept [and] we are instructed to accept brutality and return love and understanding."[28]

Carter believes that Hereford's declaration was a "watershed" moment, one in which many previously noncommittal or oppositional Whites in the community began to "move" on the issues. Hereford's statement from the bench proved significant historically, but in real time the White Pantry continued its refusal to serve Blacks. Sit-ins and picketing therefore resumed at the White Pantry on October 22, with Quesenberry again releasing insecticide in the diner.[29] The White Pantry owner doggedly served Whites only—historian Jerry Thomas described him as "something of a champion of segregationists in Huntington and West Virginia"—until the Civil Rights Act of 1964 was upheld by the U.S. Supreme Court in December. He pledged, however, that he would never serve Phil Carter. Carter let it go, declaring again that he and the others had never wanted to eat there anyway.[30]

Almost forty years later, Carter was convinced that the protesters' dignity and generosity of spirit, contrasted with the stark bigotry displayed by the White Pantry's owner, made it obvious to many previously noncommittal citizens that, as protester Frank Helvey put it, "The issue was just so morally clear-cut; there was just no way anyone could justify lining up against these demonstrators anymore. By then, you had White students who began to make some very hard decisions and to join the group. . . . By that time, you had the Tom Staffords involved and you had the Danie Stewarts involved and you were bringing in these different elements that had not been there before. Don't ask me where these guys came from. We didn't know." [31]

Carter first noticed Dan Stewart when he became an outspoken advocate for the CIP in the Student Senate, a body not historically at the forefront of civic protest. "Who was this guy?" Carter wondered, "because we never ventured across the street to the student government." [32] Stewart implored his fellow senators to endorse a resolution to boycott discriminatory businesses in town. Pat Austin wrote in the October 23 *Parthenon* that Stewart delivered "a dramatic and emotion-packed speech, which rang with sounds of the Declaration of Independence and the American ideals of the American way [yet] failed to move the emotions of the Student Senate enough Wednesday to pass a racial discrimination resolution. . . . Stewart's much praised speech even drew accolades from some of the senators who voted against the proposed anti-discrimination measure."

Political science professor Simon Perry, the "new young dude on campus" and one of Stewart's mentors, attended the Senate that day and called the speech "one of the most inspiring arguments that he'd ever heard in the name of fairness and democracy and justice." [33]

The Student Left and Labor

Tony Judt, a brilliant historian who died prematurely in 2010, had some stern words for the young European and American "New Leftists" of the 1960s and 1970s. He described them as lacking any sense of solidarity or collective purpose, as being motivated chiefly (if not totally) by "private interest and desire. . . . If something is good for me it is not incumbent upon me to ascertain whether it is good for someone else." To be on the left or to identify as "radical" in those years, he wrote, was to be mainly "self-regarding [and] self-promoting." [34]

Judt's generalization of those young activists is only partly accurate. There are many examples of young dissidents of that era who matured into older dissidents, devoting much of their lives to do exactly what Judt suggested did not happen—build solidarity and collective purpose with the powerless. That kind of commitment, admittedly, might be touched by a degree of "self-regarding [and] self-promoting," but it sometimes survived for a lifetime.

Local 1199 appealed to many young dissidents of the 1960s and 1970s *because* that union offered a vision of collective purpose combined with and structured around clear-eyed, hard-nosed pragmatism—inspirational rhetoric, sure, but the language and discipline of hard-won workplace power in equal measure. Some student radicals may have seen 1199 in romantic terms as the vehicle for working-class revolution. But over time, the union's organizers developed a nuanced analysis of what revolution was and how it could be realized. Rebellion for justice would need action in the streets—always part of the 1199 playbook—but also rigorous education in the ways power worked and how workers themselves could get it, democratize it, keep it, and pass it on.

In their history of New York City Local 1199, Leon Fink and Brian Greenberg summarize 1199's appeal for idealistic student activists and for the type of workers who were "precisely those the big unions had failed or neglected to organize." Building on their involvement in the local civil rights movement, followed by immersion in the campus antiwar movement, Stewart and Woodruff then founded the Appalachian Movement Press to connect the threads of militant class solidarity in the Appalachian coalfields of the 1930s to a radical realignment of political and economic power in the 1970s. They later carried this objective to their work as labor organizers. Could the historical memory of the tangible benefits won through those early common struggles by coal-mining families inspire marginalized West Virginia workers coming into contact with 1199 in the early 1970s? Could that legacy offset the probable cultural obstacles faced by the union when it ventured into Appalachia? Could a union identified with urban Blacks, Puerto Ricans, and Haitians find favor with Appalachian Whites? The steps taken in living one's life are usually complicated, commonly unpredictable, and often freakish, but retrospectively Stewart's and Woodruff's gravitation to a leftist, "movement" union seems logical. Consider Fink and Greenberg's observation about the appeal of Local 1199 for young activists:

> Its very being refuted the prevailing view of organized labor as a complacent, white-male dominated labor aristocracy grown conservative after years away from the struggle. . . . The hospital workers' union also consistently projected a larger social agenda. By their willing identification with social movements—from the early days of the civil rights campaign through active opposition to U.S. involvement in Vietnam . . . 1199 defined a most unconventional current in the labor movement. The very brashness of this small union, the moralistic zeal with which it operated and its flair for the dramatic and militant gesture, brought the hospital workers' union uncommon and disproportionate public attention. Amid the phenomena of hardhats attacking students,

trade union Democrats-for-Nixon, and the continuing decline of unionism within the labor force, 1199 seemed to be keeping faith with an older, more militant ideal.[35]

Hundreds of American college campuses, and some high schools, were home to chapters of the Students for a Democratic Society (SDS) in the 1960s. The organization was founded in 1962 and quickly became the most visible, vocal, publicized, and chastised student mass movement on the political left. It was originally sponsored by the socialist League for Industrial Democracy in an attempt by them to build a youth base, but most SDS members disavowed Cold War ideological discipline. Instead they reflected widespread cultural and political alienation among young middle-class Whites who were disillusioned with the country's institutions. They were impatient with the slow progress of Lyndon Johnson's War on Poverty, with the Johnson Administration's escalation of America's war in Vietnam, and with the complicity of their own colleges and universities in the war and the military-industrial complex. They wrestled with the persistence of racial discrimination and the brutalization of poor Blacks and Whites by corporate capitalism. Many were beginning to confront their own status as beneficiaries of that very system.[36]

Some Marshall students were beginning by 1965 to take notice of SDS, being familiar with its support of striking coal miners in Hazard, Kentucky, in 1963.[37] Some were probably influenced, as were many idealistic young Americans, by the principles and rhetoric articulated in the SDS 1962 founding document, known as the Port Huron Statement. The fifty-page statement, written largely by a former Freedom Rider named Tom Hayden, called for a student-led movement with a broad agenda encompassing civil rights, anti-poverty, and antiwar action. In 1966, at the annual SDS convention in Clear Lake, Iowa, the delegates reworked New Left attitudes about the revolutionary potential of working-class organizations. They adopted a resolution that SDS should "orient towards the working class as the decisive social factor in bringing about the transformation of American society."[38] This statement marked a shift in SDS circles away from an essentialist belief that organized labor was uniformly reactionary. Radicals were justifiably wary of the entrenched leadership of "Big Labor," embodied by AFL-CIO president George Meany, who delivered "one speech after another pledging labor's support to 'fighting the reds.'" But the repugnance New Leftists felt for the conservative unions' Pavlovian anticommunism did not negate the fact that labor had sponsored liberal programs and that labor's political power, its historical commitment to resisting exploitation of workers, and "its reach to the grass roots of American society, combine to make it the best candidate for civil rights, peace, and economic reform movements."[39]

Labor relations scholars remind us that the labor and civil rights movement, being "fundamentally bound by similar values, interests, tactics, and enemies," have often worked together for economic and legal reforms. The United Auto Workers supported the Montgomery Bus Boycott in 1955–1956, as did the United Packinghouse Workers of America. The UPWA lent financial support to the Southern Christian Leadership Conference (SCLC) for its pioneering voter registration drive in 1957 and also supported SNCC's voters' rights programs. In a 1961 address to the AFL-CIO, Martin Luther King Jr. declared that "our needs are identical with labor's needs . . . the duality of interests of labor and Negroes makes any crisis which lacerates you, a crisis from which we bleed." King identified one of Local 1199's crucial 1959 hospital strikes in New York as "more than a strike for union rights. . . . It is a strike for human rights and human dignity." Only three weeks before his death in April 1968, King referred to 1199, for the last time publicly, as "my favorite union." Historian Michael Honey claims that labor's support was crucial in the political fight for the Civil Rights and Voting Rights Acts of 1964 and 1965, which "ultimately broke the back of Jim Crow."[40]

The radical spirit of Don West's labor movement, as evidenced by unions like the UPWA and Local 1199, had been subsumed but not completely destroyed even by the banishing of eleven Communist-influenced unions from the CIO in the early 1950s. A dedicated noncommunist left, not unlike the Social Democratic movement in Western Europe, survived the Red Scare of the 1950s and, although weakened, had some internal influence in unions on domestic issues. The United Auto Workers (UAW), under the leadership of the staunchly anticommunist Walter Reuther, gave SDS a $10,000 grant in 1960 to hire its first full-time organizer through the League for Industrial Democracy. In 1961 the UAW financially supported the SDS Economic Research and Action Project (ERAP), a grassroots community-based organizing laboratory based on the Saul Alinsky organizing principle, "If people have the power to act, in the long run they will, most of the time, reach the right decisions."[41]

The possibility of a social revolution led by awakened workers in a progressive labor movement inspired many other campus activists like Stewart and Woodruff. One of those was Robert Muehlenkamp, a leader of Teaching Assistants' Association (TAA) at the University of Wisconsin–Madison. Following extensive internal debate, the TAA entered into a steady working relationship with the American Federation of Teachers, the AFL-CIO, and the Teamsters for Democracy between 1969 and 1974. The TAA introduced antiwar resolutions at meetings and conventions and unsuccessfully agitated for the AFL-CIO to separate itself from the American Institute for Free Labor Development, a CIA surrogate. His experience with organized labor in the TAA led Muehlenkamp to work for Local 1199 just as it was moving beyond New York in 1969. Muehlenkamp was with 1199 in Baltimore at the same time as West Virginian Larry Harless. He worked closely with Harless in the early 1970s as 1199 came to West Virginia and he, Harless, Stewart, and Woodruff trained hundreds of "member leaders" at delegates assemblies for a dozen years. Muehlenkamp became the organizing director of the National Union after the death of Elliott Godoff in 1975.[42]

The leadership of SDS, including Tom Hayden, encouraged cooperation with "younger aggressive unions such as Local 1199," which in March of 1965 spoke out forcefully against the U.S. bombing of North Vietnam. Early that same year U.S. Air Force veteran Frank Helvey and Phil Carter, graduate students at Marshall, contacted SDS at the New York office of the League for Industrial Democracy to inquire about forming a chapter on campus. Their letter set in motion the antiwar movement at Marshall and Huntington.[43]

It took two tries for the Marshall chapter of SDS to establish itself. The first attempt, in the fall of 1965, stirred little reaction among the student body, although some voices of opposition came from the Student Senate. One student warned that such a group at Marshall would soon be controlled by communists who would twist the minds of students, a position endorsed by several student legislators. Speaking for the SDS was senior Richard Diehl, who vowed that the Marshall chapter would conform to all university rules and requirements that did "not infringe on basic democratic principles." Unmoved, the Student Senate overwhelmingly passed a resolution that SDS should never be recognized as a legitimate student organization.[44]

Majority sentiment at Marshall in 1965 reflected the prevailing Cold War consensus that American capitalism and democracy should stand as the international guardian against communist totalitarianism. Some students undoubtedly opposed the war in Vietnam, if not on moral or political grounds then at least from a distaste for the military draft. But they were a tiny minority and not, as yet, very visible. When Judy Petit was elected homecoming queen in November, a referendum attached to the ballot supported U.S. intervention by a count of 1,352 to 187. Antiwar expressions were generally scorned by the student body. Senator Greg Terry equated antiwar talk with giving aid and comfort to the Vietcong and the North Vietnamese Army. Senator Dale Louther labeled antiwar protesters as "asinine and ridiculous" and claimed that average citizens did not have enough information to decide "right or wrong in

Vietnam." He recommended that male antiwar protesters should be "caught" and "drafted immediately."[45]

Louther's proposal was not uncommon. Danie Stewart's friends and allies were convinced that Stewart was drafted—into the U.S. Marine Corps— because of his political activity on campus. Being drafted into the marines was rare but not unheard of. George Q. Flynn claims that in 1969, about 17,500 recent college graduates were drafted into the U.S. Army and Marine Corps.[46] Stewart's discharge document states that he was inducted—drafted—on February 21, 1966. He was released from active duty to return to college and entered the U.S. Marine Corps Reserve as of January 17, 1968, his reserve obligation to end on February 20, 1972. He was identified as a Corporal E-4 Inventory Clerk, had been awarded the National Defense Service Medal, a Good Conduct Medal, and a Rifle Marksman's badge. He was mustered out from the U.S. Marine Base at Cherry Point, North Carolina. He was never shipped overseas, to Vietnam or anywhere else, so he did not endure the extreme and devastating circumstances faced by so many combat soldiers. Those who knew Stewart remarked that he did not talk much about his time in the marines and, according to Frank Helvey and Roger Adkins, did not seem to have been affected much at all by the experience. He returned to Huntington, rejoined his wife Jeanine and their infant daughter Emily, and was soon active again on campus.[47]

The 1965 effort to establish SDS at Marshall—in which Stewart had played a role—had dissipated quietly. But by the fall of 1968, when Stewart returned and Charleston native Tom Woodruff enrolled after two years at Wake Forest University, everything had changed. The traumas of 1968—the Tet offensive by the North Vietnamese Army and its Vietcong allies in the South, which destroyed any remaining credibility of the Johnson Administration; the assassinations of Martin Luther King and Robert Kennedy; unrest and destruction in many American cities; the emergence of the Black Power movement and police repression against it; the police riot at the Democratic National Convention in Chicago; student rebellions in France and Mexico and on U.S. campuses; the "law and order campaign" by Richard Nixon and Spiro Agnew; the Farmington Mine Disaster that killed seventy West Virginia coal miners and sparked an insurgency by dissidents within the United Mine Workers of America—had, paraphrasing Thomas Paine, begun to make the world over again.

The student body at Marshall was caught up in it. The CIPs had morphed into the Black United Students (BUS, a national network) and Freedom and Equality for Everyone (FREE). Emulating a pattern established by SNCC, these organizations adopted a stronger emphasis on Black nationalism and history than the CIP and were led exclusively by Black students. A revitalized SDS soon appeared during the fall semester 1968, and FREE, BUS, and SDS worked in coalition and had many common supporters. There was a new Marshall Free University network, inspired by the nationwide Vietnam Teach-In movement, consisting of informal meetings outside the classroom with lectures and discussions on the war and civil disobedience. As a counterpoint to the student left, there was an active Marshall branch of the most prominent student conservative organization, the Young Americans for Freedom. The YAF was the youth arm of the Republican Party, and they were enthusiastic volunteers for Barry Goldwater in 1964 and Nixon in 1968.[48]

Almost immediately upon beginning at Marshall, Woodruff, who had not been politically active at Wake Forest, got involved in antiwar work with the new Marshall SDS, which was founded on October 31, 1968. The Marshall chapter planned to hold educational forums and demonstrations to "change a few local attitudes," guided by the principles of participatory democracy outlined in the national organization's *Port Huron Statement*. They described themselves as "an association of young people on the left, [which] seeks to create a sustained community of educational and political concern; one bringing together liberals and radicals, activists and scholars, students and faculty. It maintains a *vision* of a democratic society, where at all levels the people have control of the decisions which affect them and the resources on which they are dependent."[49]

The presence of SDS on the campus caused some fanfare among the student body, but the reporting about the organization in the local newspapers aroused considerable opposition from some alarmed local citizens. The uproar over the SDS petition for formal recognition eventually dominated campus debate and local headlines during the spring semester of 1969. The controversy intruded upon the early tenure of Marshall's new president, Dr. Roland Nelson. Nelson had hoped to focus on his efforts to develop Marshall according to a concept known as the "Metroversity." Nelson envisioned the university as a "major societal force in its region: a brokerage house for ideas; a brainpower; a catalyst for action; concerned with and closely tied to the development of the region in which it is located."[50]

SDS supporters feared Nelson's Metroversity would expand corporate influence over academics, making the campus a laboratory for weapons research and American militarism, instead of a safe place for the free exchange of ideas. Ironically, Marshall's SDS recognition as a campus organization was dependent on Dr. Nelson, who as president would make the final decision on the group's petition. The SDS suspected Nelson's agenda, and Nelson was troubled by some of the violent behavior attributed to the SDS nationally, especially the torching of ROTC buildings at numerous campuses around the country. Historian Brian

Burroughs reminds us that in the winter of 1968–1969, "political violence was spreading on campuses around the country, much of it fueled by the Vietnam War's escalation and the new Nixon administration's vow to crack down on student protesters."[51]

Just as the new Marshall SDS was organizing, and doing so without any expression of violence (beyond occasional hyperbolic rhetoric), the national movement's leadership was in a downward spiral of bickering, posturing, and ideological hairsplitting. The end of SDS as a viable national organization was sealed by the ascendance of the Weathermen, a splinter group that advocated the violent overthrow of the U.S. government. Historian Ralph Young claims that the Weathermen never totaled more than two or three hundred revolutionary nihilists. The name was taken from a line in Bob Dylan's "Subterranean Homesick Blues" and was actually not adopted until June 1969, after the SDS controversy at Marshall had receded. But the faction that became the Weathermen (and later the Weather Underground) had skillfully employed the rhetoric of revolutionary violence long before that, and the core leadership had a flair for generating media notoriety wildly out of proportion to actual Weathermen numbers. Inevitably, some influential Huntington conservatives projected the perception of SDS as violent revolutionaries onto the Marshall chapter. One faculty member recalled that these citizens and the local newspaper "played this up very greatly. They *wanted* desperately to see the reflection of what was going on nationally in Huntington. And as a consequence, they did."[52]

The Parthenon reported on February 4, 1969, that six local Church of Christ ministers had organized an anticommunist campaign while the campus was closed for semester break. Their concerns were the presence of the SDS and the scheduled speaking engagement of Herbert Aptheker, a prominent Marxist historian, during a traditional spring cultural and educational festival known as Impact Week. The anti-Red campaign soon widened its scope to include not only SDS and Aptheker but, sometimes overtly and sometimes implicitly, the Marshall faculty and administrators who would allow such disloyalty on campus. The Church of Christ ministers were soon joined by Reverend Paul Warren, pastor of the Jefferson Avenue Baptist Church, who became the most powerful spokesman for the antis. Church of Christ Reverend Dewey Parr, welcoming Warren to the campaign, described him as a "Bible-loving minister and a warrior of conservatism." Warren's leadership was complemented by Mrs. E. Wyatt Payne, one of Huntington's bluebloods and well known for her civic works and radically conservative politics, who was frequently quoted by the local newspapers. Mrs. Fred Perry, president of the Woman's Club of Huntington, pledged the organization's one thousand members to a letter-writing campaign to force Nelson to deny legitimacy to the "small minority of young subversives" at Marshall. Eventually, among the hundreds of letters President Nelson received during the recognition conflict, opponents of recognition outnumbered supporters by about ten to one.[53]

The controversy peaked at a mass meeting in the Campus Christian Center on February 16. Over three hundred students and Huntingtonians crowded the center to hear speakers from the pro, anti, and "moderate" views on recognition. A contentious debate ensued. Reverend Paul Warren read from a prepared statement, attacking academia for protecting the dissemination of communist propaganda. He and Mrs. Payne each charged that the national SDS was ruled by communists who wanted to take over America's high schools and universities. Warren even criticized the Campus Christian Center, the host for the evening, as a "haven to give aid, comfort, or encouragement to the very enemies of Christian principles and ideals."[54]

Stuart Colie, associate professor of political science, said that SDS espoused "subversive ideas rather than subversive practices," and a democracy could only refute, not prohibit, subversive ideas. Economics professor William Cook, one of Stewart's mentors, pointed out that local SDS chapters had "complete autonomy" and should be judged on their merit and actions on each campus. Woodruff and Stewart both spoke for the SDS, this being Woodruff's first public appearance as a representative of the group. He defined SDS recognition, provided they abided by university rules and requirements, as first and foremost a free speech issue. Why, he asked, should ROTC, an arm of the war in Southeast Asia, have a greater right to exist than an organized group of peace activists? Woodruff later believed that the polarization on display in the Christian Center meeting was a positive thing, concluding that it helped confirm the Marshall campus as the natural location in Huntington for open debate and dissent. "Nelson and the university," he recalled, "had to deal with [the reality] that there was no basis on which to deny recognition, except as knuckling under to a right-wing, anti-intellectual and anti-university barrage."[55]

The Parthenon consistently defended the organization's right to exist and checked any impulse to over-sensationalize the issue. Editorialist Nancy Smithson wrote that the SDS "has articulated views varying from the established opinions of a conservative university." Smithson advised readers that "whether you agree with its position on issues or not, you have to admit SDS has expressed these views within the limits of civil laws and university policies." Editor-in-Chief Suzanne Wood wrote that SDS, an "unrecognized campus organization has already served a far greater purpose here than most others have managed to do in 50 years of recognition." She explained that the anti-communist reaction presented the student body with a "long-overdue" opportunity. She explained that the antis revealed a "lack of understanding as to what was the purpose of this academic community," and no doubt were an embarrassment to the majority of Huntington's church people, who understood the Bill of Rights. In a neat reversal of convention, Wood identified the Payne-Warren faction as outsiders, turning the "outside agitator" trope against the right. Wood rejected the Payne-Warren group's assumption that they had any right to determine who had First Amendment rights at the university and who did not. "SDS must be recognized at MU," said Wood, "because this is a test case of the true meaning of democracy on this campus." Both Woodruff and Suzanne Wood believed that the intrusion of this "barrage" on campus actually mobilized uncommitted students. Even many who initially opposed recognition for SDS, Wood wrote, soon supported recognition on free speech grounds.[56]

President Nelson apparently agreed. His interoffice memos and correspondence with supporters suggest that from the outset of the issue, he discerned no legitimate reason to deny SDS recognition. He saw nothing in the Marshall chapter's charter or conduct that either advocated or rationalized any form of violence. When angry alumni threatened to withhold contributions to Marshall if SDS was permitted to remain on campus, Nelson wrote Harry Sands, the director of alumni affairs, "As you and I know, alumni can never be permitted to run an institution no matter what their financial contribution to it may be."[57]

President Nelson approved university recognition of Students for a Democratic Society at Marshall on March 11, 1969, after consulting with several formal and informal faculty/student committees. Nelson reported to Donald Dedmon, dean of arts and sciences, that he acted on the basic principle that a university is a seat of knowledge and investigation, a place where opposing ideas can be presented and studied openly. He also noted that he took into account a petition to him endorsing recognition, signed by seven hundred Marshall students who were not members of SDS.[58]

Marshall's SDS survived about another year and led protests against President Nixon's invasion of Cambodia in late April of 1970. By then Stewart and Woodruff were working with the Appalachian Movement Press, and Local 1199 in New York had taken the first steps toward becoming a national union. In the fall of 1970, Larry Harless was organizing small proprietary hospitals in southern West Virginia for the new 1199WV. Speaking of the "forgotten workers" in the region, national organizing director Elliott Godoff affirmed that the union's work in West Virginia would "serve as a demonstration of the tenacity and perseverance of our union to prove that where others walk away our union will stay and try and fight and do everything in its power to succeed."[59]

Deep reserves of tenacity and perseverance would be required to build a progressive healthcare workers' union in Appalachia. Long before Harless began his work in southern West Virginia, the influential theologian Reinhold Niebuhr foretold the fate of social justice organizing. "Nothing that is worth doing can be achieved in our lifetime," he wrote in 1952. "Therefore we must be saved by hope." [60] Accordingly, when Woodruff interviewed Don West for the January 1971 issue of *Mountain Life and Work*, West had already gone on record as being unimpressed with much of what he had seen of the New Left, especially splinter groups like the Weather Underground and the Revolutionary Communist Party. They did not understand that meaningful radical struggle demanded a long haul, like his hard journey had been. Too many of the New Leftists were "bourgeoisie radicals" who believed they could "solve everything" overnight. West's sentiments were echoed by Steve Nelson, one of West's fellow organizers for the Unemployed Councils. Nelson's memoir, published in 1981, explained the essential need to meet workers within their personal circumstances rather than assaulting them with remote ideological dogma. Leftist labor activists like Davis, Godoff, West, and Nelson had an unshakable conviction that working-class people had unarticulated ideals of solidarity and social justice that could be woven into their consciousness by way of tangible improvements in their daily lives. The Unemployed Councils, Nelson said, "focused on the practical grievances brought to them by the people in communities." "It was from involvement in the daily struggles," he continued, that radicals like him could help people realize how their individual well-being demanded their involvement in collective aspirational movements for social and economic justice. This was a message that Stewart and Woodruff heard. [61]

Chapter 3

New Boundaries for Local 1199

Dr. Roland Nelson approved recognition for the Marshall SDS on March 11, 1969. Nine days later four hundred service workers at the University of South Carolina's Medical College Hospital in Charleston, South Carolina, walked off the job. The strike was called by Local 1199B, the first local formed outside New York City in 1199's campaign to organize hospital workers nationally. Representatives of the four hundred strikers, all of whom were Black, had contacted one of the union's top organizers, Henry Nicholas, for help from the union following the firing of twelve workers, allegedly without cause. Local 1199 had not intended to begin its national efforts in the South, where the labor movement had never recovered from the failure of the CIO's sweeping organizing initiative, Operation Dixie, between 1946 and 1948.[1] "But," said 1199's cultural director Moe Foner, "here were these highly motivated workers." Their walkout spread to a smaller hospital, Charleston County, on March 28. None of the total of 460 strikers was White, and only twelve were men. Both facilities were public institutions.

This strike, which lasted until June 27, was in equal parts guerilla theater, civil rights demonstration, working-class pageantry, and street brawl. Charleston's 1199B adopted the slogan "Union Power, Soul Power," which minority workers in New York had used to great effect. The hospitals secured injunctions to stop strikers and supporters—who included well-known civil rights leaders such as Andrew Young, Coretta King, James Orange, and Hosea Williams—from marching and picketing. The Charleston marches continued, however, and by the end of the strike more than one thousand demonstrators had been arrested. One of those was Leon Davis, who was jailed for ten days, along with Southern Christian Leadership Council leader Ralph Abernathy.

According to Foner, it was the work of the local Black community itself that gave the strike its energy. Black churchgoers joined the picket lines and took up collections for the strikers. Black businesses provided meals and haircuts free of charge; some strikers, said Foner, "even got help with house payments." The strikers endured when the hospitals hired an antiunion lawyer on loan from J. P. Stevens, a notorious antiunion textile company. The governor sent the

National Guard with an implied threat to forcibly put down the strike, possibly at the behest of Senator Strom Thurmond and Representative Mendel Rivers, virulent racists and vocal supporters of hospital management. Someone threw a firebomb into Henry Nicholas's (unoccupied) hotel room. Against all that, the workers held out and it appeared, at least to some, scored a victory. "The four-month long strike and the resulting administration-worker agreement," wrote Steve Hoffus, a Charleston freelance writer, "stood as a model to workers. . . . It suggested that no institution, in any state, was immune to the power of organized workers." [2]

Called the Memorandum of Agreement, the settlement included wage increases, a grievance procedure, and a commitment from the hospital management to set up a credit union to provide for voluntary dues checkoffs. The twelve workers whose firings had sparked the walkout were reinstated. But the agreement did not include recognition for 1199. To the National Union staff, this was not unexpected. Moe Foner acknowledged that they understood all along that "we weren't going to end up with a contract." [3]

The Charleston strike is remembered as a pivotal moment for the new national orientation of Local 1199. Thanks to a public relations blitz by Foner's staff, the public now knew that 1199 was *the* civil rights union and would faithfully stand with minority workers against White domination. The union produced and began to distribute a documentary about the Charleston strike, *I Am Somebody*, that was widely used in organizing campaigns. Just over a month after the Charleston strike ended, workers at five Baltimore hospitals, invoking the "Union Power, Soul Power" theme, negotiated contracts that recognized their new union, 1199E. Fink and Greenberg claim that at Johns Hopkins, "the mere threat of 'pulling another Charleston'" caused the hospital to hurriedly sign a union recognition agreement.[4]

In terms of building a union for the Charleston workers, however, the strike fell short. South Carolina had been a right-to-work state since 1954, meaning that even if a union managed to establish a core membership at a workplace it could neither require new hires to join the union (a union shop agreement) nor automatically have monthly dues checked-off from their members' paychecks. And as public employees, the workers at Medical College Hospital and Charleston County did not have a legal right to collective bargaining under South Carolina law. The immediate reason for the new National Union to get involved in Charleston was to draw attention to working conditions in the South and pressure the management at the Medical College Hospital to reinstate the twelve discharged workers. What the union hoped for, at best, was to leave a dedicated core of members, secure some benefits for the workers at the hospitals, and begin the hard work to get the state law changed, as 1199 had done in New York earlier. With these conditions, it is understandable that union veterans like Moe Foner would realize that there was at best a minute possibility for a contract.[5]

As for the workers who fought to win recognition for their union with this strike, however, they were sorely disappointed. According to historian Steve Hoffus, nurse's aide and 1199B leader Mary Moultrie acknowledged a few years after the strike that the wage increase was indeed a plus, but otherwise the Memorandum of Agreement was woefully inadequate, as was follow-up support from the National Union. "In terms of working conditions and everything, everything is basically the same," Moultrie reported. "If we had gotten union recognition and had adequate representation over there, had somebody that would be able to bargain with management, it probably would have worked. But the Memorandum of Agreement wasn't worth the paper it was printed on." As evidence, Moultrie could point to MCH's violations of its own agreement. The hospital never established the promised credit union for dues checkoff and immediately took steps to weaken the grievance procedure.[6] Moultrie herself was a gifted organizer and negotiator, but she and the other members were unsuccessful in sustaining momentum from the strike. Henry Nicholas concluded that Moultrie's gifts were magnetic—she was a "Barbara Jordan type of speaker"—but that as chapter president she proved ineffective. When she was later voted out of office, Moultrie turned away from organizing altogether.

Fink and Greenberg suggest an additional reason for the Charleston local's recession: Mary Moultrie's difficulties "revealed a basic tension between the union's metropolitan base and its provincial outpost." Similar tension would occasionally surface in the early stages of 1199's work in West Virginia.[7]

Kay (Moller) Tillow was in high school in Metropolis, Illinois, in 1959 when her Presbyterian minister gave her a copy of Anne Braden's new memoir entitled *The Wall Between*. In 1954 Braden and her husband Carl, who were White, had agreed to purchase a house in Shively, a small Louisville, Kentucky, development, and deed it over to an African American acquaintance named Andrew Wade, his wife Charlotte, and their young daughter Rosemary. *The Wall Between* is a remarkable first-person account of the citywide uproar in the aftermath of that purchase, which included the bombing of the house and the imprisonment of Carl Braden for sedition against the state of Kentucky. It also documented the tireless agitation of the Bradens for progressive interracial unionism in Louisville and their subsequent circuit-riding work for the Southern Conference Education Fund (SCEF) throughout the South. SCEF was an organization dedicated to educating and activating southern

Whites to join with Blacks in the struggle for civil rights, directed by James Dombrowski. Tillow was deeply impressed by *The Wall Between* and credits it with starting her on the road to a lifelong commitment to social justice. She later met the Bradens, and her future husband Walter, at a 1964 conference at the Highlander Center. She also briefly worked with them at SCEF.

Tillow, inspired by the persistent message of "the need to stand up" throughout *The Wall Between,* joined the NAACP as an undergraduate at the University of Illinois at Urbana–Champaign. After returning to campus in 1963 following a year in Ghana, Tillow was sent to an Atlanta civil rights meeting by her NAACP chapter. At the Atlanta event, Tillow interacted with much of the young leadership of SNCC, including John Lewis, James Forman, and Prathia Hall. She soon volunteered to join Robert Moses and other SNCC activists working for voting rights in Hattiesburg, Mississippi. Here she saw violent reaction against civil rights demonstrators for the first time. She witnessed the frightening militarization of the Hattiesburg police and learned of brutal violence committed against some jailed demonstrators in "violent, oppressive Hattiesburg." But "something was moving and shaking and turning," Tillow said, "and was not to be put back in spite of the violent opposition that it faced."[8]

"Walter came from a left background. I came from the farm."[9] That was Kay Tillow's assessment of the childhood differences between the two, but they ended up together and built their lives around principles of social and economic justice, grounded in leftist critiques of corporate capitalism. Walter was born in 1940 and raised in the Bronx, New York. His mother was an unemployment worker for the state and his father operated laundromats. As youngsters, they had been part of the Young Communist League in the 1920s but were no longer active in any kind of formal political work, although they maintained an interest in progressive and left-wing causes. When Julius and Ethel Rosenberg were executed in 1953, Walter's father took his thirteen-year-old son with him to the funeral. Tillow remembered extended family gatherings divided between radicals and conservatives, leading to sometimes heated but always informative discussions.

Walter attended Harper College, a New York state university in Endicott, where he gravitated toward unaffiliated campus politics as the sit-in movement took form in the South. His first active involvement was as a picketer at a Woolworth's in Johnson City, New York, that refused to serve Blacks, a demonstration by Harper students that incurred the disapproval of the student government and the university president. He was soon involved in campus-based protests against a required Civil Defense fallout shelter drill and in the formation of a Young Socialists party as a counterweight to the Young Republicans and the Young Democrats.

During a bruising *New York Times* compositors' strike in 1963, when Tillow was in graduate school in economic history at Cornell, he and a small group of fellow graduate students took it upon themselves to make copies of newspaper articles from the library's collection and post them around campus. Tillow was responsible for collecting and clipping pieces from the *Baltimore Afro American*, where he read an announcement for SNCC's 1963 annual meeting to be held in Atlanta. He attended, met Anne Braden there, and was soon involved in voter registration work in Fayette County, Tennessee, for SCEF. He did some work there with James Forman and Charles Sherrod and was then in Mississippi for the Freedom Summer of 1964. He worked closely with the organizers of the Mississippi Freedom Democratic Party (MFDP), mostly helping Julian Bond put out regular newsletters.

Freedom Summer ended in tragedy and disappointment. Three civil rights workers were murdered by the local Klan in Philadelphia, Mississippi. The MFDP failed to seat its delegates at the 1964 Democratic Convention in Atlantic City, where they claimed to be the rightful voice of all Mississippians and sought to unseat the segregationist regular state delegates. The MFDP did not significantly move the national Democratic Party, but it inspired civil rights activists nationwide. After the convention, said Walter Tillow, he "moved on," perhaps sensing the split that was coming to SNCC. He became active in the labor movement and eventually joined the Communist Party USA.[10]

At the time (fall 1964), Kay was editing a newsletter called "Miner's Justice" for the Appalachian Committee for Full Employment, a poor people's movement in eastern Kentucky. When Anne Braden asked Walter to organize a Highlander workshop on labor and civil rights, he pulled it together with help from the United Packinghouse Workers. Kay attended the workshop for her organization, as did delegates from SNCC, the Bradens, and James Dombrowski. Kay and Walter met at the conference and married not long after. In 1965 they both went to work as organizers for the United Electrical, Radio, and Machine Workers of America (UE). The union sent Kay to northern Pennsylvania and Walter to Detroit. They were drawn to the radical tradition and direct-action tactics of the UE, one of the leftist unions expelled by the CIO in 1950, and to its longtime director of organizing and in 1965 the general secretary, James Matles. Within a couple of years, however, Kay left the UE and moved to Pittsburgh, where she edited the *Pittsburgh Peace and Freedom News* and completed work for her college degree at the University of Pittsburgh. She was working as a teacher in the summer of 1969 when the Tillows were contacted by a friend at St. Margaret's Hospital, where workers had put together a petition to ask the newly formed 1199P to come in and organize them. Leon Davis sent organizer John Black, who was familiar with Kay's history in the civil rights and labor movements, to follow up on the St. Margaret's petition. The first organizing drive for 1199P, however, was elsewhere in Pittsburgh.[11]

> There was a sense that it was a union that was moving and cared about issues and wanted to organize. It was doing things; a lot of the labor movement was having hard times and no forward movement.
>
> In SNCC, there [had been] a feeling among the people that the public accommodations fight was just the very beginning, that the real issues of inequality were economic issues. That solutions took something that related to the labor movement, with organizing and putting people into motion.
>
> In 1969 I was put on staff of 1199 but told not to go to St. Margaret because that was small . . . they wanted a big one. So I was sent to Presbyterian-University Hospital.[12]

Henry Nicholas joined Tillow for the Presbyterian campaign in the fall of 1969. Once again the union applied the "Union Power, Soul Power" mobilization tactics of the civil rights movement, but the approximately seven hundred service and maintenance workers at Presbyterian, which Kay Tillow estimated were fifty-fifty White and Black, never built the militant solidarity which had been on display in Charleston and the Baltimore campaigns. Fink and Greenberg unequivocally describe the Pittsburgh organizing drive, which lasted from September 1969 into March 1970, as a "major defeat in the national campaign." Tillow agrees that in the central objective of organizing Presbyterian, the "big one," the union fell short. But as we will see she is not willing to write off this early struggle by 1199P quite so sweepingly as Fink and Greenberg.[13]

One hospital executive dismissed the popular mobilization tactics 1199P used at Presbyterian as "a bewildering blend of old-style union organizing and the tactics of the SDS and Black militants." Another critic disparaged Henry Nicholas for running union meetings "like down home revivals." In Pittsburgh, the "movement" tactics of high-visibility demonstrations failed to generate much enthusiasm or public support. Likewise, the practice of eliciting testimonials from prominent civil rights activists, unless they were directly connected to the city, proved ineffective. In retrospect, some 1199P officers and organizers concluded that what was missing was a rigorous enough effort to organize Presbyterian workers rather than to mobilize them for direct action. By these accounts, the union allegedly portrayed hospital administrators, who held fast in their refusal to accept a recognition election, as villainous elites squeezing poor workers with "poverty wages." Hospital management, however, was prepared to offer wage increases and in fact did so on the day before the union struck for an election on March 20, a common preemptive tactic to block union momentum. As it happens, the hospital had also apparently been working with a powerful management consultant team from Philadelphia to devise a wage equalization ("Operation WE") plan for just such an occasion as the 1199P drive. When the recognition strike began, only a relative handful of supportive workers came out to picket. When a local judge offered to mediate a truce, the hospital and 1199P consented. The hospital allowed striking workers to return to their jobs without reprisals and promised not to oppose a state labor law guaranteeing hospital workers the right to a union election.[14]

Here Kay Tillow confirmed the underlying weaknesses of the Presbyterian effort: "But Presbyterian Hospital wasn't moving, so by March we threatened a strike and there was indeed a strike in March of 1970. We had a rally the night before the strike. Coretta King came in, and Moe Foner. We could always get Coretta King to come. It was a crazy time, I remember there was a bomb threat where we had the rally. And the next morning it was really clear that we didn't have a majority of the people out. That we had a substantial minority but not enough to give the hospital trouble. Before it dwindled [the] strikers got a pledge of no retaliation. We went back without a contract."

As momentum around the Presbyterian campaign sputtered, however, the union succeeded in organizing Pittsburgh's Jewish Home and Hospital for the Aged, a private nonprofit. Tillow and 1199P members at the home held a sit-in on Christmas Eve 1969 and requested an election. The administration agreed to set up an election, and Rabbi Walter Jacob, whom Tillow knew from the local antiwar movement, was asked to monitor the vote. "We won and that was our (1199P's) first contract."[15]

The loss at Presbyterian inevitably raised the question as to whether 1199, under the banner of "Union Power, Soul Power," would be able to succeed in a shop where workers were largely or predominantly White. Moreover, as Henry Nicholas came to realize, if 1199 was going to survive in an industry that was becoming increasingly specialized, the union must be able to attract professional as well as service employees. Professional hospital workers, even in communities with sizeable minority populations, were mostly White, a function of the racially biased educational and occupational legacies that prevailed in America. As the union expanded geographically, it would more and more be dealing with local and worker populations of majority White, in both professional and service sectors. Organizing director Elliott Godoff declared that "you can't organize White America with the bosses pushing an image of 1199 as a 'militant Black union.' "[16]

Godoff suspected that as 1199 moved into predominantly White communities, race would commonly be exploited by hospital management to try and discredit the union. He was right. The racist tropes against the union were rarely blatant. Instead they were coded, with leaflets or letters to the editor identifying 1199 as "urban," "militant," or "prone to violent strikes." The power of such coded messages is explained by Ibram X. Kendi in his book, *Stamped from the Beginning*. They help in understanding how 1199 anticipated potential White reticence as the union approached overwhelmingly White communities and workplaces. The union's commitment to racial equality was essential but could face challenges: "There was nothing simple or straightforward or predictable about racist ideas, and thus their history. Frankly speaking, for generations of Americans, racist ideas have been their common sense. The simple logic of racist ideas has manipulated millions over the years, muffling the more complex antiracist reality again and again."[17]

Some industrial unions, notably the United Mine Workers of America (UMWA) from its inception in 1890, had early on recognized that the expanding number of African Americans in industry demanded an elemental shift in race relations within the labor movement. Consequently, Blacks were welcome in the UMWA, partly for pragmatic reasons and, for at least some leaders and members, antiracist principles. But the traditional craft basis of AFL unions had systematically excluded Blacks from membership, a circumstance that industrial leaders often exploited by bringing in African Americans to break strikes. By the mid-1930s the CIO unions, recognizing the obsolescence of the exclusionary craft system in an age of mass production, organized on the basis of racial and ethnic inclusiveness. Led to a great degree by the very left-led unions that the federation would later expel, the CIO became, according to W. E. B. DuBois, "the greatest and most effective effort toward interracial understanding among the working masses. . . . Probably no movement in the last 30 years has been so successful in softening race prejudice among the masses." The record of the CIO unions was not pristine. Michael Yates cites the example of how the United Steelworkers of America "abandoned the theme of racial unity" once the industry was organized by the time of World War II, later reclaiming its rights consciousness in the 1960s. It was the unions with a committed left-wing leadership, like the UE and 1199, that "set the standard by which unions could be . . . judged in terms of racial solidarity."[18]

Anne Braden, in her aforementioned memoir *The Wall Between*, explained how the United Farm Equipment Workers confronted the "simple logic of racist ideas" at an International Harvester Plant in Louisville, Kentucky, in 1949.

She and her husband Carl were employed as publicists by Local 236 of the FE, which competed with its much larger CIO rival, the United Auto Workers, for the loyalties of farm equipment workers. Its major locus of power was in Harvester plants. Braden analyzes the interdependence of self-respect, dignity, and racial justice in the workplace (I am leaving the language of 1958 intact) that characterized Local 236:

> I know the union carried on a constant campaign to convince the white workers that only by solidarity of Negro and white could the union be strong, and this undoubtedly had an effect. But probably the most effective thing of all was the hard, pragmatic fact that under the conditions and circumstances that existed the workers did not need their prejudices anymore.
>
> For the white workers, this new sense of dignity and security meant they no longer needed the Negro as an object of scorn, no longer needed him for the inflation of their own egos and as an outlet for their frustration and worries; for the Negro workers it meant they could look at the white workers without bitterness. The results in terms of human relations were startling.[19]

The key to internalizing the ideal of racial justice and equality, said Braden, was to remove "inner feelings of insecurity and inferiority" on the part of all workers. "In our present society this kind of development most often occurs under the impact of some union struggle."[20]

As 1199 ventured into majority White Appalachia, its identity as a minority rights union would be reworked but the moral force of its argument for human dignity and respect would remain. The "dignity and security" of a democratic union could fundamentally restructure power relationships at work and interpersonal relationships in the larger community.

In this regard, appeals grounded in interracial class solidarity had a greater force of moral argument than did management promises for a little more pay. The union must appeal to workers on the basis of respect as a human right. Once workers believed that the union was the means to securing that human right, they could be inoculated from any race-baiting or "outsider" language from management. According to sociologist Rick Fantasia in an influential study of worker consciousness and solidarity, a union should not be defined merely as "a bureaucratic structure" with a grievance procedure but a "democratically organized configuration of workers that can effectively contest for power in the workplace." If a little better wage was all the boss had to offer, the union offered a lot more than that. Many White workers eventually embraced 1199's "Union Power, Soul Power" history as a point of pride. Still, they acknowledged that ideas about race were deeply culturally embedded and must be commonly aired and worked on at local meetings and delegate (steward) trainings. It would be naïve in the extreme, of course, to assume that somehow Local 1199 was pristine among American institutions in terms of racism, sexism, and paternalism. "It was and is a great Union," one 1199 staffer wrote me, "but we are clearly not immune to these same troubles."[21]

Shortly after the defeat at Presbyterian University in Pittsburgh, the Pennsylvania Legislature did pass a collective bargaining law for public employees. This legislative fight had been in progress before the Presbyterian strike, led by the American Federation of State, County, and Municipal Employees (AFSME) for a while. It was the Presbyterian strike, however, that compelled the Pennsylvania lawmakers to broaden the legislation to include hospital workers. Kay Tillow saw that as a significant victory coming out of the Presbyterian loss. Soon she was involved in a string of organizing victories for 1199P that demonstrated that a "Black union" could appeal to White workers.[22]

These victories came in rapid succession by June 1971. At Lewistown, 1199P got its first win under the new Pennsylvania Public Employee Relations Act. At Mercy Hospital in Wilkes-Barre, 1199P won by a large majority, losing only one of five bargaining units. The registered nurses went union in spite of a class-based appeal by the nuns who operated the hospital, who pleaded that joining a union would undermine the professional status that the RNs had worked so hard to attain. Why would they endanger that professional prestige when they had struggled to prove that they were not just "coal crackers," a pejorative term for coal-mining families? "So that made the nurses furious," Tillow remembered, "because almost everybody's father or grandfather had worked in the anthracite mines. They were furious [the nuns] would try to divide them. So the nuns helped us. We won that overwhelmingly."

The workers at Lewistown and Wilkes-Barre were practically all White, and one of the union's biggest supporters was an African American doctor:

> Here we were in Pennsylvania organizing White workers. That was a joy, because the company made it known that this Black union, you know, that we could overcome that [talk].
>
> We had a lot of success in these small industrial towns that were union through and through. There was a union tradition. And then in '73 I worked on the Washington, Pennsylvania hospital. There was steel and coal there. In fact Washington Hospital was where they took the

bodies when they shot Yablonski. But Washington was a huge victory, majority White. [We got] the service and maintenance people. It put 1199P on the map.[23]

When Local 1199 came to West Virginia (1199WV) in 1970, it did not start out by taking on a big public hospital like 1199P had in Pittsburgh. Although the union worked assiduously throughout its entire early history in the state (1970–1989, before its merger with the Service Employees International Union), 1199WV and its labor and political allies were never able to compel the West Virginia legislature to approve a public employee collective bargaining law. Regardless of this obstacle, a significant percentage of 1199's Appalachian membership was comprised of public employees. As regional membership grew between 1970 and 1980, 1199 organized municipal, state, and private hospitals, and, beginning in 1978, nursing homes in West Virginia and Kentucky. Some of these struggles will be a focus of later chapters.

Leon Davis and Eliott Godoff at the National Union office in New York sent West Virginia native Larry Harless, a veteran of 1199 campaigns in New York and Baltimore, to his home state to start building the union in 1970. The objective was to organize workers at the many small, privately owned (proprietary or "fee-for-service") hospitals that dotted the southern counties of the state. Davis and Harless surmised that workers in these facilities in rural and small-town West Virginia might be receptive to unionization, particularly in light of the steady decline in coal employment due to the rapid mechanization of the industry.

Proprietary hospitals, you will recall, were covered by the National Labor Relations Act (NLRA). The original intent of the NLRA/NLRB framework in 1935 was to promote collective bargaining in order to minimize instability and conflict at the workplace. The NLRA (or Wagner Act) did indeed protect the masses of industrial workers who built the labor movement between 1935 and 1947. It worked so well that labor's traditional opponents, who took control of Congress in 1947, were committed to dismantling the law. The Republican "class of '47," over President Harry Truman's veto, passed the Labor Management Relations Act, usually referred to as Taft-Hartley. Written largely by lobbyists for the National Association of Manufacturers, the law outlawed the closed shop and secondary boycotts, two of labor's most effective weapons, and included loyalty clauses designed to push out any residual communist sympathizers. Taft-Hartley authorized the states to pass right-to-work legislation, forbidding a union to require union membership or dues payments by workers covered by a collective bargaining contract.

Over time, the NLRA became as much an obstacle as a help to workers' self-organization. One labor relations scholar describes the post-1947 management rights structure as "legal but asymmetrical," protecting employers' power to resist unionization more than it protected workers' rights to organize. Another, summarizing the steady drift of the NLRB away from labor and toward management, concluded that after Taft-Hartley unions were "increasingly entrapped within a formalistic and legalistic structure of rules" deliberately written to favor management. As practiced, NLRB oversight "became positively unhelpful in certain areas." [24] Taft-Hartley even took away unionization rights from workers in not-for-profit hospitals, who had been covered by the original NLRA. Ironically, the restoration of NLRA coverage to workers in not-for-profits in 1974, as we will see, brought unforeseen obstacles for 1199 and other healthcare unions. Its rules both protected and restricted workers trying to form a union. They also protected the ownership or management of a hospital in resisting unionization.

Although unionized healthcare workers were uncommon in Appalachia and the South, there was a significant exception. Union workers staffed hospitals and clinics operated by the UMWA Welfare and Retirement Fund, which had been providing care for union miners and their families since 1947. Miners' health benefits were jointly funded by operator and UMWA contributions under the terms of that year's National Bituminous Coal Wage Agreement. Additional funding based on royalties paid by operators into the fund was included in the Love-Lewis Agreement of 1950, negotiated by the union with the Bituminous Coal Operators Association. In exchange for these added resources, John L. Lewis agreed that the UMWA would not resist mechanization in the mines. Miners working with a UMWA contract would be well compensated, but the inevitable reduction in numbers of miners in "inefficient" mines, even as production increased, soon began to weaken the bargaining power of the union. According to one historian, "this agreement set the stage for the human tragedy in the coalfields during the 1950s and 1960s brought on by massive technological unemployment" and outmigration. Declining UMWA membership and a series of ill-advised financial transactions by the fund's managers eroded its reserves, leading to cutbacks in programs for unemployed and disabled miners and miners' widows. By the early 1960s, the fund was in dire straits, and the union agreed to sell its network of ten Miners Memorial Hospitals in West Virginia and Kentucky. In 1963 the transfer was made to the United Presbyterian Church, USA, a nonprofit corporation, and the hospitals were rechristened the Appalachian Regional Hospitals. The United Steelworkers of America and the West Virginia and Kentucky Nurses Association replaced the UMWA as the bargaining agents for the employees in the system. [25]

Larry Harless knew, then, that a significant portion of working-class families in the southern West Virginia coalfields owed what property and security they had to hard-won union membership. Many knew about or even experienced the struggles in the 1920s and 1930s that prepared the ground for better times. But the likelihood of steady work with a union contract in the mining industry was disappearing by 1970. Younger workers, given the shortage of occupational choices in their communities, might consider themselves fortunate at the prospect of steady work in the local hospital.

In an era of growing rights consciousness, many workers in chronically low-wage hospitals and nursing homes (1199WV began organizing nursing homes in 1978) were inclined to rebel against the deeply embedded paternalism, condescension, and authoritarianism that was built into the culture of that work. The conventional perception of rural and small-town Appalachians, reinforced by influential popular and academic sources, was that they were remote, isolated, and fatalistic about their condition and their future. Most, however, were fully aware of the wider world's social and cultural upheavals and the struggles of marginalized people to have better lives. Political scientist Stephen L. Fisher and others remind us that since the 1960s, Appalachian activists have organized an extensive network of grassroots organizations to "rid the region of oppressive structures and practices." Historian Jessica Wilkerson contends that Appalachians "stood at the nexus of mid-twentieth-century social movements." Wilkerson studied the leadership roles of women in the 1960s and 1970s antipoverty programs, welfare rights organizations, community health work, environmental justice protests, and unionization campaigns. They joined forces with rank-and-file miners in the Disabled Miners and Widows of Southern West Virginia, the Black Lung Association, and the Miners for Democracy, leading to the expulsion of corrupt UMWA leadership and the passage of the Federal Coal Mine Health and Safety Act, all between 1968 and 1972. Moreover, small towns like the ones Harless began to frequent in 1970 disproportionately gave up their sons to the war in Vietnam. Residents of these communities were well schooled in the culture and politics of rich and poor, the dynamics of power and powerlessness, and the imperative for collective action.[26] It is not surprising that Harless was optimistic that 1199 might take hold in West Virginia.

Harless was twenty-nine, a native of Pineville, West Virginia, and a U.S. Army veteran when he began work, alongside one other organizer, Wendell Drake, in Boone, Logan, McDowell, and Fayette Counties. By the time Harless and Drake arrived, the few jobs available in coal and timber were usually sporadic and lacking union benefits. Operating heavy equipment on a strip mine site or driving coal trucks required only a handful of workers and, occasional energy boomlets notwithstanding, the economic vitality of these formerly bustling coal towns was gone. Jobs in the small, locally owned hospitals (they, too, were destined for extinction) were important sources of income in these towns. In many cases 1199WV, with its promise of respect at work and a better standard of living, got a fair hearing from the people. Why, they might logically ask, should the work of nurses and nurses' aides, orderlies, technicians, maintenance workers, office clerks, housekeepers, and kitchen workers not be accorded the same worth and dignity that miners had secured through organizing?[27]

Harless took up residence in the Boone County hamlet of Peytona, hard by the Big Coal River, as his base for the West Virginia campaign. The November 1970 issue of *1199 News* announced the impending rumblings within the West Virginia healthcare system by announcing that "organizer Larry Harless reported that four proprietary hospitals in the southern part of the state had filed petitions for representation elections through the National Labor Relations Board." At each of the four facilities—Doctors Memorial in Welch, Madison General in Madison, Guyan Valley in Logan, and Oak Hill Hospital in Oak Hill—new members of 1199 WV had staged "high noon demonstrations," being mass rallies on hospital property to demonstrate workers' demands for union recognition.[28] The December issue carried this feature, under the title "First in State to Vote in 1199":

> Forty employees at Madison General Hospital in Madison, W. Va. became the first hospital workers in their state to win Local 1199 W. Va. representation when they chose the union overwhelmingly in a card count.
>
> The unit includes RNs, LPNs, technicians and service and maintenance workers, reports organizer Larry Harless. Conditions at the hospital include $1.45 [$9.59 in 2019] an hour pay for all services, $300 [$1,980.09] a month for practical nurses; no sick leave or uniform allowance; maximum of two weeks' vacation; and no on-call pay for orderlies who sleep on-call at the hospital after their shift ends.
>
> Madison General is a proprietary hospital located in the mountainous southwestern part of West Virginia. This is a coal mining area where automation has produced extremely high rates of unemployment.[29]

The "card count" reference means that the management of Madison General, after being presented with signed union authorization cards by employees, consented to negotiate a contract without going through the NLRB election process. In order to petition the NLRB for a union election, the law requires a union to secure signatures from at least 30 percent of the affected employees, but no union will petition without at least 50–60 percent signed cards. If there is majority support, the employer can voluntarily recognize the union, bypassing the NLRB electoral process. That was the case at Madison General. The hospital agreed that about forty employees, excluding clerical workers and supervisors, represented an "appropriate unit for the purposes of collective bargaining," and that 1199WV would be recognized by the hospital as those workers' sole bargaining agent.[30]

The first victory by way of an NLRB election was early in 1971 at Doctor's Memorial Hospital in Welch, the county seat of McDowell County. Situated in the narrow confines of the Elkhorn Creek and Tug Fork valley, Welch became a thriving commercial center due to its proximity to the main line of the Norfolk and Western Railroad. Incorporated in 1895, the town provided goods and services for the numerous local mining communities and, with the migration of African Americans into West Virginia's southern coalfields, McDowell County became a thriving residential and cultural center for Black families. Keystone, whose Black population was around 40 percent during the boom years, was an important social and political center for African Americans, who were able to leverage considerable power through the state Republican Party during the industrial era. One of the leading coal-producing counties in the country, McDowell was devastated, as were other coal towns, with the mechanization of the industry in the 1950s.[31]

Doctors Memorial Hospital was a proprietary hospital owned by the Wisconsin Shoe Company of Kansas City, Missouri, which also owned two other hospitals in West Virginia. African Americans comprised about 25 percent of the hospital's work force, and 1199WV members claimed that during the election drive the hospital management tried to exploit racial differences between the workers. An important element of the union's education of new members, however, was to alert them as to how their employer might try to create and exploit racial divisiveness. "Union education dealt with race head on," said David Cormier, an organizer with 1199P from 1975–1989, "and trumped the more nativist attitudes" that resided in some White members. On February 10, 1971, deflecting any race-baiting, the LPNs and service and maintenance workers voted 108–41 to be represented by the union.[32]

As per the National Labor Relations Act, the hospital and the union were required to enter into "good faith" bargaining for the purpose of negotiating a collective bargaining contract. But though the law requires bargaining, it does *not* require that the parties arrive at an agreement. Doctors Memorial negotiators therefore stalled contract talks, a common tactic by which management seeks to engender discontent and frustration with the newly elected union. Because Larry Harless and Wendell Drake took steps to instruct the members on such company tactics and relied on the rank-and-file members on the bargaining committee to educate their coworkers about the process, the hospital's delaying tactic was ineffective. Charging the hospital with not bargaining in good faith, an unfair labor practice under NLRB provisions, the members authorized a strike on April 15 to force the issue. There were some tense moments during the strike, although details are scarce. United Mine Workers of America members joined 1199ers on the picket line, and some witnesses claimed that a hospital official sprayed mace on picketers and bystanders. Governor Arch Moore dispatched thirty-five West Virginia state troopers to the scene, an action that was "blasted" by state AFL-CIO president Miles Stanley as a sign of Moore's "union-busting" sentiments. The hospital finally relented after twelve days and agreed to a first contract. The contract included a 40 percent pay raise for LPNs and service and maintenance workers, medical care provided by the hospital for workers and families, holiday and vacation improvements, a grievance structure, and a pension plan.[33]

Local 1199WV, as did all of the chapters and districts in the expanding union (a chapter or combined chapters, referred to as "areas," could petition the national Local 1199 to become a district once they had one thousand members), incorporated language from the national's constitution into their by-laws. Nondiscrimination, democratic processes within the union, a commitment to the establishment not only of a just workplace but a just society, and more are enumerated in the constitution. Such aspirational ideals were not exceptional in union language; no one would outwardly contradict such a vision. The challenge was to build a union that lived up to them. For that, Local 1199 chapters vowed to "facilitate and stimulate the broadest possible rank and file participation in the formulation and execution of the program of the District and to encourage development of the most effective leadership."[34]

The key (or the "bedrock," say Fink and Greenberg) to rank-and-file participation in Local 1199 was the delegate (equivalent to shop steward) system.[35] Each bargaining unit in a chapter was entitled to one delegate for each twenty-five members. If a unit had less than twenty-five members, as was not uncommon in the facilities in southern West Virginia, units could combine for purposes of delegate allocation. Delegates often serve on contract negotiation committees or recommend others for that duty, remembering that in every negotiation, "We're trying to get something and they're trying to take something away." Delegates and the rank and file are responsible for educating new members, always keeping in mind that "everything they have can be taken away politically."

These passages from *1199 Hotline*, a newsletter published by members at Cabell Huntington Hospital (organized in 1974–1975), summarize the role of delegates in every 1199 chapter:

> There is no more important position in the National Hospital Union than that of delegate. Elected by the membership from each department and classification at every institution, the delegate plays the key role in the day to day function of the Union. They must communicate with members daily. They inform members of their contract rights and help defend members against a boss who tries to infringe any of these rights. They lend members help in confronting management about problems as they occur.
>
> Being a delegate is a difficult and often time-consuming job. And without strong delegates, the Union cannot function. There are over 50 1199 delegates in this area. Each elected by the members they serve, delegates attend training classes conducted by the National Union. But their real training comes through the "school of hard knocks." In handling grievances at the 1st and 2nd step. In educating new members about the Union and their contract rights. And in helping members decide how to solve a problem when it arises.[36]

The centrality of the delegate system, wrote Moe Foner, evolved from 1199's earliest organizing struggles in New York pharmacies and drugstores. The union's survival depended on assertive, educated rank-and-file leaders within the system of the decentralized retail drugstore business. And if members were going to work hard for the union, said Foner, "you can't easily exclude them from decisions on union policy. So member participation was linked to internal democracy."[37] The union's ideological and practical reliance on member involvement migrated naturally to 1199WV's efforts in the small hospitals in West Virginia. It was more than rhetorical posturing. It was essential for the union's survival.

Delegate training, therefore, was the cornerstone of the union's solidarity, education, and effectiveness. On September 7–9, 1971, delegates from the new chapter at Doctors Memorial in Welch attended their first delegate training. Here the delegates—LPNs, nurses aides, orderlies, and a laundry worker—expanded on their knowledge of the time-consuming and often mundane life's blood of organization building and contract administration. They and Harless invited Robert Muehlenkamp, from 1199E in Baltimore, to oversee the training. He and Harless had both worked on the 1969 campaigns in Baltimore. Muehlenkamp wrote national organizing director Elliott Godoff that "we ran through several skits with the Delegates talking with New Hires about signing check-off cards and becoming Union members. So far the delegates are doing a good job. . . . Generally, the Delegates are very smart and totally dedicated to the Union. I think with the little classroom training we were able to get in and procedures we set up that they will be able to get along pretty well on their own most of the time."

The attendees also set up a system whereby delegates themselves would take over some of the "administrative duties," including keeping track of new employees coming in, documenting who and who had not signed up for card-check, and communicating with hospital management on the card-check requirement in the contract and other routine affairs. They would regularly report to Harless, their union representative. These were essential steps in the emergence of a natural leadership in each work center and on every shift at the hospital.

Muehlenkamp also told Godoff that "I hope that we accomplished enough so Larry can be 'freed' of that administrative burden. I think that Larry feels better about it—feels that he can leave Doctors' Memorial except for the regular meetings and emergencies. . . . He is anxious to get things started again." [38]

Harless had in fact already gotten things started again, having been working on a major new organizing drive at Beckley Hospital in Beckley, West Virginia. There were a lot of new members "totally dedicated to the union" there also, and working hard to get their employer to recognize 1199WV and sit down at the bargaining table. They were facing formidable concerted obstruction, however, from the owners and administration of the hospital, who included Beckley's mayor and a former governor of the state.

Chapter 4

"1199 Comes to Appalachia"

Established in 1838, Beckley, Virginia, was a small agricultural settlement, distinguished as the county seat of Raleigh County when the Virginia county was formed in 1850. Beckley became part of the new state of West Virginia in 1863 and was positioned on the "doorstep" of a massive bituminous coalfield encompassing western Raleigh and eastern Wyoming counties, where small mining operations opened in the 1890s. The C&O reached Beckley in 1901, and the Winding Gulf coalfield, named after a tributary of the Guyandotte River, began large-scale production in 1907. When the Virginian Railway built a new line to the ports of Virginia, coal production expanded dramatically. The Winding Gulf became known as the "Billion Dollar Coalfield," and Beckley prospered as a commercial and service center for the dozens of mining communities that dotted the field. It was more insulated from the long post–World War II decline in coal employment than were the surrounding coal camps, partly because it was at the southern portal of the busy West Virginia Turnpike and partly because of its status as the county seat.

For a town of its size (about twenty thousand in 1970), Beckley was well served by healthcare facilities. In addition to Beckley Hospital, some of whose workers had contacted Larry Harless, Beckley was served by one of the Appalachian Regional Hospitals owned by Presbyterian Church USA, Pinecrest Hospital (a former tuberculosis sanitorium, which in 1970 was mainly a care center for elderly patients), a Veterans Administration Hospital, and Raleigh General Hospital. In 1969, Raleigh General had been purchased by the Hospital Corporation of America, identified by financial historian Maggie Mahar as "the nation's first investor-owned hospital chain."[1]

Beckley Hospital had about 130 employees in 1971, 75 percent White and 25 percent Black. Harless began signing up members at the hospital around February 12, shortly after the successful election at Doctor's Memorial in Welch. He soon requested that the hospital ownership voluntarily recognize 1199WV and negotiate a contract. The hospital trustees refused, declaring their preference to work the issue through the NLRB election machinery. Administrator Albert Tieche and Beckley mayor John McCulloch, both of whom were part owners of the facility, told the *Raleigh Register* that the hospital would prefer "guidance" through NLRB hearings to determine employees' eligibility to vote on collective bargaining representation. They claimed that Harless sought voluntary recognition because he feared that 1199WV could not win an NLRB vote.[2]

Harless accused the hospital of delaying tactics with the intent of frightening employees away from support for the union so that by the time an NLRB election could be held, 1199WV's momentum would have stalled. Harless scoffed at the hospital's deferral to the NLRB in the *Beckley Post-Herald*, since the NLRB itself encouraged "consent agreements" without the "red tape" of its time-consuming election structure. The hospital repeatedly refused even to meet with Harless and union members, claiming that a meeting "could be interpreted that the hospital acknowledges the union, which it does not." Through a union lawyer, Harless did file an election petition with the NLRB dated February 19. Albert Tieche mailed letters to hospital workers, apologizing that planned pay increases could not be implemented "while the union matter was being discussed."[3]

Threatening employees with wage punishment for exercising their right to organize, however consolingly expressed, is an unfair labor practice as defined by the NLRA. The union could protest such violations to the NLRB, but decisions by the board could take months or years. A ruling favorable to the union might result in the board ordering remedial action by the company, but the board could take no punitive action. Harless was well aware that the employer could exploit the NLRB election machinery to delay a representation vote, and one role of the organizer was to educate the members about delaying tactics. Management had the right of unlimited access to workers at work during a recognition election campaign, defined as the employer's "freedom of speech" and implemented through one-on-one or group "captive meetings." Union representatives, however, were denied access to company property during the election process. That made "worker-to-worker" communication at work crucial—but those practices, too, were tightly proscribed, with penalties for any worker suspected of "talking union" on company time.[4]

On February 22, Administrator Albert Tieche tipped his hand by summarily shutting down the hospital's third-floor obstetrics-gynecology (OB-GYN) ward and dismissing its twenty employees, practically all of whom had already signed union cards. Tieche insisted that the closing of the OB-GYN ward and the firing of its workers was an economic decision that had long been under consideration; it was strictly a coincidence that the closure came when those workers signed union cards. A local pediatrician said he was disappointed with the closing and it "would take away beds he really needed." He had heard about possible plans to close the ward but was surprised at the suddenness of the action. Within hours after the shutdown, the new 1199WV members at the hospital, most of whom were women, voted to walk off the job and set up pickets outside the hospital the next day.[5]

Beckley Hospital officials soon reconfirmed Harless's expectations of calculated obstruction and intimidation. While waiting for "guidance" from the NLRB, supervisors reportedly were instructed to tell their workers that "we have large stacks of applications, and workers who support the union can get into trouble and lose their jobs because of the union." Only two days after the February 23 walkout began, John McCulloch said that the hospital was replacing workers who did not report for work. The hospital was "hiring permanent replacements," he said, "in accordance with procedures approved by the NLRB." The presence of police cruisers at the hospital entrances appeared to heighten rather than relieve the tension between striking picketers and nonstriking employees heading to work. The cruisers were obviously there to intimidate picketers, said Harless, at the order of Mayor McCulloch. A hospital spokesman claimed the police had been posted because "many employees have been threatened by the pickets" and were afraid to come in to work. The spokesman, Assistant Administrator L. B. Carper, began driving skittish workers to the hospital and at one point was accused by Wanda Stover, a picketing nurses' aide, of deliberately trying to run over some of the pickets. Carper said that "to his knowledge this was not true."[6]

The National Union believed a victory at Beckley, following closely on the heels of the victory at Doctor's Hospital, might generate considerable momentum for the Appalachian campaign. Accordingly, Moe Foner, editor of the union's *1199 News* monthly journal, sent staffer and contributing editor Dan North to Beckley to do a feature story on the Beckley strikers for the 1199 readership. North interviewed some of the thirty-one strikers who had been arrested during a March 9 "march on the boss" and sit-in at Albert Tieche's office. North's lengthy photo essay and narrative, which he titled "1199 Comes to Appalachia," appeared in the May 1971 issue of *1199 News*. While the story was not free of the paternalism that infected most journalism about the region, North effectively documented the hard fight into which the Beckley workers had willingly thrown themselves.

The opening pages included a pleasant family portrait of James and Mary Polk and two of their ten children. The Polks resided in rural Raleigh County, and readers learned that Mary, a nurse's aide at Beckley Hospital, provided a critical portion of the family income, especially since James had suffered a debilitating spinal injury in a coal tipple accident in 1969. They also learned that Mary's wages ($1.64 an hour, or $10.37 in 2019 terms) had been cut off when she walked out on strike, and that she had been among those arrested in the sit-in at Tieche's office.

James Polk, by virtue of his long membership in the United Mine Workers of America, was guaranteed a disability check each month. "I'm 100 percent behind my wife and all the others on the picket line," he said. "Anyone who works should have a union." Mary agreed, vowing that "we'll stay on the line as long as we have to." Mary's fellow striker Helen Bragg hoped that whatever trouble she and her coworkers faced would leave a legacy of hope and occupational dignity for their children. "The poverty wage we have here comes down through the generations. More than likely my kids will have to work here, but if we get a union they won't have to work for any $1.64 an hour." Dan North described the Beckley Hospital strike as another "grim chapter in the long history of bitter labor struggles in this harsh home of mountains, coal, and poverty."[7]

The hospital management and trustees were adamant in their refusal to negotiate voluntarily and told Harless his only recourse was the NLRB election. After hearings, the board scheduled an election. Their decision came on July 2, five months into the strike. The election was scheduled for August 2, six months into the picketing. By that time some influential forces, led by the hospital Board of Trustees, had tipped the balance against 1199WV. Union supporter Ruby Keeler summarized the odds with her statement, "The same bunch that owns the hospital owns the whole town."[8]

Beckley's power structure in 1971 was reflected in the composition of the Beckley Hospital trustees and major stockholders. Four of these men represented influential families in the town—Smith, McCulloch, Tieche, and Sayres. Among the enterprises they and their kin controlled were a bank, a radio station, a hotel, a printing company, insurance and real estate agencies, and a Chevrolet dealership. Former West Virginia governor Hulett C. Smith was a stockholder and treasurer of the hospital and still active politically as a national Democratic committeeman. As already mentioned, hospital vice president John McCulloch was the mayor of Beckley. It was he who ordered police cruisers either to protect "loyal" workers or intimidate picketers, depending on one's sympathies. His duty, said McCulloch, "is to maintain law and order." Albert Tieche, as we have seen, was the hospital administrator. A "local attorney associated with labor law," hospital trustee Floyd Sayre, advised both sides in the dispute to "remain silent and await the decision of the board." Other Beckley lawyers warned picketers that their action "can be termed illegal and harm the efforts of the union." Despite the warnings, picketing continued, both at the hospital and at business establishments owned by the Smith, Tieche, and McCulloch families.[9]

Smith, the state's twenty-seventh governor from 1965 to 1969, was the most prominent of the hospital's leadership. He was a Beckley native, born in 1918, and was immersed in business and politics from childhood. His father was Joe L. Smith, who owned a newspaper and was at various times a bank president, mayor of Beckley, a state senator, a U.S. congressman, and chairman of the West Virginia Democratic Party. Hulett graduated from the Wharton School at the University of Pennsylvania at age twenty and married Mary Alice Tieche in 1942. After serving in the navy during World War II, Smith returned to his hometown to build his business portfolio in the family ventures. In addition to being a stockholder and trustee at Beckley and Oak Hill Hospitals, he was a director of the Bank of Raleigh and vice president of Beckley College, a private junior college that had opened in 1933. He began his political career in 1951 as chairman of the Beckley Democratic Committee and worked his way up the Democratic ladder. He lost the Democratic primary for governor in 1960 to W. W. Barron but won the nomination and defeated former (and future) Republican governor Cecil Underwood in 1964.[10]

As governor, Smith had often professed his belief in "peace and harmony in labor-management relations." Smith had been supported by organized labor in West Virginia, including getting an endorsement from the state AFL-CIO, when he ran for governor. While in office he had served as chairman of the National Governor's Conference Committee on Labor-Management Relations in the Public Sector. But as reported in the *West Virginia AFL-CIO Observer*, the former governor "has been persistent in a campaign aimed at busting labor at the Beckley Hospital." In a press release dated May 14, 1971, West Virginia AFL-CIO president Miles Stanley chastised the hospital directors for their obstructionist behavior. Stanley was especially "shocked by the apparent apathy of former governor Hulett C. Smith and the present Mayor of Beckley, John McCulloch" toward the workers at the hospital. The management had rejected several attempts by the union to negotiate a settlement, Stanley charged. The closing of the third-floor OB-GYN ward and the firing of its staff was "an obvious attempt to head off the unionization of the employees of Beckley Hospital." Smith and McCulloch, Stanley continued, were violating the principles of "social and economic justice," which "are not based on political platitudes but on practical application of such principles in our dealings with our fellowman." When Eliott Godoff thanked Stanley, Stanley replied, "Unfortunately, thus far our intervention has been to no avail and the strike continues. Management is very recalcitrant and is going all out to protect their family interest."[11]

As the Beckley strike continued, so did periodic confrontations between picketers and hospital administrators, picketers and police, and strikers and nonstrikers. In addition to the arrests of Mary Polk and her fellow strikers,

Harless and four others, accused of picketing on company property, were arrested by city police and jailed overnight, even though they insisted they had secured authorization to picket on that site. They also claimed they were denied phone calls while jailed, an accusation that Mayor McCulloch denied. The most serious incident occurred when a carload of nonstriking workers drove past a picket line and unloaded at a hospital entrance, only to have the driver return to the line, stop his car, jump out, and sucker-punch Harless. The injury broke three bones in Harless's face and was serious enough for the union to fly Harless to Johns Hopkins for surgery. His attacker was tried for assault in municipal court and fined $10. Aside from the serious attack on Harless, described by Elliott Godoff as "cowardly, sneaky, and vicious," there apparently was no serious physical violence from either side for the duration of the six-month standoff. A newspaper account affirmed that the strike was a bitter interlude but marked primarily by "arrests, harassment from both sides, and allegations thrown back and forth." Meanwhile, some of the strikers had taken other jobs to support themselves.[12]

Hospital officials insisted that neither a majority of the employees, nor the hospital's patients, had any sympathy for the strikers. Testimonials appeared in the *Beckley Post-Herald*, including that of a patient who said, "I resent, as do several of the other patients, having to hear from the employees how badly they are being treated. If they have complaints, they should talk to Mr. Tieche, not the patients." That logical recommendation, of course, was problematic in that Mr. Tieche was not willing to talk to them. Assistant Administrator Carper claimed that hospital operations had continued "without too much difficulty," and he was heartened by Beckley citizens who had been "calling us and saying they will come and help at no charge. There was one housekeeper with 33 years' experience who called and said she did not want any union and that she would come and help, be there for 18 hours without any pay if necessary."[13]

As the August 12 date for the NLRB election approached, hospital management claimed it was "quite confident" that their union troubles would soon go away. The NLRB delivered the union a body blow by rejecting its claim that the OB-GYN ward shutdown was in direct response to 1199WV's presence at the hospital. This decision meant that the seventeen union members among the workers fired from that unit were ineligible to vote. The NLRB also turned down the union's claim that the hospitals forty-five imported replacement workers were temporary and therefore not eligible to vote. In public comments the day after the election, as ballots challenged by the union were being reviewed by the board, Harless seemed to know the union had lost. He insisted that before management closed the third floor (on February 22), "we had a clear majority. But after they got rid of 17 union sympathizers and hired about 40 additional employees, it changed." He added that "the NLRB bureaucracy is stacked in favor of the employer. . . . The same kind of people who control the hospital also control the labor board." As if to redouble the demoralization among the strikers, the hospital publicly announced that it was "highly unlikely" that striking employees would be brought back to work if the union lost the election.[14] The union challenged thirty-nine ballots on grounds that the replacements were temporary, but the board had already decided for the hospital on that issue. Minus the challenged ballots, which would undoubtedly be mostly "no" votes anyway, the vote was 64–43 in favor of the hospital.[15]

Local 1199WV did have a later victory in Beckley, although not at Beckley Hospital. In 1980, despite a "fierce" antiunion campaign by the ownership, workers at Heartland of Beckley nursing home voted 71–38 for the union. Organizer Dan Stewart claimed that the home, part of a chain of fourteen facilities, spent $65,000 on "union avoidance" materials and intimidation tactics.[16]

Sharon Harless drove her husband to prison on May 14, 1974. Turning Larry over to officials at Wise Correctional Unit in Coeburn, Virginia, there to serve a four-month sentence, "was the most difficult thing I ever did." Larry's incarceration punctuated a bittersweet struggle for 1199WV. It "left an emptiness in our lives," said Sharon, referring to herself and the couple's six children.[17]

About a year before Harless began serving his sentence, the members of Local 1199 at the Clinch Valley Clinic Hospital in Richlands, Virginia (1199V), had improbably won recognition and signed a first contract at the hospital, a private for-profit facility owned by Bluefield Sanitarium. For more than four months in late 1972 and early 1973, after the hospital's maintenance workers, housekeepers, and LPNs voted to unionize in an NLRB election, hospital management had stalled contract negotiations. The union, charging the hospital with refusal to abide by the NLRA requirement to bargain in good faith with the duly elected agent of the workers, finally went on strike on February 13, 1973.

The hospital immediately secured an antipicketing injunction from the Circuit Court of Tazewell County, an injunction the union insisted was illegal. By the end of the day, over one hundred picketers had been arrested and jailed in Richlands and nearby Grundy, Virginia, in Buchanan County. The court granted limited picketing rights the next day, and three weeks into the strike the hospital and Local 1199WV reached a two-year agreement, ending the strike and beginning a short era of union representation for these workers in a right-to-work state. These were the preconditions leading to Larry Harless's imprisonment a year later.

Like many communities in central Appalachia, the industrial history of Richlands, Virginia, was founded upon railroads and coal. In 1887 the Norfolk and Western Railroad (N&W) built a branch line from Bluefield, Virginia (then called Graham), to a spot on the banks of the Clinch River, near the river's source in Tazewell County. In 1891 the N&W extended that line to meet up with the Louisville and Western line at Prince's Flat, Virginia, which later was renamed Norton.[18] Forward-looking English and Philadelphia investors purchased thirty thousand acres of coal, timber, and iron prosperities. To exploit these resources, they bought and combined seven small existing operations to form the Clinch Valley Coal and Iron Company. Aware of guaranteed rail connections, in 1891 they incorporated the town of Richlands, intent on creating "the Pittsburgh of the South." The company sold town lots at reasonable prices and recruited coal diggers and artisans from England and continental Europe to labor in the new Richlands industrial economy. The company's rolling mill manufactured iron and steel, fed by the settlement's surrounding coalfields. The iron and steel workers worked and lived in a section called Puddler's Row, and skilled glassblowers worked and lived in Glass Row. The yards and shops of the N&W provided employment for hundreds of workers.[19]

The crash of 1893–1897 destroyed the Clinch Valley Coal and Iron Company and the entrepreneurial dream of Richlands as a thriving industrial center. The town itself survived as a service center for regional farm families, and the N&W and scattered coal operations provided some work. After the Love-Lewis agreement mechanized the mines, bootleg truck mining operations cropped up here and there. In 1970 the population of Richlands was 4,843, with about 18 percent of the population living below the poverty line. Richlands rallied temporarily during the energy crisis of the early 1970s, when coal markets expanded because of an increase in oil prices. The town's population increased by nearly 20 percent during the decade to 5,800. Deindustrialization in the 1980s, however, resulted in a 20 percent reversal of that growth, taking the population down to 4,456 in 1990.[20]

In 1972 the Clinch Valley Clinic Hospital (CVCH, later the Clinch Valley Medical Center) in Richlands was a proprietary hospital owned by Bluefield (West Virginia) Sanitarium, Inc. The operation was comprised of the "Clinic," which specialized in outpatient services, and the "Hospital," which provided inpatient treatment. The clinic doctors worked on a contractual system, while all other workers were employed by the CVCH.[21] The idea of healthcare workers wanting a union seemed suspicious to some of the power brokers in Richlands. "It is impossible to say when the seeds of discontent began growing," reported to the *Richlands News-Press*, "but one could possibly date the beginning of the

union when Larry Harless distributed some union literature to employees."
Now, Harless was certainly an agitator, and he was an "outsider" in Richlands,
but worker discontent must have been approaching a boil for some time. It is
possible that Harless traveled to Richlands on a hunch and initiated contact
with some workers. But it is unlikely that Harless would walk into a situation
cold and begin to agitate for a union—there were not enough resources for
that and, particularly in Virginia, a right-to-work state, the chances for success
were slim. It is more plausible that someone from the CVCH contacted Harless or the national office and asked for an organizer. Without an invitation, it
would be difficult for an organizer to earn the trust of the workers.[22]

Harless met with Clinch Valley workers throughout the summer of 1972,
and sufficient numbers signed union cards for 1199V to petition the NLRB.
The board scheduled an election for October, authorizing two bargaining units:
service/maintenance and licensed practical nurses (LPNs). The union won con-
vincingly with a 77–23 vote.[23] Hospital Administrator Homer E. Allen claimed
to be surprised by the union drive, since "he had thought salaries and fringe
benefits for these employees were among the best in the area." That could have
been a true statement but did not necessarily mean that those wages were fair
or adequate. One housekeeper was making $1.99 ($12.19) an hour, with only
fourteen cents in raises in eight years. She spoke of a female coworker who had
been at the hospital for three years, with her wage rising from $1.83 to $1.86.
"Our take-home pay is so low," she continued, "that most of us fall below the
official 'poverty levels' in our incomes."[24]

As the two sides sat down to bargain, it soon became apparent that there
were wide disparities on many issues. Negotiations dragged on for thirteen
grueling weeks, with management claiming that the last obstacle was over
a union demand that the employer accept a voluntary checkoff clause in the
contract—that is, members could agree to having the employer deduct dues
from their pay and send the dues to the union. Virginia's right-to-work law,
of course, meant that a checkoff agreement was not a mandatory subject of
bargaining. While theoretically possible, a checkoff would require voluntary
dues payment by each worker covered by a contract that was legally bound to
represent them anyway. The employer had no inclination to relieve the union
in any way of its obligation to collect dues individually from each member.
"It's the union's job to collect its own dues," said hospital spokesman Paul
Hudgins. Harless claimed that "misunderstandings" about health insurance
and contractual seniority rights were also delaying a settlement. On February
9, Harless joined some eighty union members who marched on Homer Allen's
office to vocally reject the hospital's latest offer. They were stopped by police,
and Harless was kicked off hospital grounds.[25]

At that point the union members decided that the hospital was bargaining in bad faith and voted to strike. When nearly one hundred 1199ers set up a picket line outside the hospital at 5:30 a.m. on February 13, they were embarking on the first-ever hospital workers strike in Virginia. Within hours the hospital personnel director, Joe Sereno, who was a municipal judge, secured an injunction from his colleague Judge Vincent Sexton in Tazewell County Circuit Court, which not only enjoined strikers from disrupting the hospital's routine business but also prohibited "picketing in any manner about plaintiff's premises." The judge also pronounced, in a declaration that formed the basis of a lengthy legal struggle by the National Union for 1199V, that the strike was "contrary to the public policy of Virginia." Sexton based his ruling on a Virginia state law that outlawed strikes in nonprofit hospitals. Clinch Valley, of course, was a for-profit business.[26]

The next morning, Wednesday, February 14, "dozens of workers" reestablished a picket line. Harless was quoted as saying, "We are not going to obey the injunction. We are not going to have an effective strike made ineffective by an illegal injunction." That morning, about sixty strikers, mostly women, were arrested and held in the Richlands city building until they were bailed out at noon. On Thursday, the pickets were back, and again about sixty strikers were arrested, this time sent to jails in Tazewell and Grundy. Together these incidents made up the largest mass arrests in the history of Tazewell County. On Thursday afternoon, acting on an appeal from Local 1199V, the U.S. District in Roanoke amended the Circuit Court injunction to allow limited picketing at hospital entrances. Picketing continued daily throughout the remainder of the twenty-one-day strike. Whatever messages the hospital and Judge Sexton were hoping to send to striking nurses' aides, maintenance men, and housekeepers, they probably were not happy with the public response to the arrests. "The big mistake," said one striker, "was when they arrested everyone's wives, mothers, and grandmothers. . . . The miners didn't like that."[27]

Indeed, they did not. UMWA president Arnold Miller, having recently ousted the corrupt Tony Boyle in a special election ordered by the Department of Labor, traveled to Richlands in early March in a show of support for the Clinch Valley strikers. "I had the privilege of walking the picket line with your members during the strike at [the] Richlands, Virginia hospital," Miller wrote to Dan Stewart in 1976, "and UMWA members were proud to join in that successful organizing effort." A big part of that support came when five thousand rank-and-file miners shut down eighteen mines in a one-day walkout to bolster the morale of the Clinch Valley workers. For good measure, Miller threatened to withdraw UMWA financial support for the hospital unless the employer settled the strike favorably. Faced with escalating resistance from both Local 1199V members and the wider public, the hospital at last recognized the union at Clinch Valley and signed a contract.[28]

The Clinch Valley members ratified a two-year agreement including seniority rights, a fifty-cent raise over the life of the contract, sick leave and hospital benefits, and a guarantee from the employer to pay employees' health insurance and outpatient expenses. All but eight of the striking workers—from the dietary, housekeeping, and nurses' aide departments—returned to work on March 6. Paul Hudgins reported that these eight had just been "replaced" and would be rehired at a later date. This factor figured prominently in a dispute that Harless had with Leon Davis and the National Union, which is addressed below. As for the agreement in sum, Harless declared a "definite victory," even though the members had to face "illegal arrests and a one-sided injunction."[29]

Resisting authority, particularly when risking arrest, tended to have a liberating effect on workers, especially women stepping across societal and institutional lines. Jessica Wilkerson contends that the cultural role of women as family "caregivers" quite logically extended into their dedication to community well-being, either as unpaid or "public" (wage) laborers. Antipoverty activist Edith Easterling recalled that "becoming politically active and speaking out against injustice made one 'feel like a free person.'"[30]

Teresa Ball, who became an organizer for Local 1199WV/KY in 1982, once worked at a Kerr Glass plant in Huntington, West Virginia. It was a union shop, and as a new employee Ball was working on "probation"; that is, she had not yet been sworn in to union membership.[31] She was working a night shift on an inspection and packing line for gallon jars when one of her coworkers told her "we're going to walk"—in other words, stage a wildcat strike, a spontaneous work stoppage not authorized by the union and expressly forbidden by the contract. Ball could not remember the specific issues involved, but she vividly recalled walking out, and within an hour the issue was settled. "It was really the first time I realized the power of the workers," Ball said.[32]

Joyce Lunsford, a registered nurse at Fairmont General Hospital in Fairmont, West Virginia, referring to a union victory there in 1978, proclaimed: "If we hadn't broken the law, we wouldn't have a union." Anna May Jenkins was arrested three times during a strike at Cabell Huntington Hospital in 1977. "We were so sick of being treated unfairly, of not getting a raise, and just being treated with no dignity, no respect, anything they wanted to do to you they did," said Jenkins. "If they didn't like the way you combed your hair or who you went out with the night before; that's the way it was." Loretta Williams was arrested for blocking an entrance to the Hazard Nursing Home in

Hazard, Kentucky, in 1984. "I didn't know what [getting arrested] was all about at first," said Williams. "But I'm proud of it. It's not hard if you truly believe what you're fighting for." [33]

Each of these women made a conscious decision to transgress the rules and laws that governed them—and the norms that prescribed women's behavior. Ball by violating her contract, Lunsford and her coworkers by participating in an illegal strike, and Jenkins and Williams by trespassing were fully aware of possible consequences for their actions. Ball jeopardized her job and her provisional union status, and the others faced arrest and possible jail time. When Mary Polk and her coworkers occupied the lobby of Beckley Hospital, they also knew they faced arrest, as did the youthful dissidents of the Civic Interest Progressives when they protested segregation in Huntington.

The picketers at Clinch Valley also knew that they might be charged with striking illegally or arrested for trespassing and violating Judge Sexton's injunction. They acted in self-interest, of course, but that self-interest was entwined with their coworkers' collective pursuit of better lives. Purposefully or not, by willingly taking such risks they were also involving themselves in a long tradition of protest and civil disobedience, which, according to the writer Wendell Berry, become "properly a part of a citizen's life and work after political and legal processes have failed." Meaningful and enduring protest, Berry wrote, is moved by more than a hope for public notoriety or guaranteed results. It is moved by "the hope of preserving qualities in one's own heart and spirit that would be destroyed by acquiescence." It is not an easy or an inconsequential decision to, as Thoreau said, "let your life be a counter friction to stop the machine." All who undertake civil disobedience, Berry wrote, "have felt intensely and complexly the seriousness of it." [34]

Here is how some of the strikers described their protests and arrests during the Clinch Valley actions:

Audrey Helpert, LPN:

Feb. 15, 1973 was quite an experience for me and my fellow co-workers as we went out on the picket line against the Clinch Valley Clinic. I don't suppose we were there more than five minutes when we were arrested and put in a convict bus and hauled to the Richlands Court House until they could process us and take us to separate jails.

Then eight men and seven women were loaded in State Police cars and taken to Grundy. The rest went to Tazewell. In all, there were 65 of us.

Mr. Harless, our union organizer, was handcuffed and pushed around. When they brought him into Grundy jail, someone there in the Town Hall asked him what he had done. We told them that he hadn't done any more than we had, which was nothing. We were not violent. We did not resist arrest, we had a job to do and we were determined to do it.

Well, Grundy is a nice place to be in jail, if you can call a jail a nice place to be. It was clean and they gave us what we needed, like toilet paper, soap, clean towels, aspirin, paper cups, coffee, and a very nice hot dinner. They even let us have our transistor radio. Everyone was nice to us and told us they knew we hadn't done anything to be ashamed of, so I suppose that's the reason they treated us with respect instead of like criminals.

They locked all the women together and we kept each other company singing and talking. Two of the girls even danced to the music from the transistor. We had visitors who insisted that we hold up for our rights. One thing we found out is that we have a lot of support from the Buchanan County coal country.

Gertie Boyd, LPN:

As an LPN on strike at C.V.C., I would like to say that I am not ashamed, but proud, that I went to jail. I was not behind bars for committing a crime out of anger or for non-support to someone for whom I am responsible. I was behind bars for standing up for what I believe in.

Some say a hospital is no place for a union. I do not agree. I feel that more is accomplished when people, even hospital workers, are united.

Judy Breedlove, LPN:

We, the members of Local 1199, have been arrested, spent time in a cold, damp jail cell, walked the picket line during snow and rain and we believe we stood up for what we believe is right, which is seniority, better health care, better wages, etc. . . . . There has been no violence on the picket line or elsewhere during the strike. Nobody resisted an arrest.

Caroline Newberry:

There is no hate from Union 1199. We are standing together for the sake of one another in the justice of equality and we need your support![35]

The willingness of the Clinch Valley workers to challenge the law and transcend their traditional boundaries emanated from a tradition of resistance that hospital and healthcare workers would need to hold on to in the coming era when, in the words of Maggie Mahar, "laser-eyed entrepreneurs saw an opportunity to turn the hospital business into a moneymaking proposition." Workers were on the verge of stepping into the new era of neoliberal economics, when public policy in the United States followed a playbook emphasizing deregulation, the erosion of historical social contracts, antiunionism, and corporate consolidation. The nature *of* work and relationships *at* work would be changing dramatically in the 1970s and 1980s. If workers were to live decent lives, and if unions were to survive the new order, they would have to prepare themselves to "mobilize in an effective way despite existing legal sanctions," just as " 'illegal' factory occupations forced employers to recognize industrial unions in the 1930s." This context provides the backdrop for the remaining chapters in this book.[36]

According to testimony presented in the Circuit Court of Tazewell County, on March 16, 1973, Bob Muehlenkamp of the National Union[37] and a small group of 1199V members were present on February 13 when Larry Harless allegedly destroyed Judge Sexton's injunction notice, which had been posted at the Clinch Valley Clinic Hospital's main entrance near the strikers' picket line. Homer A. Croom Jr., a supervisor for a private security firm from Martinsville, Virginia, testified that at about 5:45 p.m. on that day Harless told the group that the injunction was illegal; as he walked away from the site, "he reached back with his left hand and tore the posted injunction off the column and stuck it in his left hand pocket." He was almost immediately arrested by two Richlands city police officers, one of whom, Charles Vencill, corroborated Homer Croom's account.

The National Union sent a New York attorney named Harry Weinstock to assist two Norton, Virginia, lawyers as counsels for the defense. In addition to Harless and Muehlenkamp, three 1199V members, Gertie Boyd, Kate Smith, and Gloria Regan, were in court on charges of contempt for violating the injunction, specifically for being present when the posted notice was destroyed.[38]

Based on his opening statement to the Circuit Court, Harry Weinstock and the National Union were in court not only to challenge the contempt charges against Harless and the others but to use the charges as a wedge into challenging the constitutionality of the so-called Virginia Hospital Statute. Weinstock began by avowing that the Virginia law clearly violated Sections 2 and 7 of the National Labor Relations Act. Clinch Valley Clinic Hospital was a private, for-profit hospital subject to the jurisdiction of the NLRA. Workers at private for-profit hospitals were guaranteed, as paraphrased by Weinstock, the "right to picket, the right to exert economic pressure by picketing and other concerted activity in the event of an impasse in negotiations, or even in the absence of an impasse in negotiations." The picketing at the hospital was peaceful and lawful, he claimed, and guaranteed by the First Amendment, even though "it was picketing the plaintiffs did not like." The Virginia Hospital Statute, which outlawed picketing and strikes as a matter of public policy, "must necessarily fall and is unconstitutional." CVCH conducted an NLRB election, so there could be no question that the NLRA exercised jurisdiction "over this particular hospital." Moreover, seeing as how the Virginia law was unconstitutional, the injunction issued by the Tazewell court was not lawful. "Consequently," Weinstock continued, "if it is void, there can be no contempt proceeding based upon a void order."

Bluefield West Virginia attorney Paul Hudgins, speaking for the Hospital, argued that Weinstock's claim that the NLRA "pre-empted" the Virginia Hospital Statute was a violation of the state's right-to-work law, although he did not clarify precisely how. He also argued that the pickets prohibited people from exercising their constitutional right to enter the hospital for treatment, which at least indirectly had some merit. Although there was no documented evidence of picketers prohibiting patients from entering the hospital, some could plausibly have been intimidated by a picket line. Hudgins's central claim was that since the U.S. Supreme Court had never invoked preemption in "the critical area of public health," then neither attorneys nor litigants had the right to question whether the Virginia Legislature, "in all of its wisdom," had the power to "legislate constitutionally in a critical area such as public health." Neither Judge Sexton nor the U.S. District Court for the Western District of Virginia, nor the Supreme Court of Virginia, nor, as reported, the U.S. Supreme Court wished to tackle the constitutional issues raised by either Hudgins or Weinstock, beyond an implied endorsement of Hudgins's position.[39]

The proceedings ended when Judge Sexton fined Muehlenkamp $500.00 and Boyd, Regan, and Smith $25.00 each plus court costs. Harless was fined $500.00 and sentenced to four months in jail. The sentences were stayed for sixty days pending appeal, and all were released on bond. The union did appeal the convictions, all the way to the U.S. Supreme Court, which dismissed the union's final appeal for "want of jurisdiction." Back in Tazewell County Circuit Court, Judge Sexton denied a motion by Harless's attorneys to suspend his sentence, and he was ordered to begin serving it, as we have seen, at the Wise Correctional Unit on May 14, 1974.[40]

By the time his sentence began, Harless's relationship to the National Union had begun to unravel. The aftermath of the CVCH strike led to a serious falling out between Harless and Leon Davis, probably contributing to Harless's resignation from the National Union staff in 1975. The conflict was rooted in the organizer's pledge to continue strike benefits to eight members whose jobs had been filled by CVCH when the strike began. During bargaining, the employer promised to bring them back to work as soon as possible after the strike ended, claiming this was the best CVCH could do. If the union could not accept this promise, the negotiations might collapse. Harless explained the caveat to the membership, assuring them that the National Union's strike fund would pay the eight workers until they were called back or took other work. The members voted to accept the proposal.

For about three months, the National Union provided funds to pay the eight members on the basis of their prestrike wages. Then the payments stopped. Harless apparently was confident that he had a commitment from the National Union to send payments to the eight workers until they returned to work. He assumed so on the basis of a clearance he and Muhelenkamp, as the National's assistant organizing director, secured from Elliott Godoff. Quoting Harless directly, in a letter he sent to Godoff on July 21, 1973, he said the following: "Bob and I . . . consulted with you about what our response should be to this proposal. It was decided that we would recommend to the strikers that they accept the contract offer with its attendant terms regarding the 8 employees, *and that the Union would pay the full weekly wages of these 8 employees until they returned to work at the Hospital.* There were no limitations or qualifications placed upon this commitment, nor was this even discussed" (emphasis added). When the payments stopped, Harless complained to Godoff that "we are obligated to keep our commitments." He further told Godoff that the cessation of the payments "has not helped the morale of the other employees and their trust in the Union and myself. I personally am used to being called a liar, but not by our own members, when that is surely one way you can look at it." He authorized Godoff to share the letter with Leon Davis.[41]

Godoff did share the letter with Davis, and Davis was not pleased. The leadership structure of the National Union was highly centralized, although, as pointed out by Fink and Greenberg, "the basic directive to young organizers was 'sink or swim.' " The day-to-day existence of an 1199 organizer was one of constant pressure to perform and took an emotional and physical toll. Turnover was high; in fact, turnover among union organizers in general is high. Harless had been operating under such pressure since he joined the union staff in 1968. He had been to jail several times and was slated to go again, he had suffered many beatings, he had a large family to look after, and he was underpaid.[42] Burdened by such pressure, Harless may have overcommitted the union. He assumed that Davis would not object to payments to the eight strikers, especially if he feared the contract negotiations collapsed. Since the National Union had already paid the costs for "organizers, meeting halls, transportation, telephones, and other expenses," including, as we have seen, legal fees, would its leadership object to extending financial help to eight strikers for the duration of, hopefully, a short period of time?

Yes, it would and did. Davis harshly chastised his organizer for violating the National Union's constitution. "You are laboring under a misconception about the obligation of our Union to strikers in general," Davis wrote, while complimenting him on "honorable motives":

> Considering the fact that the Clinch Valley Hospital strikers never paid dues to the National Union and consequently made no contribution to the strike fund—they have received very generous financial support from the National Union Strike and Defense Fund. . . . Contributions to workers who never paid any dues must be considered as an act of solidarity extended to workers who are struggling to build a Union.
>
> The National Union does not make agreements with workers who are being organized and no representative should even give the impression that in the event of a strike or the loss of a job that the National Union assumes any financial responsibility to a worker or to strikers. We do, as you know, extend whatever assistance we can to workers who may be victimized in the course of Union organization.

Davis acknowledged that Godoff had told him that as part of the Clinch Valley settlement, a few workers were told that the Union would help them out until they were called back to work. But then, implying a serious misjudgment by Harless, he told the organizer that "no one who has any experience would assume that the commitment would be open-ended and continue indefinitely or forever."[43]

It would not be fair to condemn Davis for upholding the National's constitution, which did serve as the central governing document for all of the 1199 locals and districts. It is arguable that Harless was careless in not speaking directly with Davis about the payments to the eight workers. But Davis did apparently agree to some payments in discussion with Godoff. In retrospect, it is clear that Harless and Davis should have agreed on a clear time frame for the payments. Why didn't they? Did Harless assume that Godoff could speak for Davis on a policy issue like this? (Foner, Fink, and Greenberg certainly do not suggest that.) Was Harless clear with Godoff that he had told the membership and the eight workers that the payments were open ended? Without engaging in overspeculation, in reading and rereading this correspondence between the two many times over, there is a sense in Harless's writing that he feels like he has been undercut by his union's leadership. Two years later, after working on a few more organizing drives, he left 1199 for law school at West Virginia University, where he was described by one of his professors as "the most interesting character I ever met. He was brilliant." Harless graduated at the top of his class.[44]

When the Clinch Valley workers approved their contract, *Mountain Life and Work: The Magazine of the Appalachian South* celebrated "a great victory" and predicted a possible wave of unionization at other Virginia hospitals "as the spirit of the union and this strike spreads." That did not develop, and in a sobering development, some CVHC workers filed a petition with the NLRB to "decertify" 1199V as their bargaining agent.

Just as the NLRB establishes a framework for voting a union in, it also has a process for voting a union out, or decertification. The union and the employer negotiated a one-year contract after the expiration of the first two-year agreement; at some point during that second contract at CVCH, some employees in the LPN unit covered by the contract began circulating a petition for a decertification election. By law the employer cannot file for a decertification election but sometimes will claim that the union is not fairly representing the membership and will refuse to bargain for a new contract. This makes the employer subject to unfair labor practice charges, but to some it is worth the risk. The employer can suggest a decertification to workers and can actively campaign against the union, although it is not supposed to provide any money for any "no union" campaign.[45]

According to Tom Woodruff, who at the time was the Clinch Valley union representative, 1199V had been in a precarious position from the beginning. The core of militant union activists did a fantastic job, he said, keeping the union alive by the exhaustive process of one-to-one "hand collection of dues." Some clinic doctors had vowed never to work with striking LPNs again, calling their actions "unprofessional." Although the NLRB ordered CVCH to put those LPNs back to work at their prestigious clinic assignments, that never happened, and morale among the LPNs weakened. It may be that the conflict between Davis and Harless did mortal damage, as Harless feared, to the fragile trust that the union had established with the membership. At some time,

Woodruff said, "you have got to get a real good contract." The determination of management at CVCH to kill the union ultimately made that impossible. The level of employer opposition was "just vicious," Woodruff said. "They were not going to allow the union to stay." After the LPNs voted 27–26 to leave the union, even the core militants could not keep it going. The logic of right to work won out—why pay dues voluntarily to a union that can't get a "real good contract?" Within four years after the beginning of the long struggle, 1199V was busted at Clinch Valley.[46]

Chapter 5

Law, Busting Unions, Building Unions

When the Sherman Antitrust Act became law in 1890, American workers believed that the U.S. Congress was on their side. Their understanding of the act was that it was to use the power of government to break up monopolies or "trusts." American Federation of Labor president Samuel Gompers had been assured by members of Congress that the regulation of big business, or any combination that acted "in restraint of trade or commerce among the several states," was the object of the law.

Within three years, the original intent of the act had been turned on its head. A federal court in Louisiana established the precedent for invoking the Sherman Act to justify sweeping injunctions against labor unions. True enough, said the court, the Sherman Act "had its origin in the evil of massed capital." But the scope of the law could legitimately be "so broadened" that it could be used to stifle the "excesses" of labor. Workers' organizations could be seen as equivalent "combinations in restraint of trade" to the trusts.[1]

Enter the unanticipated consequences for healthcare workers from the long-awaited Nonprofit Hospital Amendment to the Taft-Hartley Act. One of Richard Nixon's final acts as president was his signing of the amendment (Public Law 93–360), which expanded the jurisdiction of the National Labor Relations Board to include workers in private not-for-profit hospitals. In 1974, private nonprofits comprised the largest segment of the hospital industry, with about 1.5 million workers, or 56 percent of all hospital employees. When the 1974 law took effect, Leon Davis noted, "It was hailed as a new day for hospital and healthcare workers. However, our expectations were unrealistic. What we didn't reckon with is that to pass a law is one thing, but to have it administered impartially is something altogether different."[2] Davis was primarily alluding to the rapid expansion of, in the words of labor writer Steven Greenhouse, "one of America's stealthiest, least-known industries. It euphemistically calls itself 'the union-avoidance industry.' Others call it union busting." Practitioners in this field were adept at using the letter of the law to do their work.[3]

The logic for expanding the role of the federal government in hospital labor relations through Public Law 93–360 followed that of the 1935 Wagner Act. Senator Robert Wagner and his legislative allies believed that federal administration of labor-management relations was imperative in order to protect workers from exploitation and assert control over a confrontational industrial system that had caused a wave of militant and sometimes violent strikes in 1934. When workers and bosses were bound by rules equalizing bargaining power, the thinking went, both the autocratic tendencies of employers and the radical leanings of working-class activists would be supplanted by industrial democracy. The establishment of permanent institutions based on negotiation, compromise, and, when necessary, third-party mediation, says labor relations historian Howell Harris, would "be conducive to industrial peace."[4]

Critics of the Wagner Act on the right feared regulatory overreach by a centralized national government. Such a system, they believed, would undermine property rights and the time-honored sanctity of individual contracts freely negotiated by employer and employee without "third-party" interference. Critics on the left had concerns that federal oversight of union elections and negotiations would separate workers from their most effective tools for putting pressure on employers. They warned that strikes, sympathy strikes, spontaneous work stoppages, and a working-class vision for social justice beyond the shop floor would be diluted or eliminated by the strictures of the NLRB process. Some feared that the advocates of "responsible unionism" actually intended for Wagner to legitimate a "top-down" system to "control the rank-and-file."[5] Nevertheless, Wagner was welcomed in most prounion circles as, at least potentially, a long-overdue formula for balancing power at the workplace.

The Roosevelt administration gambled that rights and rules backed up by the federal government would weaken the working-class radicalism so prevalent in the Depression era. A generation later, given that unionization in not-for-profit hospitals increased by 90 percent between 1961 and 1967, it seemed logical policy to simply extend existing government regulation to assertive workers in a rights-conscious age. Labor's supporters of the 1974 amendments believed, as Leon Davis remarked, that the expanded labor law could check employer abuses and promote worker-employer harmony in the hospital industry. Conservative advocates agreed, contending that the outdated exemption for private nonprofits had virtually guaranteed disruptions such as recognition strikes and picketing by prounion employees. Expanded coverage under the act, says William A. Rothman, "should completely eliminate the need for any such activity, since the procedures of the Act will be available to resolve organizational and recognition disputes." [6] Hospital strikes were not outlawed by the act, but unions were required to submit a series of advance notices to management, given the possible interruption in patient care. The designation of bargaining units in public hospital elections, although not covered by the new law, generally followed those outlined for private facilities in Public Law 93-60. But the composition of bargaining units, either by the NLRB or by municipal hospital boards, was fluid and often worked to the disadvantage of labor. In 1987, officers of the National Union reported that "thirteen years after the federal government recognized the rights of hospital workers to organize, we still don't know what the appropriate bargaining units are." The report contended that "different groups of workers are entitled to their own bargaining units . . . in groups they, the workers, choose." The bargaining unit issue played a significant role in the 1975 Cabell Huntington election, as we will see. [7]

Healthcare unions faced several "cooling off" requirements before a recognition strike. The union was legally required to give a nonunion hospital a thirty-day notice before picketing or striking for voluntary recognition, followed by a ten-day advance strike notice if no settlement has been reached. If a collective bargaining contract was in place and due for renewal talks, then both the union and the hospital must commit to new negotiations ninety days before the expiration of the agreement. In the event of a bargaining impasse, the Federal Mediation and Conciliation Service (FMCS) would be called in to mediate. Both parties must notify the FMCS at least thirty days before a possible impasse and agree to a sixty-day extension of the existing contract at the time of that notification. Finally, if there were still no settlement when all the mandatory steps have been taken, the union must provide the hospital with a ten-day notice if the members call for a strike. [8]

Public Law 93-360 was only one of several federal interventions into the healthcare industry after World War II, with significant implications for the Appalachian region. In 1946, for example, lobbying by the United Mine Workers of America helped persuade the U.S. Department of the Interior to issue the Boone Report, an extensive survey of coal-mining regions. The report documented the scarcity of basic health services, high infant mortality, and physician shortages in rural Appalachian communities. These findings compelled Congress to pass the Hill-Burton Act, which subsidized the construction or expansion of modern hospitals in underserved areas. The cost-sharing requirement of Hill-Burton, however, left out those rural communities that could not generate the revenue to cover the cost share, and many small proprietary hospitals eventually shut down. The benefactors of the program tended to be towns and cities with relatively large populations. According to one account,

Hill-Burton financed about 90 percent of a $10-million expansion of Fairmont General Hospital (FGH), then a public hospital in Fairmont, West Virginia, in the mid-1960s.[9]

Hill-Burton contributed to the emergence of what Paul Starr defines as the "medical industrial complex" in the postwar decades. Two of the most significant structural developments were advances in medical technology and the infusion of third-party hospitalization benefits. Private health insurance plans (often an outcome of union contracts) and government spending through Medicare and Medicaid combined to provide hospitalization coverage to over 80 percent of the civilian population by 1967. Between 1965 and 1989, Medicare and Medicaid spending grew from $28 million to $256 million. The dramatic expansion of healthcare expenditures resulted in "an immense medical research establishment" of scientifically advanced hospitals and community health centers, "comprising one of the nation's largest industries." [10]

The expansion of the industry, of course, required more employees, and those employees required ever more extensive training in their respective technical, service, and professional occupations. Already by 1973, wrote an industry analyst, technological sophistication required highly skilled personnel "who, in turn, want correspondingly higher wages." The Fair Labor Standards Act of 1967 required hospitals to pay "premium wages for overtime," and other personnel costs—hospitalization, outpatient benefits, family coverage, vacation and holiday benefits, training—were high on the agendas of the "aggressive unionization" campaigns by 1199 and other healthcare unions. In part, that aggressive posture was driven by a structural shift between the 1960s and 1980s, away from organizing in the shrinking industrial sector and toward white-collar professional and service occupations. "Faced with its own waning strength and influence," said historian Barbara Melosh, "organized labor began to look to these new and active constituencies." Melosh put particular emphasis on the intersection of the civil rights and women's movements with healthcare unionism, factors around which 1199 was historically well positioned to build. Traditionally underrepresented workers, whether in service, professional, technical, or clerical occupations, faced increasing pressures associated with the technological requirements and routinization of work in a competitive environment. Union representation was a "mechanism that might gain them a degree of control over the work environment," providing in equal measure more respect, a better standard of living, and a clear voice for improving the quality of patient care.[11]

Union avoidance consultants warned hospital administrators that women workers, especially, who comprised roughly three-quarters of the nation's healthcare employees, "are beginning to look at unions as the possible solutions to some of the unique problems they *feel they face as women workers*, including equal pay, comparable worth, sex harassment, pregnancy-related benefits, and child care" (italics added). Jessica Wilkerson wrote that poor and working-class Appalachian women "bore responsibility for caregiving in their communities." They lived in a society "that assigned them that social position through institutions, culture, and law." Many women working in the Appalachian healthcare industry concluded they could optimize the quality of care they provided for their expanded community of patients and coworkers by building a union to help resolve their "unique problems."[12]

The industrial harmony envisioned by advocates of the 1974 healthcare amendments did not materialize. Whatever gains 1199 made after 1974 were not cultivated in a garden of mutual peace. As healthcare unions mobilized in anticipation of new organizing campaigns, industry analysts cautioned hospital administrators that the major consequence of a union contract is the lessening of managerial control. Management professor Jonathon Rakich surmised that the "perceived threat of unionization of hospitals" presented hospital personnel management with two possible options: the first was an adversarial environment based on "conflict and confrontation." The second was a "collaborative and cooperative relationship" designed to allow the "employee and the organization a chance to accomplish objectives together," persuading workers to internalize "a sense of obligation to the organization." Ideally, this sense of obligation would undermine the appeal of unions, so management would be spared "the repulsive thought that management will lose control of the operation of the institution."[13]

In the 1950s and 1960s, the strength of organized labor insulated millions of workers, union and nonunion, from the type of employer assaults and intimidation that had marked an earlier generation. According to many labor economists, powerful corporations and powerful unions in basic industries negotiated a post–World War II "labor-management accord" or "social compact" anchored by industrywide collective bargaining agreements that had a ripple effect, benefiting all working families and communities. In exchange for retention of managerial control of production and business matters, corporate executives consented to generous compensation packages for their employees. If the accord broke down, serious consequences, like the 116-day 1959 steel strike, could occur, but eventually a settlement would restore industrial peace. Advocates of the social compact consensus therefore claimed that the rise of vigorous management resistance to unionism in the 1970s, prelude to a frontal assault against labor in the 1980s, was a departure from established labor relations.[14]

Labor rights activist and historian Kim Moody believes that the enlightened industrial relations ethos of the social compact was overstated, and indeed many analysts have challenged the social compact consensus in recent years.[15] Moody contends that the American labor accord of the 1950s was embraced by corporate leaders because it was a weak alternative to the more thoroughly social democratic industrial relations in Western Europe. "American capital," he argues, "has never accepted unions or collective bargaining." The Taft-Hartley Act laid the foundation for a more sophisticated framework of "union avoidance" than that of the pre–New Deal era, and American businesses' "fundamental opposition to worker organization . . . with only the rarest of exceptions, has been and remains a constant in US industrial relations." The post-Vietnam decline of the U.S. industrial sector also weakened the labor movement, allowing businesses' fundamental antiunionism free rein. Industrial relations specialist John Logan claimed that by the mid-1980s, more than three-quarters of employers facing organizing campaigns brought in union-avoidance consultants. The multimillion-dollar industry "has not only enabled employers to resist unionization; it has also allowed them to undermine union strength or unload existing unions."[16]

The hard fights waged by 1199 in Appalachia after 1974 support Moody's national thesis on a regional scale. As noted in the opening chapter, 1199WV and 1199KY merged in 1980; in 1982, 1199 in southern Ohio joined these two and established 1199WV/KY/OH. From 1974 until the 1989 merger with the Service Employees International Union, in practically every campaign 1199 ran, it faced determined management opposition. If workers won an election and signed a first contract, they had better expect and prepare for redoubled opposition when contract expiration approached. In 1977 at Cabell Huntington Hospital, in 1981 at Highlands Regional Medical Center in Kentucky, and in 1987 at Fairmont General Hospital in West Virginia, the employers forced strikes with the intention of breaking the union that their workers had built in the mid-to-late 1970s. Much of the rest of this study will examine the contexts of such conflicts.

Martin Levitt made a fortune working for Modern Management Methods (3M), the most powerful management consulting firm in the country. In 1993 Levitt released a penitential memoir of his work at 3M entitled *Confessions of a Union Buster*. He documented the alarm that plagued healthcare managers as their workers turned to unionization:

> During the 1960s administrators of hospitals and nursing homes across the country watched with horror as their housekeepers, cooks, and

nurses' aides took to the streets by the thousands in virulent protest of the poverty and indignity imposed on them by their employers. In 1974, with the blessing of the American Hospital Association, which wanted to end the devastating chaos within its industry, President Nixon signed the NLRA amendment into law, giving employees at the nonprofits the right to collective bargaining.

Then the union-busting door burst open. Although 1199 and other unions had organized a great number of nonprofits before passage of the law, the amendment acted as a catalyst of fear on hospital administrators, particularly those in charge of small facilities where workers had felt they didn't have the strength in numbers to force union recognition, as did workers in huge hospitals. [The various areas and districts of] Local 1199 filed thousands of organizing petitions in the wake of the 1974 amendment. That, of course, meant thousands of jobs for anti-union consultants.[17]

Union avoidance campaigns could be directed by pricey consulting firms such as 3M, by local or nearby law firms with labor relations or labor law specialists on staff, or independently by hospital or nursing home administrators who could rely on the ready availability of antiunion strategies found in guidebooks and industry literature. Medical professional associations and trade journals sponsored supervisory and management conferences and seminars that featured sessions on union avoidance. *Hospital Topics* and other journals featured prescriptive articles with titles like "Employee Participation as an Alternative to Unions," "Chronology of a Hospital Union Campaign," "Health Care Labor Relations Today," "Unionization in Hospitals: Causes, Effects, and Preventive Strategies," "Union Avoidance in Hospitals," and "How to Preserve the Union-Free Status of Your Facility by Practicing Preventive Labor Relations." For employers in a unionized facility, how-to-guides for getting rid of the union were accessible, including *How to De-Certify a Union: The Procedural and Practical Guidebook to Decertification*, by Memphis-based management lawyer Ted Yeiser.[18]

In testimony before a subcommittee of the Committee on Education and Labor in 1979, Alan Kistler of the AFL-CIO identified management consultants as "the new technicians of a new movement for totalitarian control." Professional associations and universities, said Kistler, train management representatives to "exploit the fears of workers and convert those fears into a rejection of collective bargaining." He estimated that labor-management consultants were involved in two-thirds of all NLRB elections. At the same hearing, Robert Muhlenkamp documented in minute detail the campaigns run by 3M against 1199 locals in Uniontown, Pennsylvania; Kenosha, Wisconsin; and at a half-dozen other facilities in Wisconsin, Ohio, and Maine. In all of the 1199 districts, he concluded, workers in recognition drives and contract negotiations were confronted by "delay, intimidation, saturation propaganda campaigns, efforts to destroy rank-and-file leadership by transfer, promotion, firing or character assassination; and efforts to control local mass media and politicians." [19] Labor organizer William Roel contended that healthcare managers attended labor-management seminars to reinforce a "network of opposition" to unions. He also commented that decertification drives had "reached a level I never dreamed would exist." Looking over the list of individuals attending the consultants' seminars, one does not find only names of representatives from plants or hospitals which are not organized, but also finds names of lower, middle, and sometimes upper-management people who have had contracts in their plants and hospitals for a long time. [20]

As if to demonstrate Roel's point, the union at Butler County Memorial Hospital in Pennsylvania, which Kay Tillow had helped organize for 1199P in the early 1970s, faced a relentless cycle of decertification campaigns between 1974 and 1978. Monsignor Charles Rice, a prolabor but self-confessed and repentant Red Scare–era red-baiting priest from Pittsburgh, wrote that 1199P "was the victim of a shrewd but heavy-handed decertification drive" by hospital management. The Butler local defeated decertification in 1974 and again in 1978, by a thin margin. The hospital demanded another vote on the grounds that the NLRB's election officer was late (by ten minutes, according to Msgr. Rice) for the balloting. The board conceded and ordered a new election in six months, by which time "fifty new workers were hired and captive audience meetings held." Management stonewalled on a new contract and allegedly promised workers a "retroactive raise" if they voted to decertify. On March 2, 1979, 1199P was decertified at Butler—by fifty votes. The employer was represented by "the well-known union-busting law firm of Reed, Smith, Shaw, and McClay." A dejected Msgr. Rice claimed that the board's "incredible rulings" for the hospital proved that it had become "almost a management tool." [21]

The language of employer antiunion propaganda in 1199's West Virginia and eastern Kentucky campaigns was so interchangeable one might assume that all of the administrators attended the same seminars. It might be moderate and paternalistic, or it might indulge in character assassination and intimidation. The tactics, entreaties, and veiled threats were so nearly uniform from hospital to hospital that the union's organizers sometimes appeared prophetic to new members. Hospital administrators "did everything possible to try to turn us against the union," said Larry Daniels, a medical technician at Highlands Regional Medical Center when he and others approached 1199 in 1975. Highlands Regional hired a well-known consulting and security firm, Southeastern Employers Service Corporation (SESCO), to beat the union. "I think this union-busting consulting firm thought the people in eastern Kentucky were just dumb hillbillies," said Daniels. "They thought they had their strategy down pat, that we'd vote no." But Daniels and his coworkers absorbed their own lessons in "consultant avoidance," under the tutelage of Dan Stewart, their chief organizer. "Dan Stewart was brilliant," said Daniels a quarter-century later. "I could never figure out how he knew what management was up to before they did it. And I asked him one day, 'How do you know?' 'Well,' he said, 'I've been through this before. Once you know the strategy of a union buster you've got it down.' "[22] What follows are common tactics of union avoidance campaigns against 1199 in the period covered in this study:

- Send a letter to employees explaining the hospital's position on unions and card signing
- Inform the workers that they should avoid "union salesmen"
- Advise supervisors and department heads as to the reasons the hospital should remain "union free"
- Inform workers that the hospital prefers to deal with them directly, as independent individuals, rather than through an outside "third party"
- Inform workers that a union will mean strikes, picket line duty, monthly union dues, and strike assessments, even for strikes at other hospitals
- Tell workers that the hospital will provide better wages and benefits than a union contract will
- Tell workers they may lose their jobs in the event of an economic strike because the law permits the hospital to hire permanent replacements during economic strikes
- Tell workers they may be ordered around by a few militant coworkers who want power for themselves
- Praise "loyal" workers who reject unionism
- Tell them that union dues will go into the pockets of "labor fat cats"
- Portray the union as violent and "strike-happy"
- Suggest that a union in a hospital will imperil the well-being of patients. This factor is an element of "Nightingalism," or self-sacrifice, invoked by hospital or nursing home management whenever nurses or nurses' aides contemplate a work stoppage. This is further explored in chapter 6.

- Tell them that unions do not value rewarding individual merit
- Tell workers that the friendly relations through which employees and management handle complaints will disappear
- Require small group and one-on-one meetings to lobby against the union
- [In dealing with 1199, it was common for employers to emphasize the Communist history of Leon Davis, the SDS affiliation of Woodruff and Stewart, and send a message that the National 1199 was primarily a union for racial minorities in "urban settings"][23]

Cabell Huntington was a public hospital with approximately three hundred beds when Tom Woodruff began handing out union leaflets and sign-up cards in August of 1974. At the time, Woodruff was volunteering for the union while still working with the Appalachian Movement Press, but by the late fall of 1974 he had joined the National Union staff as a full-time organizer. Making first contact with workers by leafleting is now usually seen as archaic and inefficient, and even in 1974 it was not often practiced by 1199. But since Cabell Huntington was just down the street from the local's Huntington office, leafleting seemed a logical step. "You wouldn't organize that way today" says Woodruff, but "we got a good response. Probably a week after, you know, we had one or two meetings with workers quickly, [and] within a week or ten days—the strategy was to call a meeting, get volunteers as a committee, send people back in to sign more cards, pull back for a meeting as long as you were expanding."[24]

Anna (Davis) Jenkins was just short of eighteen when she went to work at Cabell Huntington in 1962, starting out in Food Services and retiring as a histology technician forty-two years later. She had been working in a laundry near the hospital for $0.67 an hour ($5.68). After three months on that job, she crossed the street to Cabell Huntington during a lunch break and started her new job that afternoon; "That's how easy it was to get a job." Her pay was $0.86 an hour ($7.29) and "I thought I was rich." Jenkins recalled that on her first day at work, the supervisor in Food Services "looked at me and she said, 'You don't have any objection to working with Black people, do you? We have to hire 'em.' That's what she said. I said 'no.' "[25] African Americans made up about 5 percent of the hospital's workforce.

Jenkins's father had a union job at American Car and Foundry (ACF) in Huntington, an East Third Avenue railway car manufacturer founded in 1872, which in 1962 employed over fifteen hundred workers. Jenkins was well aware of the type of purchasing power, security, and respect a union contract could guarantee. She also knew that cultural and racial biases had to give way to class solidarity in order for a union to be effective.

> The big difference is respect. Everyone wants to be treated with respect. That's the biggest thing a union can give you, respect. The union gave us a voice to stand up for yourself, and other people. Without a union you don't have that. Before the union, myself and everyone else was treated like dirt. We didn't get raises—if you got a raise, it was a "merit raise." In other words, if the boss liked you, you got a raise. If the boss didn't like you, you didn't get a raise. It didn't matter what kind of work you'd done.[26]

When she ran into Tom Woodruff outside the hospital in late summer of 1974 she was working as a nurses' aide. She had just received a good evaluation and was due an automatic pay raise, which she did not get. She complained to the nursing supervisor who, as Jenkins recalled, told her " 'Well, Miss Davis'—I was Miss Davis at the time—'if you're not satisfied, find other employment.' That's what she said to me. The *next day* Tom Woodruff was standing out back passing out union cards—timing couldn't have been better. And he said 'Do you want a card?' and I said, 'Give me a whole damn handful.' "[27]

Woodruff and the early membership assumed that Cabell Huntington was covered under the 1974 amendment. Hospital spokespeople were telling them otherwise, and research at the County Courthouse revealed that "in fact the members of the [hospital Board of Trustees] were appointed by a number of organizations including the city and the county, and there was enough of a public connection" to support the hospital's contention that it was not a private hospital. When the hospital and the union consulted with the NLRB, the board agreed with the trustees that Cabell Huntington was indeed "a government instrumentality" and exempt from the NLRA.[28]

Thus began a six-month-long struggle by 1199WV to pressure the Board of Trustees to authorize an election. Union supporters adopted a strategy of mobilizing pressure from the public and from other local unions in, at that time, a heavily unionized community. As many as sixty-five union loyalists packed each monthly meeting of the Board of Trustees. Over one hundred Cabell Huntington employees "jammed Huntington City Council chambers" October 19, successfully lobbying the council to adopt a resolution calling upon the hospital trustees to schedule an election. At the October 21 meeting of the Board of Trustees, however, the hospital's lawyer, William Beatty, assured the trustees that they were under no obligation ever to deal with the union unless they adopted a policy to do that. At that time, the trustees voted 8 to 2 not to recognize the union or agree to a meeting to talk about a consent election. The dissenting votes were cast by Wilbirt Ward, who was appointed to the board by the Huntington District Labor Council, and Charles Spurlock, appointed by the AFL-CIO. These two were immediately charged by another trustee for "conflict of interest." Board president Paul Pancake announced that the hospital was in the midst of adopting personnel policies to "improve employee conditions" without "turning the job over to a third party." Anticipating such an argument, a basic educational objective of 1199 for new members was to convince them that "there are only two parties: there are bosses and there are workers, and when the workers unite they have a union and there still are two parties— there are bosses and there are workers who are now united." [29]

The refusal of the trustees to approve an election elicited a charge of hypocrisy from 1199 member Manton Speaks, who pointed out that other public employees in the city, including sanitation workers and city clerks, had secured the right to elections from their agencies. Speaks claimed that his union would be "taking our cause to the people of our community in an attempt to persuade the trustees to respect our rights and the democratic process." Speaks hoped there would not be any interruption of services at the hospital, "but we feel that in their irresponsibility," the trustees "are forcing us into this course of action." [30] True to his promise, a seventy-five-member organizing committee at Cabell Huntington developed a plan to leverage community pressure on the trustees to hold an election. A local newspaper conceded that the hospital trustees had historically operated Cabell Huntington as a "closed corporation," responsible to no one, "least of all the public." At the same time, the paper castigated organized labor for focusing on public employees, particularly hospital workers, as "prime targets." Invoking "third-partyism," the paper charged that the union movement at Cabell Huntington "hardly has been spontaneous but rather has been carefully orchestrated by professional union organizers." An implication that poorly paid and overworked employees in a "closed corporation" would act only at the urging of outsider agitation was clear. [31]

Act they did. The Cabell Huntington organizing committee, working with Woodruff and Dan Stewart, helped out by Larry Harless, set out to solidify public support. The Huntington Ministerial Association joined in a resolution by the City Council and the County Court calling for an election, urging the Board of Trustees to bargain in good faith if the union should win. At a time when nearly one-third of West Virginia's workers were unionized, the Cabell Huntington committee had endorsements from Huntington's AFL-CIO Labor Council, the International Brotherhood of Electrical Workers Local 317, United Steelworkers Locals 37 and 40, the American Federation of State, County, and Municipal Employees (AFSCME), the Fraternal Order of Police, the International Firefighters Association, the International Ladies Garment Workers Union, and others of the city's more than twenty unions. The membership also hearkened back to the White Pantry days by picketing local businesses operated by members of the Board of Trustees, notably the real estate office of Paul Pancake.[32]

> Well, we had an aggressive campaign with the trustees; that thing went from October to February month-to-month, and I don't remember all those votes, but it started like 10 to 2 against us, then it might have gone 9 to 4 and 8 to 6 and then we finally flipped it, and a lot of that was just pressure, you know, we picketed in front of Pancake Realty— he never flipped. We kept the pressure on, you know, we went to City Council, they passed a resolution supporting the right to vote, we went to County Commission, they passed a resolution to support—now all that took political work, you know, there was opposition; the workers were very actively involved, we'd take 150 people to the City Council meeting, or the County Commission meeting, we did all the political work. I think we might have eventually got the support of the newspaper on the right to vote.[33]

The organizing committee was particularly effective in refuting the hospital administration's effort to cast 1199WV as outsiders. Bringing civic groups, municipal governing bodies, churches, and other unions into the campaign put the hospital in the awkward position of labeling a healthy cross-section of Huntington's people as third parties. Recruiting supporters not only from inside the hospital but also from the neighborhoods where they lived, shopped, and worshipped established the unionists as part of a "whole people" rather than as a special interest. As the mobilization campaign gathered momentum, the employer made several overtures to its workers in mid-November in an attempt to weaken the union's case. Recently hired administrator Kenneth Wood promised pay raises for all 850 employees at Cabell Huntington. Wood also promised a "merit pay" pool, extended sick leave, a wage-differential policy for night shift and on-call work, and "a new grievance procedure so employees can discuss their problems without fear of reprisal" (from whom, he didn't say). Without elaborating, Wood claimed that the Board of Trustees had "activated a new philosophy toward personnel administration," then proceeded to insist that "we simply don't want to deal with our employees through a third bargaining agent." Wood accurately claimed that several of these enhancements had been under consideration by the trustees since August, but Woodruff pointed out that the plan had only been revealed to the workers after they began signing union cards.[34]

Wood's entreaties did little to fend off public pressure to allow Cabell Huntington workers a choice. The perception that the hospital was a "closed corporation" was not likely to change if its employees were denied this fundamental democratic right, a point the union and its backers repeatedly made in the papers and at public meetings. Mayor Harold Frankel, an ex officio member of the Board of Trustees, urged the board to hold an election on these grounds. The organizing committee published a broadside in the local papers with "Some Open Questions for the Cabell-Huntington Board of Trustees," invoking "the American Way." In a democracy, how could seven board members deny the right to vote to the people who kept the hospital running and took care of Huntington's sick and injured? Seven people (this was after the board voted 7 to 5 against the election at its November 25 meeting) "who claim to be public officials refuse to do what the public wants. This certainly is not democracy!" The board's recalcitrance—in total, the trustees rejected an election four times—frustrated the editors of the *Herald-Dispatch*. Making clear that the paper did not think highly of unionized public employees, especially in a hospital, the editors nevertheless could not justify denying workers the right to vote. Cabell Huntington workers "are deluded when they think that by unionizing they're going to solve all their problems," the paper warned, ignoring the fact that no worker thought that. But, even without a legal obligation to hold an election, the hospital board had "a clear moral obligation to grant the [organizing] committee's request for an election."[35]

Perhaps sensing that the trustees were wavering, Kenneth Wood claimed he had a letter from ninety employees who wanted nothing to do with a union. The Cabell Huntington medical staff opposed a union vote in a January 16 resolution. But at last the Board of Trustees realized that the union was not going away and, as Woodruff said, "would continue to apply pressure every way possible." The board approved an election at its January 1975 meeting, with the caveat that supervisors be included in the voting unit. Woodruff protested and remarked that "there was no way supervisory people could be represented by Local 1199," and the organizing committee rejected this condition outright. On February 17 the trustees approved an election without supervisors, to be monitored by the American Arbitration Association. The 10 to 2 vote was decisive, but there was still a catch, to which the union reluctantly agreed.[36]

From the beginning of 1199WV's Cabell Huntington campaign it was apparent that the broadest support for a union was with the service and maintenance workers, the licensed practical nurses, and the technicians. It was for these units that the union petitioned for an election, but before finally acquiescing the Board of Trustees insisted that *all* nonsupervisory employees be included in the election, expanding the number of eligible voters from 450 to over 800. Was this maneuver adopted to cut into 1199's chance for a majority, or simply as a tribute to democracy? Woodruff was unaware of the "behind the scenes politickin' [sic] of the board members," but noted "it's logical to believe that the administration of the hospital wanted to stack it as much as it could." If the organizing committee objected to this arrangement, even though one of the purposes of the bargaining unit structure was to prevent such "stacking," it would have to explain denying the right to vote to hundreds of workers. Objection to the sweeping eligibility provision was justifiable, says Woodruff, but "we'd been on a six-month campaign to give people the right to vote." Trying to argue about "such inside baseball" in order to *prohibit* some workers from voting would most probably erode community support, and the trustees were adamant about including all nonsupervisory workers in the election. Better to persuade the registered nurses and clerical/technical workers who were now eligible to vote that their interests would best be served by union representation.[37]

As the April 2, 1975, election approached, the Cabell Huntington organizing committee redoubled efforts to recruit their coworkers. Stewart, Woodruff, and the rank-and-file members continued to identify and educate new leadership, committed to learning about every worker in every unit, "jumping on every mistake the boss makes," and distributing union buttons and self-produced flyers, newsletters, and song sheets with folk and labor songs adapted to the Cabell Huntington scene. Licensed Practical Nurse Judy Siders, responsible for the care of her mother and her three children on wages of $1.75 ($9.11) an hour, listened closely when Stewart and Woodruff outlined the benefits the workers could demand if they were unified—especially better wages and hospitalization insurance. Siders had been "kind of bashful when I started working there" in 1970. "I wouldn't talk back to my charge nurse. She was sort of like a sergeant. After being there a week I thought I was in the army. I went out of there every day all tired and sometimes crying it was so bad . . . so when the union came around I was ready for them." Most of her fellow LPNs were afraid of losing their jobs, said Siders, but she listened to the organizers and "I believed them."

> Before the union if you wanted a weekend off you had to work ten straight days to get it; also the patient load. When they hand you ten patients, when eight of those patients can't do anything for themselves, are 'complete patients,' it's impossible to take good care of the patients. The [nurses'] aide helped a lot but we had to do a lot.
>
> Had it not been for the community we would probably not have been organized at all. We went to the churches and leafleted, put things

on the windshields of the people at the churches; talked to the ministers, told them our problems, of the hospital CEO salaries and how much we were not making.[38]

Siders approached coworkers in the cafeteria and furtively during breaks on her floor. "I hid behind a lot of doors. I still did my work but I hid behind a lot of doors and talked to a lot of people. I did a lot of talking. There were a lot of people in the situation that I was in." The National Union supplied the new Cabell Huntington local with some organizing funds. Dues would start being collected only if and when a contract took effect, and the National's contribution to expenses was sparse. "We rented a little shack down on Charleston Avenue and I think we paid about $60 or $70 a month rent, 'cause we didn't have any money." Interested workers would be recruited to attend meetings at the shack "to find people to help organize."[39]

The Cabell Huntington administration adopted an avoidance campaign that incorporated the bullet points from the industry's prescriptive literature. Workers received a "question and answer" pamphlet in their early March pay envelopes warning against the "rule from New York City." Many of the union's "demands" would destroy the hospital's ability to survive in a competitive industry. An economic strike could cost you your job. A collective bargaining contract will lead to a "loss of individual freedom to deal directly with administration." The employer repeatedly played the third-party card, as in a letter from Kenneth Wood to the employees dated only two days before the April 2 election, in which the administrator said, "I sincerely hope and trust that our current relationship will continue. It will be a sad day when we can no longer talk with each other and must communicate through an outside third party who is not even a member of our hospital family."[40]

Woodruff and Stewart believed that the hospital did "not a have a team of consultants to come in and really work the supervisors over," instead probably relying on a single consultant training administrative staff who in turn "worked their supervisors themselves." The membership suspected that the hospital was working with groups from Charleston and Columbus, perhaps professional hospital associations, to keep Cabell Huntington "union-free." They were also suspicious of a man whom Kenneth Wood had "pulled in" to be the hospital's new personnel director, rather than hiring a trusted female candidate with long experience at the hospital.[41]

Kenneth Wood's sad day came true when the hospital workers voted 389 to 327 to be represented by 1199WV, at the time the largest unit of hospital workers to ever vote union in the state. Voter turnout was very high at 93 percent, and it is highly likely that the approximately three hundred workers added to the initial service/maintenance and LPN units inflated the opposition total. The registered nurses (RNs) and technical and clerical workers whom the hospital had resolved to add to the original units had never shown much support for the union from the beginning. In fact, many of the RNs let it be known that they wanted no part of the union. This became a problem as 1199WV struggled to survive at Cabell Huntington.[42]

As the union's newly formed bargaining committee began negotiations with the employer, it appeared that the "family" Kenneth Wood spoke of was dysfunctional. It became obvious to the committee that the hospital was going to stonewall on the negotiations, perhaps with the intention of dragging them out until the union collapsed. After nearly four months of sporadic negotiations, the hospital finally agreed to a 3 percent wage increase, which the membership derided as "so unfair that it is ridiculous." At the same time the hospital laid off thirty-five workers without discussing layoff rules or procedure with the union. In a statement to the public, the union claimed, "There is a crisis at Cabell Huntington Hospital." The membership voted to strike and issued the required thirty-day strike notice, even though Woodruff believed a strike would be disastrous. The new Cabell Huntington chapter, with a long and stressful election campaign behind it, was losing its sense of internal unity as the contentious contract talks dragged on. Apparently, the employer concluded that getting the union to sign a weak agreement was less risky than a strike—an ineffective union very possibly could lose a decertification vote in two years. The two sides ultimately agreed to a "very mediocre two-year contract" with small wage increases and a grievance procedure. The union was not able to get an automatic dues checkoff agreement, so at least for the duration of the two-year contract the dues would have to be collected voluntarily from each member, a tiresome and draining burden. Woodruff later noted that owing to the difficulties with the inflated bargaining unit and the hospital's stonewalling, "people did very well to get a union at all."[43]

Other factors contributed to the union's acquiescence to a poor contract. The optimistic rush of organizing by 1199 and other healthcare unions in the wake of the 1974 law, as we have seen, was met by forcible management resistance. The "West Virginia campaign" of 1974–1975, begun with great expectations by Leon Davis and the West Virginia staff of only five organizers statewide (a new staffer, David Harrington, had joined Drake, Harless, Stewart, and Woodruff), stalled after the election win at Cabell Huntington. Consent elections were held at two major hospitals, Charleston Area Medical Center and United Hospital Center in Clarksburg, only days after Cabell Huntington, and at each of these the hospital management had waged "fierce, well-organized, total" resistance resulting in decisive losses for 1199WV. It is likely that these crushing disappointments shook the Cabell Huntington workers, contributing to the wavering morale suggested by Woodruff as their negotiations bogged down.[44]

The stress put on organizers and new members in this organizing wave— organizers typically put in sixteen-hour days and many members essentially took on a second (and unpaid) job in these situations—made 1199's universal battle cry of "organize or die" sound only slightly hyperbolic. The National Union's organizing report for 1975 observed that "as in the past in West Virginia, we spread ourselves too thin." It was in the aftermath of this period that Harless resigned from his job, removing the union's senior organizer from the field. But the beat rolled on—even as the Cabell Huntington members did the hard work of piecing together their first contract, Dan Stewart had answered a call from workers at Highlands Regional Medical Center in Prestonsburg, Kentucky. The union was about to embark on a new stage of growth, maturation, and management reaction.[45]

Cabell Huntington workers rally in front of the hospital during the 1977 contract renewal strike. (Photo by Lee Bernard. Courtesy of Huntington *Herald-Dispatch*)

President Arnold Miller and other UMWA officers join the Clinch Valley Hospital Clinic picket line during the 1973 first contract strike. (Courtesy of SEIU District 1199WV/KY/OH)

PROGRESS THROUGH STRUGGLE

The 1199 story in West Virginia, Kentucky and Ohio

A report on members in motion 1986-88.

District 1199WV/KY/OH's more than 8,000 members in over 40 chapters in West Virginia, Kentucky and Ohio have made immense gains in the past decade. It hasn't been easy. More and more, when people think of 1199 they think of health care workers involved in their union, pushing management for better pay and working conditions, pushing management for decent patient care, pushing management for respect and dignity on the job. It's paid off. Many of 1199WV/KY/OH's recent gains are summarized on the following pages.

Rally for West Virginia state employees near the capitol building in Charleston, 1986 or 1987. Larry Daniels of Highlands Regional Medical Center in front with sign. (From the "Progress through Struggle" brochure for members. Courtesy of SEIU District 1199WV/KY/OH)

Cincinnati members from nursing home and hospital locals, about 1983–1985. (Courtesy of SEIU District 1199WV/KY/OH)

Cincinnati members with iconic 1199 flags. (Courtesy of SEIU District 1199 WV/KY/OH)

Cabell Huntington striker, 1977. (Courtesy of *1199 News*, Larry Daniels, and SEIU District 1199WV/KY/OH)

Chapter 6

A Kentucky Saga and a Strike for Survival

Prestonsburg, Kentucky, established as the county seat of Floyd County in 1799, became a booming commercial center due to early steamboat traffic on the Big Sandy River. Following the familiar industrial pattern, the arrival of the Chesapeake and Ohio Railroad in 1904 placed Floyd County at the center of a flourishing modern timber and coal-producing region. Never densely populated, the town lost some citizens due to the mechanization of the coal industry in the 1950s. Its status as county seat moderated outmigration, however, as did its role as a service center for surrounding towns and hamlets. In 1964 the University of Kentucky opened a Community College branch in Prestonsburg, and the population stood at 3,422 in 1970. Highlands Regional Medical Center (HRMC) began operations in 1972 as a private not-for-profit facility with capacity for 150 patients. Highlands Regional, with over 300 employees, was a major employer in Prestonsburg.[1]

In early August of 1975, Jo Anna Martin (later Risner), a licensed practical nurse at Highlands Regional, received a letter and a couple of leaflets from New York City, setting in motion a sequence of events that changed the lives of her and her coworkers forever. The material came from Robert Muehlenkamp, assistant director of organizing for the National Union. Muehlenkamp informed Martin that "tens of thousands of hospital workers in twenty-two states" had joined 1199 in the past year. He encouraged Martin to talk to employees in the different departments of the hospital and contact him if the workers at Highlands Regional were interested in organizing.[2]

Jo Anna Martin was born in prison in 1938. Her mother was incarcerated in the new Kentucky Correctional Institution for Women near Peewee Valley in Shelby County, sentenced for shooting her drunken husband to death when he began beating her. Three months pregnant at the time, Martin's mother pleaded self-defense and was sentenced to "two or three years." Martin believed the only reason her mother was imprisoned was because the judge thought she would be safe from her dead husband's relatives, who had sworn they would kill her. Martin grew up in Salyersville, Kentucky, and earned a practical nursing degree from Mayo Vocational School in Paintsville. After working at a UMWA hospital in South Williamson, Kentucky, and at a Paintsville nursing home and clinic, she went to work at HRMC when it opened in 1972.[3]

Martin had written to the National Union concerning grievances she and her coworkers had about working conditions at the hospital. She had complained to supervisors on several occasions about being undercompensated for overtime work. She and other LPNs and nurses' aides were pressured to work double shifts, with a clear implication that noncooperation could lead to dismissal. Martin recalled one stretch in which she worked two shifts for thirty-six consecutive days. When she appealed for some time off, her supervisor answered with a common insult at HRMC: "I was working two shifts. I was working the day shift on the fourth floor and hoot owl shift on the second floor. That's from 11 to 7. That's when nobody's up but the hoot owls. And so I worked the hoot owl shift and the day shift and they had me working 36 days, two shifts, without a day off and when I would complain about it they told me, well, if I didn't like it, don't let the door hit my ass as I left."

Martin's moment of truth came when she arrived a few minutes late for a fourth-floor day shift after completing paperwork on a patient who had died on her second-floor night shift: "The charge nurse told me I would be docked for being late and I had a fit, of course. So when she told me if you don't like it don't let the front door hit my ass as I left, and I looked at her and said 'You have told me that for the last time. You can be rest assured that something will be done that you will not tell me that anymore. I will guarantee you that.'"

Although the hospital administrator at the time, a Mr. Frasier, intervened to relieve Martin of the crush of double shifts, the practice continued with other nurses. The exhausting schedule, compounding what Martin described as a complete lack of appreciation from the employer for the workers, finally got Martin thinking about a union: "I had a girlfriend [Brenda] who worked as a ward clerk there at the hospital and she [had] worked in Baltimore, Maryland, at Johns-Hopkins and 1199 had represented them, and she was telling me about 1199 and I asked her if she thought that 1199 would come to Prestonsburg at Highlands and represent us, and she didn't seem to think so. She didn't seem to think they would come to a small place like this."

Dismissing her friend's skepticism, and unaware that 1199WV was already active in bordering West Virginia, Martin contacted the National Union directly, telling only Brenda. Martin was confident that if the union would commit to sending a representative to Prestonsburg, many of her coworkers would want to hear the union's message. Muehlenkamp's letter encouraged her to "call us collect" if she was able to identify coworkers "who actively want to organize." Risner was aware that nearly all of their families had union histories; "They knew all about unions from the coal mines. So, I talked to a few of the girls that I knew were good, strong backbone girls that would stand up for themselves and the other people."

Martin visited the various hospital departments, talking with workers she knew as respected organic leaders among their coworkers, individuals "that people paid attention to and listened to, kind of the carrier of that department. I talked with each one of them and told them what I had done and told them that I had gotten an answer and told them that representation was on the way and they were like me. They were in awe that this would really happen." [4]

As Martin canvassed the employees, a large majority of whom were women, widespread discontent with the overall administration of the hospital and its new administrator, Gene Divine, became evident. Workers harbored muted but growing resentment over basic issues of respect from supervisors and specific employment practices under Divine, including poor wages, cutbacks on personal and sick days, inadequate medical coverage, and no pension plan. "What little we had he was trying to take away," according to Medical Technician Larry Daniels. "We had no voice at all."

> We would ask for these things. We would ask for a pension plan to be established at our hospital and they would say, "Well, okay, we're working on one." And we'd say, "Well, how long will it take you to work on getting us a pension plan?" And they'd say, "Well, six months." And we'd say, "Okay, great." Well, six months we'd wait and go back and say, "Well, your six months is up. Where do we stand? What is the status of our pension plan?" And they'd say, "Well, we're still working on it, but it's going to take a little bit longer." And we'd say, "How much longer?" And they'd say, "Six more months." So, we just kept playing these games. [5]

"We had some choices to make at Highlands Regional Medical Center," said Daniels, whose father worked as a coal miner for Island Creek Coal for over forty years, covered by UMWA contracts. "We either had to quit our jobs or we had to stay here and fight this person." Daniels echoed Martin's recollection of the management rejoinder "don't let the door hit you on the way out." "That was like fighting words to us," he said. "That really got us kind of riled up." Most of the employees were longtime residents of and had family in the Prestonsburg area. They had homes and working spouses and children or grandchildren in local schools. They anticipated staying at HRMC for their entire working lives, "so we decided to fight back." [6]

Encouraged by the feedback she got from her coworkers, Martin called

Muehlenkamp and asked him to send a union representative to meet with them. They booked a banquet room in Prestonsburg's Plantation Motel, whose management was prounion and supported their objective. "Everyone was union in the area," said Daniels, although unionized hospital workers were "just unheard of." But "the UMWA was already here. The American Standard [plant] was organized. West Virginia/Kentucky Gas company was organized. Of course, the railroad had their own union structure. So everybody up and down our highway was union at that time." The Plantation Motel meeting began at 3:00 on a sweltering August afternoon. An estimated two hundred workers and family members packed the banquet room, with some people "crawling through the windows to get in because there were so many standing at the doorway that they couldn't get in the doors." "Whenever two hundred people get together," said Daniels, "something is bad wrong."[7]

Unaware that 1199WV even existed, the crowd was expecting an organizer from New York City. Muehlenkamp had directed Dan Stewart to meet with the HRMC group and, typical of usual first contacts, Stewart expected a small delegation. "I will never forget this guy's face when he opened the door" and saw the crowd, said Daniels. "He opened the door and he about fell backwards because he thought he was coming down to talk to two or three people." Stewart soon overcame his initial shock and, in spite of what had to be a chaotic, albeit energizing confluence of questions, comments, and possibly argument, out of the Plantation Motel meeting came a consensus that 1199, specializing as it did in representing healthcare workers, should be invited to help organize HRMC. Learning that the 1199WV local was not far removed in New York City, had been at work in neighboring West Virginia for five years, and that the workers at Cabell Huntington were in the midst of their contract negotiations after a hard-won struggle for recognition convinced the Highlands Regional workers that 1199WV could probably be trusted. Workers were impressed that Stewart made clear that the National Union and 1199WV would work with them but they would be expected to run their own local. Ward Clerk Penny Burchett remembered that she and others at the meeting went from being scared about even being there to "being really excited" about the prospect of building a union. "It was just a real good atmosphere," she said.[8]

From the Plantation Motel and subsequent small meetings, a core of rank-and-file organizers coalesced, including Martin, Burchett, Daniels, Pat Stambaugh, Garnet Cox, and a half-dozen others who set out to build their local. They encouraged their coworkers to wear union badges en masse, as a sign to the employer that worker solidarity was widespread. "They couldn't fire all of us at one time," said Martin. "We put our little badges on and wore them so proudly. We got the cards signed and had our badges on and, of course, they brought in the union busters. . . . We started writing poems and nursery rhymes and we posted them up everywhere. We put them up on ceilings. You'd open up a cabinet door and there'd be a sign."[9]

In late August, the chapter organizing committee requested voluntary recognition from the employer at HRMC. Jo Anna Martin, acting for the new local's Press and Public Relations Committee, reported that they also filed an election petition with the NLRB regional office in Cincinnati, in the likely event that the hospital would deny their recognition plea. As expected, administrator Gene Divine rejected their request, preferring instead a secret ballot election "with all parties fully informed." Divine declared that affordable and "high-grade" medical services for HRMC's five-county service area would best be served if the hospital remained nonunion. "All discussions and actions related to the unionization move," he said, would be handled by the hospital's attorney, Phil Damron.[10]

The hospital administrators immediately embarked on a textbook union avoidance campaign, but they met resistance at every turn. Phil Damron secured preelection hearing delays from the NLRB three times, the objective being to erode the union's initial momentum. Finally, a group of workers publicly announced a bus trip to march on the NLRB regional office in Cincinnati. On the eve of their trip, word came from the board that the election was scheduled for November 13. Jo Anna Martin collected the management's antiunion leaflets in a paper bag with the intention of delivering it as "1199's trash" to Divine's office. Her supervisor intervened and demanded that she relinquish her trash bag; when Martin refused, she was suspended. About a dozen of her coworkers began collecting their own antiunion "trash" to empty in Divine's office. Martin was hastily reinstated, and her coworkers took up a collection to cover her missed shifts. Garnet Cox and Ollie Sweeney were promised substantial pay raises if they would abandon the union; they immediately reported the bribe attempt to their coworkers, to the embarrassment of the bosses. Penny Burchett recalled the union's tactic for resisting group "captive meetings," conducted by supervisors, under the tutelage of Southeastern Employers Service Organization, management consultants ("union busters," said Daniels and Burchett), from Bristol, Tennessee. "We always had someone planted in the [meetings], you know, who would give the high sign that it's time for everybody to get up and leave," said Burchett. "Somebody would say, 'Let's go,' and everybody would just get up and leave the room." The captive meetings stopped.[11]

At the time the Highlands Regional campaign got under way, 1199WV did not represent any workers in the state of Kentucky. The employer attempted to capitalize on the Prestonsburg community's unfamiliarity with the union by consistently invoking the "third-party" argument, including charges that the New York Local 1199 had a history of violent strikes, Communist Party ties, and being a "nigger union," according to several HRMC members. "Their big thing was there's no blacks in this area, very few now, I mean, even in 1998," said Burchett. "There's very few blacks in this area and there were almost no blacks in 1975, so their big thing was 'Do you all really want to belong to a black union? This is a black union.' . . . They would show us pictures of Leon Davis addressing an entire black caucus of people," a tactic suggesting black domination of the union, and "that would really offend me because I never think like that or believe like that," said Daniels. This ploy fell especially flat with the workers, he continued, as it was one of many such devices that Stewart and their contacts at Cabell Huntington had warned them about.[12]

Newspapers in Prestonsburg and Paintsville ran several stories identifying 1199 as a "militant union," a coded message implying "dangerous black people." The papers also ran sensationalized accounts of strikes by the New York local, alleging "assaults on physicians and medical transport trucks attempting to service the strike-bound institutions." This story was paired with one reporting a peaceable arrest of Dan Stewart during a spontaneous rally in the hospital parking lot, as he was "reading to workers a review of their rights." With television cameras "whirring," Kentucky state troopers summoned by the employer escorted the organizer to jail. Highlands Regional acted within the law in having Stewart removed from its property but apparently did not foresee that the arrest of a union organizer for reading about workers' rights, when played on the evening news, might not go over too well in a region that was densely populated by United Mine Workers, Teamsters, and United Steel Workers. A UMWA member, in fact, followed Stewart to jail and posted his bond.[13]

As the election approached, the organizing committee recruited members for an informal speakers' bureau to have teach-ins with local community organizations and other union meetings, getting particularly strong support from UMWA Local 30. Martin claimed that despite the hospital's plea to local ministers to tell their congregations that "God didn't want us to have a union," most did not talk antiunionism from the pulpit. They rejected the administrators, Martin said, telling them that "only the people who worked there knew what was needed to be done."[14]

About a week before the November 13 NLRB election, the *Floyd County Times* carried a feature story from the *New York Times* documenting a strike by the New York 1199 that idled thirty thousand hospital workers and necessitated the transfer of patients from several struck facilities. Workers had walked off the job to protest the refusal of President Nixon's Cost of Living Council to authorize a 7.5 percent pay increase under terms of a new contract.

Yet Richard Nixon had been out of office for over a year by November 1975, and the council had disbanded before his resignation in 1974. Remarkably, the Floyd County paper ran a *1973* story one week before the 1975 election at Highlands Regional, dramatizing the disruption associated with the New York strike, as if it were a contemporaneous event.[15]

Stewart responded with a letter to the Paintsville and Prestonsburg papers, pointing out the time warp and charging that the story had been planted by the management at Highlands Regional. As specified in 1974's Public Law 93-360, he explained, a hospital strike in the NLRB system could legally transpire only after a union's adherence to a complex progression of notices and "cooling off" periods. Stewart wrote, accurately, that in any event the New York incident had "absolutely no relation to our [1199K] organizing campaign." In short, Stewart was charging Highlands Regional with calculated scare tactics just before the union vote. The hospital management, he wrote, not the HRMC employees, "are the only people talking strike." The union, on the other hand, was looking forward to a fair election and, if successful, the beginning of good-faith bargaining. He accused the newspapers with betraying their public trust "by placing stories from long ago and far away" in its columns.[16]

The election on November 13, held during morning and afternoon shifts in the hospital's second-floor lounge, drew over 80 percent of the 259 union-eligible employees. Service and maintenance workers voted union 95 to 49, with LPNs and technicians voting 38 to 16 for 1199. The registered nurses voted 8 to 5 against. The kitchen staff voted union in spite of intense intimidation from their supervisors, according to Jo Anna Martin. "Despite the brainwashing and harassment, we stuck together," technician Rebecca Wells told *1199 News*. "The hospital really campaigned dirty, but we sent their union busters packing." Wells, Martin, Burchett, Daniels, and fifteen others then went to work on the bargaining committee.[17]

Contract talks began in December and continued for nearly three months. Negotiations stalled on several bargaining issues, including differences over wages, shift assignments, a grievance and arbitration structure, union concerns over subcontracting, a health and welfare plan, and union security. In several reports the local newspapers insisted that 1199K was holding out for a "closed shop." This accusation reflected either unintentional or willful ignorance, since closed shop provisions, meaning an employer cannot hire workers who are not already members in the union, were outlawed by Section 8(b)(2), a provision of the 1947 Taft-Hartley Act. For example, on March 10, the *Paintsville Herald* claimed that "one of the key issues apparently is the union demand for a 'closed shop,' in which all present and future employees in union classifications would be required to join the union." What the newspaper actually described was a "union shop," in which new hires are required to join the union after a probationary period and to maintain their membership as a condition of employment. An "agency shop" is one in which individuals may opt out of union membership but must pay a periodic fee for the benefits of union representation. Still another variation, one favored by HRMC management, was a "maintenance of membership" agreement, in which no employee would be required to join the union but those who did must maintain membership for the duration of the contract. These various forms of "union security," or ways to protect the union as an institution at the workplace, could be contentious issues in collective bargaining.[18]

Neither the union nor the employer was willing to move from their position on the security issue, and the union sent HRMC and the Federal Mediation and Conciliation Service (FMCS) the required thirty-day strike notice. A Board of Inquiry from the FMCS was unable to get the two sides to agree on a contract, so the National Union, through Leon Davis, filed a formal ten-day-to-two-week strike notice with the FMCS on March 10. The hospital made plans to begin the transfer of patients, with the announced intent of shutting down the facility if a strike ensued. The union also formed strike awareness committees to alert the community of a possible walkout and held a March 18 rally that drew three hundred supporters. The hospital quit admitting new patients, but a last-minute negotiating session just before the March 22 strike deadline resulted in a two-year settlement. Union security was established in a modified maintenance of membership agreement, in which current employees did not have to join the union, but all future hires would. Dan Stewart praised the agreement for serving the "interests of the community and of the hospital workers," while administrator Gene Divine urged all parties to "all put our efforts into constant improvements of the hospital." Divine moved on from HRMC a few months later.[19]

The contract signed at Highlands Regional was the first for 1199 in Kentucky. Before the formation of the WV/KY district in 1980, the Kentucky "area" of 1199 was occasionally referred to in union literature as 1199K or 1199KY. The HRMC victory was especially significant after the discouraging outcomes of the campaigns at Clarksburg's United Hospital and the Charleston Area Medical Center. Within the space of one year, the victories at Cabell Huntington and HRMC helped enhance the credibility of 1199 in Appalachia. The workers at HRMC won significant wage increases across the board as well as improved Blue Cross-Blue Shield coverage, additional holidays, improved on-call pay, and the dues checkoff, signifying that "the union is recognized and here to stay." Stewart remarked on the workers' "toughness" versus a determined adversary, and physical therapist Donald Hurt was delighted that "we've got a union here now—a union that's alive and well."

Jo Anna Martin was justifiably proud of what had come of her letter to the National Union and of the militant commitment of her coworkers. She was aware that other Kentucky healthcare workers were following the HRMC struggle closely. "We didn't want to appear too rebellious," she recalled, "while still showing we were willing to bargain hard and stand up for our rights, partly as an example to the others." She noted another important lesson for other workers: "The fact that we were ready to strike is what got us this settlement." [20]

Leon Davis had a reputation for irascibility within 1199, not toward workers but occasionally with the staff. Tom Woodruff was also known to show his temper now and then ("he could be volatile," said one former organizer), sometimes for effect in negotiations. It is therefore not surprising that these two assertive personalities might clash at some point. Such was the case in the spring of 1976, when Woodruff excoriated Davis over the National Union's withholding of strike pay for three workers at Doctor's Memorial in Welch who had been fired for strike activity during a recent unauthorized walkout at the hospital. Apparently for Davis, the issue was union discipline; reportedly the Welch action was the first wildcat strike in the union's history. For Woodruff, the issue was loyalty to workers who had built a union at Welch for five hard years. Davis had refused to cover the three fired workers for the period until their case came up for arbitration. Woodruff wrote Davis to protest

> against this crime committed by the union against the workers. Apparently, it is the feeling in New York that these workers didn't need to strike, and that they should be punished as much as possible for doing so. Strange that that is the boss's attitude. These workers can beat the boss. It is harder to beat the union.
>
> If the National office plans to make every decision from 500 miles away, without knowing the facts, without knowing the workers, without in any way being a part of the struggle, then they ought to import another flunky to do the dirty work. [21]

This is the extent of my knowledge about this conflict, although Davis and Woodruff appear to have reconciled (or suspended) their differences by mid-July, when Davis delivered a presidential address at the first formal 1199WV and 1199/KY Delegates Assembly in Huntington. Bob Muehlenkamp, who became the national director of organizing after the February 1975 death of Elliott Godoff, also participated in the assembly. The keynote speaker was Ken

Hechler, Democratic representative from West Virginia's Fourth Congressional District. Hechler, a former political science professor at Marshall, had been the leading national legislator in the successful battle for the Coal Mine Health and Safety Act of 1969. Special guests included a delegation of service and maintenance workers from Fairmont General Hospital. They were members of Local 550 of the RWDSU, 1199's international parent, who had been organized at the hospital since 1965. Nearly seventy delegates attended from Holden Hospital, Doctor's Memorial in Welch, Cabell Huntington, and Highlands Regional. The theme of the assembly was inspired by Frederick Douglass's 1860 declaration that "if there is no struggle, there is no progress." [22]

Workshops for the delegates concentrated on two central issues: contract administration and organizing new employees. For a new and struggling local like that at Cabell Huntington, whose members knew they had accepted a poor first contract, such education would be crucial for the union's survival when contract renewal talks arrived in 1977. In the midst of the first Cabell Huntington contract talks in 1975, the National Union's education director, Marshall Dubin, had discerned the members' depth of commitment to their new local, which they would need to develop in order to survive. The setting was a basic delegates' training conducted by Woodruff and Wendell Drake:

> The delegates are very conscious of the need to sign up a majority in the bargaining unit. Accordingly, considerable class time was devoted to the fine art of refuting anti-union arguments and signing up the workers.
>
> The delegates had been subjected to anti-New York propaganda by management during the recent elections. They rejected it on the grounds that, over the years, they had learned to disbelieve anything management said. . . . There is a noticeable feeling of friendship and solidarity among the delegates. This included the three black delegates present. (Tom Woodruff estimates that 5 percent of the workers in the bargaining unit are black.)
>
> There is a strong union tradition among these delegates. A number have union backgrounds or are wives or mothers of steel workers. One was the wife of the president of a steelworkers local.
>
> The delegates of Cabell Huntington have a very healthy hatred and contempt for their management. Some delegates commented that the greatest barrier to organization was fear among the workers. This, they say, is definitely changing. [23]

The contempt for management was well founded from the standpoint of union members. Judy Siders recalled that the workers who had gone through the contract talks in 1975 had no illusions about the employer's intentions as the bargaining sessions for contract renewal got under way in the fall of 1977: "We had a CEO named Ken Wood. He talked the Board of Trustees into bustin' us. He was gonna bust us. He was a good CEO and was gonna bust the union. So I remember what we got when we was at the table: it was a bulletin board and a three-cent raise. Three pennies. So that's kind of a sign that they wanted us to go out on strike and we certainly did. We had a three-week strike." [24]

Not only Siders and her coworkers but also the National Union had a great interest in keeping the Cabell Huntington local on a firm footing. Contract gains at Cabell Huntington, the largest organized hospital in Appalachia, would "help lead the way in organizing hospitals throughout the region," according to *1199 News*. The Cabell Huntington workers took a measure of pride in being called "the largest organized [public] hospital south of the Mason-Dixon line." To them, their workplace's symbolic status was significant in understanding the employer's determination to disable the union. The union's newsletter at Cabell Huntington contended that "breaking the union was important to them as well as a whole lot of other hospital administrations through the region." [25]

As expiration of the 1975 contract approached, the employer and the union were far apart in their negotiations. The union issued the mandatory strike notices and three days before the October 1 expiration date formed an emergency care committee providing for strikers to "reenter the hospital" for emergency patient care. The membership voted overwhelmingly to strike if no agreement could be reached. The negotiating committee had permission to tentatively approve an acceptable offer from the hospital, but none came as the parties remained at odds over health care, wages, job bidding, and union security issues. The *Herald-Dispatch* scolded both parties, declaring that a hospital strike was "an outrage this community should not be asked to tolerate." The paper reminded readers that the hospital's stubborn resistance to unionization in 1975 eventually aroused community opposition and suggested that public pressure might again be necessary. The hospital's Board of Trustees had resurrected the "bad habit" of sometimes meeting in secret session, the paper noted, a violation of the state's open meeting law. At one such "Special Board Meeting" on September 15,

> Mr. Wood asked the Board that, if a strike notice was received, he be given the authority to bring in additional security personnel as well as an outside consultant to assist the Administration in preparing for the strike and in keeping the hospital going. This item was discussed at length as to the necessity of hiring an outsider, and Mr. Wood was asked to state the duties of the consultant. It was pointed out that *the*

consultant was very beneficial during the last contract, especially since the supervisors, as well as administration, had never experienced an actual strike situation before and having an experienced consultant to give direction would add much to the security of the remaining personnel. (Italics added)

Wood repeated his request at a subsequent meeting, noting that the fee would be $400 per day plus expenses. The board authorized him to proceed with hiring the consultant in the event of a strike. Curiously, the minutes recorded the vote on Wood's request passed "with no abstentions" and acknowledged no opposition to the motion, even though it seems likely that the prolabor members would have opposed it.[26]

By this point, a strike appeared unavoidable. Continuing talks seemed to be merely a formality, with the hospital offering contract language nearly identical to 1975's "lousy" agreement. The hospital's legal counsel, William Beatty, declared that a strike against the hospital, a public agency, was illegal. Grant Crandall, one of the union's go-to lawyers in West Virginia, claimed the hospital was a "quasi-public" body and that West Virginia law was indefinite on public workers' right to strike. Legal or not, it was clear the union had no intention of lessening strike pressure without a settlement. Administrator Kenneth Wood announced that "no one out on an illegal strike will have job protection." Wood brought in a dozen extra security guards "to protect hospital employees under strike conditions" and arranged for Marshall University to provide nursing and medical school students as "replacement workers." Plans were put in place for transportation of nonstriking employees and to house working employees "on a 24-hour basis." The employer defended such actions as simply being prepared. The union saw them as provocations. It was "astounding," said Woodruff, "that these guys want to force us out on strike." The old contract expired at midnight on September 30, and at 6:00 a.m. on Saturday, October 1, picketing strikers appeared at the hospital. When two hundred picketers returned on Sunday, October 2, they marched in violation of a preliminary injunction issued by Circuit Court judge Robert Conaty.[27]

Judge Conaty had issued the injunction at the request of Beatty and Richard Bolen as the hospital's attorneys, early on Saturday afternoon. Conaty, approached by Beatty as he painted his house, descended his forty-foot ladder to hear Beatty's plea. A close friend of the judge, Beatty presented a complaint and decree for Conaty's signature, claiming that the strike would "seriously impair" the hospital's operation and possibly lead to the "loss of limb, life, and property." He asked that Conaty prohibit picketing at the hospital. Conaty informed Beatty and Bolen that the court usually did not issue temporary injunctions without a hearing on the merits of the complaint, but seeing as this matter was an "emergency," and it was the weekend, he "reluctantly" signed the decree without informing the union or hearing their case. Because of this diversion from common practice, because of Conaty's close friendship with Beatty, and because his brother was a practicing physician at the hospital, the union later demanded (and received) Judge Conaty's voluntary recusal from the case. On Sunday the two hundred 1199WV and 1199KY picketers showed up at the hospital, violating Conaty's order. From then until October 7, picketers marched in violation of the injunction until County judge Dan Robinson, appointed by Justice Fred Caplan of the West Virginia Supreme Court to take Conaty's place, vacated the injunction and allowed limited picketing and ordered neutral zones between strikers and hospital security. From the union's perspective, Robinson's rule on picketing was a tacit admission by the county that the strike was legal.[28]

Kenneth Wood announced that the hospital had cobbled together a working force of 250–300 employees from supervisory and nonstriking personnel, most of them covered by the 1975 contract but refusing to pay dues. It should be remembered that the trustees had successfully lobbied to include some employees in the bargaining unit whom 1199WV had deemed unlikely to support the union. When the contract expired and the strike began, many of these workers kept working, in twelve-hour shifts, and Wood estimated that between 150 and 200 spent nights at the hospital as the strike continued. Dan Stewart claimed that about eighty covered workers who had not paid dues, however, were now supporting the union and "staying off the job in sympathy" with the strike.[29]

A majority of the hospital's registered nurses, although covered by the 1975 contract, had opposed unionization. Indeed, Wood told the Board of Trustees that about 130 of the hospital's 150 RNs would not honor the strike and would report for work. Their opposition suggested some of the obstacles to the industrial organization of a modern hospital. The organizing principle of all 1199 locals was based on the idea of a community of all workers within what Barbara and John Ehrenreich called "the American health empire." Doctors, social workers, RNs, LPNs, nurses' aides, housekeepers, laboratory technicians, food service workers, maintenance personnel, drivers, and janitors shared a common identity as industrial workers to 1199. This model was, not surprisingly, often problematic in workplace settings that were historically divided into occupational and class hierarchies. Highly professionalized employees with specialized skills, especially physicians and registered nurses, frequently resisted the notion that they were part of a working class. As a concession to such "separateness," the massive New York Local 1199 had formed a "guild" division for professional members in the mid-1960s. This was a logical option in New York, with thousands of professional members at large facilities, but it was not adopted by 1199WV and 1199KY.[30]

Kenneth Kruger and Norman Metzgar have written that hospital managers and healthcare analysts often complain that nurses "cannot make up their minds as to whether they wish to be recognized as health care professionals or as unionists." Registered nurses in modern hospitals, many with four-year professional degrees and two to four years of training, functioned in managerial positions themselves. According to Barbara Melosh, they supervised a "hierarchy of nurses" yet also worked at patients' bedsides along with orderlies, LPNs, and aides. Depending on the individual, the RN might internalize a sense of separation from fellow workers. Or, an RN might embrace 1199's organizing principle that there need be no artificial barrier between healthcare "professionals" and "workers," that all have a common interest in bettering working conditions. Regardless of nurses' occupational or class identity, there was also a debate as to whether nurses should ever go out on strike. This thinking was reflected in the *Herald-Dispatch's* contention that the community "should not be asked to tolerate a strike" from hospital workers. But the collective bargaining process loses much of its effectiveness if the possibility of a strike is removed. In 1968 the American Nurses Association, acknowledging that strikes could sometimes be necessary, rescinded a no-strike pledge that had been in effect since 1950. The association's rationale was telling: a no-strike policy assumes that employers would negotiate with nurses' representatives in good will and good faith. Unfortunately, with a few exceptions, "nurses' employers proved to be as unwilling as most other employers to negotiate with employee groups."[31]

The disdain that some of the RNs at Cabell Huntington harbored toward healthcare unions conveyed an attitude to prounionists that these RNs saw themselves as "too good type of people to be involved in a union." But some nonstrikers simply believed that their role as healers precluded any possible disruption that might intrude on patient care. "Most of us who come to work in a hospital realize that we're not in a highly-paid industry and we are trying to help people who need help, often desperately," said one nonstriking medical technologist in a letter endorsed by ten of her coworkers. Referring to alleged harassment of nonstrikers by pickets, she continued: "We cannot allow other people to interfere physically with those of us continuing to supply health care, nor with people who need hospital services." In a closed meeting of the Board of Trustees, a member of the hospital's medical staff reported that several of the staff physicians had declared the strike, and the union itself, "abominations."[32]

Even among strong unionists, said Melosh, "hospital strikes raised serious ethical questions for many nurses," who worried about depriving patients even as "they defended their own rights as workers and fought for conditions that would improve patient care." A pledge by 1199WV to provide necessary emergency care at Cabell Huntington mediated some of the worry that striking LPNs and aides had about "abandoning" patients. Without the protection of a better contract, they argued, they would not have the staffing or the protection to compel management to maintain the best possible care for the community. Moreover, in addition to the many "frontline" workers most visible to the public, such as nurses, orderlies, and aides, there were hundreds of "invisible" workers whose lives would be improved with a better contract. These included more than forty job classifications among the hospital's lowest-paid and vulnerable workers in maintenance, food service, housekeeping, and laundry jobs.[33]

Occupational class distinctions and the hospital's charge that strikers were forsaking needy people intersected in a vignette reported by *Herald-Dispatch* reporter Jack Seamonds. As a surgical nurse chastised the strikers, Kenneth Wood spoke with reporters while standing in front of the hospital's newborn nursery:

> In surgery, a tough-talking nurse stands with her hands firmly on her hips. "I was telling the doctors this morning that this was probably for the best," she said. "At least the professional people, the dedicated people, are here working. The doctors might get to like it."
>
> Minutes later, executive director Wood is standing in front of the nursery. "We have 39 new babies in here right now," he says to no one in particular. He sighs. "This is what I can't understand. How the hell do you walk out on babies?"
>
> And outside, the sky is still gray and the rain is still pouring down and the employees still are marching with signs demanding they be paid what they deserve.[34]

This passage implies that the Cabell Huntington strike was strictly about wages. True, 1199WV sought wage increases, but also struck for other quality of work life issues such as adequate staffing, scheduling, training and promotion, job control, health insurance, union security, and respect. By specifying only wages the *Herald-Dispatch* reporter, consciously or not, reinforced a historical theme that management sought to instill in the public mind. According to this durable perception, healthcare providers are public servants, not workers. A strike therefore violated a public trust. Healthcare historian Dave Lindorff observes that the 1970s and 1980s was a time when most people still coveted a nineteenth-century ideal that a hospital was a philanthropic institution. "They were founded to care for the poor. It's hard to accept the idea" says Lindorff, that "hospitals are becoming just another business. But they are." It was logical for the employer at Cabell Huntington, indeed at all the facilities in this study, to perpetuate the myth that modern hospitals were places where "the few toil ceaselessly that the many might live," rather than corporate organizations subsidized by massive public expenditures. Undergirding the myth was the idea that nurses were enveloped in an "aura of selflessness." Their work was not just a job or a profession, "but a ministry." This way of thinking explains why many of the "professional people" at Cabell Huntington believed the walkout was "an abdication of responsibility."[35]

One need not be a cynic to presume that Kenneth Wood's lament to reporters outside the nursery might have been as much for effect as for compassion. Wood was reminding anyone within earshot that hospital work was exceptional, distinct from manufacturing, mining, construction, and banking. He was defining a hospital as "a special institution where life and death are linked to a reliable and loyal workforce." He was invoking an enduring ideal of selflessness known as "Nightingalism," named for the nineteenth-century pioneer of modern nursing. Florence Nightingale's 1860 nursing manual linked nursing with women's domestic roles even as nursing became established as specialized work for pay. The domestic ethos of nursing persisted, one doctor declaring in 1925 that a hospital was a home for the sick, and "there can be no home unless there is a woman at the head of it." Nightingalism's ideal of "womanly service," says Barbara Melosh, survived even in "the esoteric technological setting" of modern hospitals. In the emerging modern healthcare system of the 1970s, what Jessica Wilkerson calls the "expropriation of caregiving labor" was a critical component of capitalist production.[36]

Nightingalism underlay Wood's reference to the abandonment of the newborns. Loyalty and productivity in this sense derived from selfless obedience and sacrifice. From the perspective of 1199WV, however, loyalty and productivity derived from a sense of workers' self-respect, a belief that one's labor and loyalty deserved a fair return in terms of wages and security. When healthcare workers (women and men) unionized, they were "politicizing caregiving labor" and struggling to control the "extraction of their work" within the framework of market capitalism. Leon Davis explained that the union was the means for workers to know that their job is important. "If you see yourself as a more useful person," he said, the work will be done well. That sentiment explains the Cabell Huntington strike.[37]

The 1977 strike lasted three weeks. It was marked by scuffles and property damage carried out by both sides, usually involving picketers and security guards. Anna (Davis) Jenkins was arrested for obstructing traffic and Stewart was arrested twice, once for unlawful assembly and disorderly conduct, again for assault when he got in a fight with a nonstriking hospital orderly. Woodruff, Muehlenkamp, and more than forty picketers were cited for violating Judge Conaty's injunction, charges that were dropped after the injunction was overturned. As the strike entered its second week, Federal Mediation and Conciliation mediator Lee Skillman agreed to enter the negotiations after both sides charged bad-faith bargaining. By then it was clear that the issue transcended wages and benefits. "The issue in this strike," said Muehlenkamp, "is the survival of the union and collective bargaining." [38]

When on October 12 the hospital offered only small on-call raises and no across-the-board wage or benefit adjustments, the membership refused the offer and continued the strike, bolstered by $5,000 in strike aid provided by the National Union. Local 40 of the United Steelworkers at Huntington Alloys Inc. donated $500 and sent picket-line support. Union drivers from Heiner's Bakery dropped off bread, cakes, and donuts at the union office. Jenkins recalled, "We had all kinds of unions that walked the picket line with us, especially when they found out how we were being treated on the picket line . . . because the police were very down on us. They were union, too, but they were doing what they were told. It wasn't a good strike. The first strike was a bad strike, because we were fighting for our jobs, literally fighting for our jobs, and it wasn't pretty."

To Anna Jenkins, the solidarity among Huntington's labor movement created a wave effect that threatened to hurt business at the hospital, eventually forcing the employer to deal in good faith: "That hospital was a ghost town. And, you find out you're in a union town and you've got a picket line all around the hospital, burning barrels, shacks, everything else, you know you've got to survive, it was cold, it was October, it was rainy. And you [a patient] drive up to that hospital and you're union anyway, and someone informs you that this hospital is on strike, you're more likely to turn around and go to St. Mary's [Hospital]." Jenkins claimed that the strike had the support of many of the patients at the hospital who had comprehensive health insurance due to a union contract. "Most people that get to choose their health care have a union. People that don't have health care usually don't have a union, so you don't have a choice." [39]

The Board of Trustees grew restive as the strike wore on. Huntington businessman Ted Johnson reported that "everyone in the community was very concerned." He had talked with "a lot of dedicated people out on the picket lines," who assured him that the trouble was with the administration. Edmund Marshall volunteered that a major concern of the strikers was the "shabby" way the hospital was being run, and he "was told that over half of the picketers would return to the hospital" if Kenneth Wood and two other administrators were fired. Concerned that they were not receiving full reports on the contract negotiations, the trustees voted to assign two board members to sit in on the sessions. Wilbert Ward from the Huntington AFL-CIO was especially critical of the hospital administration, claiming that it had pressured supervisors "to harass the union people until there was no way out." He further believed that Ken Wood's $400 a day consultant had actually redoubled the resolve of the union to survive. The administration "had been trying to break the union for two years," Ward said, "and now a settlement must be made." [40]

The strike ended when the membership accepted a settlement on October 22. The new two-year contract (it was renewed without a strike in 1979) included a maintenance of membership clause requiring new hires to join the union after a ninety-day probationary period and, significantly, a dues checkoff agreement. It also provided for pay raises of sixty-five cents an hour (fifty cents for X-ray technicians), shift differential pay, a rationalized job bidding process, and a step system by which the hospital would pay 80 percent of employee Blue Cross and Blue Shield by 1979. In a controversial giveback, Woodruff asked the negotiating team to accept a "carve out" of the registered nurses, who ended their membership in the union. Decades later, Judy Siders still considered this provision to be "one of the downfalls of the 1977 strike." Some of the RNs had gone out on strike, she said, defying both the hospital management and the majority of their department. Siders realized the union conceded the RN carve out so the strike would end but believed it should have held out. "Tom gave 'em up," she said, "which was a very big mistake. We tried to organize them three times after that. They never got organized." To keep the loyalty of the RNs, however, the administration felt pressured to maintain wages and benefits for them on par with the union contract. During the strike, one issue the trustees addressed was how to arrive at an appropriate level of compensation for "loyal employees." [41]

The union and collective bargaining *had* survived. The new contract established organized labor as a more equitable force in the balance-of-power equation at the hospital than previously. The workers had mobilized themselves and the local labor movement to withstand "some of the most powerful elements in this city" and "have built a solid union." "Management," said Muehlenkamp, "is going to have to learn to live with you as a union." Hopefully "management has learned its lesson, and next time they will bargain in good faith." [42]

The improved contract encouraged workers' greater sense of dignity in their work. In 1979, someone washing dishes for a living in most small Southern cities was probably making the minimum wage (I was, anyway). The minimum then was $2.90 per hour, or $10.03 in 2018 dollars. The 1977–1979 contract at Cabell Huntington Hospital paid beginning dishwashers $3.51 ($12.40). A dishwasher with ten years' experience was paid $4.08 ($14.42). A living wage, health security, and job protection were, as Leon Davis said, essential elements for social progress and justice.[43]

Chapter 7

Big Win and Tough Losses, 1976–1980

The district's organizing and educational staff greatly expanded between 1976 and 1988, as healthcare workers mobilized to protect themselves in a rapidly changing industry. Some organizers were hired by the National Union, others directly by the district with the National's approval. At the time, 1199 had a rule that no organizer or staff could be paid more than the highest-paid union member, so as Moe Foner put it, "No one ever got rich working at 1199." Organizers in the late 1970s and 1980s, some of whom had long careers with the union, included Laura Batt, Bob Callahan, Lisa Watson, Dan Strahinich, Teresa Ball, Al Bacon, Dave Mott, Shirley Mullet, Harold Schlechtweg, Barry Smith, Patty Freeland, and David Freeland. Also on the staff was a legendary West Virginia community organizer named Linda Meade. Originally working from a garage on Charleston Avenue, the West Virginia/Kentucky staff moved to a larger office on Eighth Avenue in Huntington, and the district opened an office in Columbus in 1982.

The growth and survival of 1199WV and 1199KY in Appalachia amidst widespread business and political attacks on unionism included hard-won victories at two major hospitals, Fairmont General in West Virginia in 1978 and King's Daughters in Ashland, Kentucky, in 1980. Ohio's 1199 merged with the newly established WV/KY District in 1982 to form 1199WV/KY/OH.[1] And as documented in this chapter, the membership became toughened through losing hard fights as well, especially at Martins Ferry, Ohio (1976), and Wetzel County Hospital in New Martinsville, 1979–1980. During the Reagan years, the union stood down major union-busting efforts at Highlands Regional in 1981 and Fairmont in 1987 and fought off management's plans for draconian staff cuts at Cabell Huntington and King's Daughters in 1983–1984. These struggles are covered in chapters 8 and 9.

A 1976 organizing campaign at Martin's Ferry Hospital, in an industrial town of about ten thousand just across the Ohio River from Wheeling, ran into a firestorm of resistance from a determined hospital management. During the campaign, the employer promised a retirement pension so that any worker retiring with more than ten years' service would be guaranteed at least $100 a month. Following the union's loss, one worker observed that when she retired in 1977 after sixteen years on the job, the hospital set her pension payments at $125 per month. The hospital later notified this worker, however, that she was being overpaid and held back payments for a year. "Now," she wrote in October 1978, "they give me $11.67 a month. If there is a place on this earth that needs a union, this hospital needs one bad." [2]

When Tom Woodruff arrived in Martin's Ferry in early August of 1976, he and the workers at Martin's Ferry Hospital who had invited him expected management opposition. Those workers included an X-ray orderly named Norman Davis, who decided to fight back after fourteen years of low pay, no benefits, and no grievance procedure. The Wheeling-Pittsburgh steelworkers and coal miners in northern West Virginia and eastern Ohio had a history of unionism, and Davis saw no reason that hospital workers should continue without it. He was one of over three hundred service and maintenance workers, LPNs, and clerical workers at the hospital, three-quarters of whom signed union cards by mid-September. As the hospital was privately owned, the union filed an election request with the NLRB. Immediately the employer began an antiunion drive that Leon Davis described as an "extraordinary campaign of fear and coercion. We've had dirty campaigns used against us before. But the intensity of this one was highly unusual." Norman Davis said that he and his fellow union supporters "never expected all this stuff management did." Woodruff suspected that the country's most powerful union-busting firm, Modern Management Methods (3M), was the union avoidance consultant at Martin's Ferry.[3]

The NLRB election was duly scheduled for December 16. While it does not appear that the hospital management did much in the way of delaying tactics, its other tactics included some of the most distasteful in the union-busting playbook. The bosses began with regular leafleting that attacked 1199's history of civil rights activism and its defense of African American radicals such as Black Power icon Angela Davis. The union was denigrated for its New York roots, accused of relishing violence, and Red-baited for its early Communist affiliations. Leon Davis's 1948 congressional testimony, in which he defended Communism's contributions to the labor movement, was invoked in management literature. A city official saw a picture of Davis posted on the police department's bulletin board with the caption, "He is a card-carrying Communist. If the union wins the election, he will be here Monday to stir up trouble." [4]

The hospital's avoidance campaign was overseen by administrator Frank Fulton until he suddenly resigned in mid-October, attributing divisiveness brought on by the "actions of outsiders whose motives are, in my opinion, highly suspect." The hospital hired Brent A. Marsteller, a Huntington native and Marshall University graduate, on an interim basis. The Board of Trustees was sufficiently impressed with Marsteller's work that he was promoted to hospital administrator within a few weeks. The board, chaired by Martins Ferry's mayor John Laslo, hired lawyers from Columbus to direct the attack against outsiders. Laslo was also the publisher of the *Times-Leader*, where according to sympathetic reporters they were forbidden from publishing favorable news about 1199OH (Ohio). The *Times-Leader* refused to run a prounion ad purchased by 150 workers who donated a dollar apiece. Union supporters claimed that Laslo's political and editorial leverage intimidated local civic and labor leaders, who shied away from endorsing the campaign. Only the Steelworkers Local provided consistent support for the Martins Ferry workers.

Laslo sent a letter to every hospital worker, admonishing them to reject the "outsiders from New York." Management's "extraordinary campaign of fear and coercion," according to Leon Davis, succeeded in driving out 1199OH and two other unions that were on the ballot, the SEIU and the Ohio Licensed Practical Nurses Association (LPNA), both of whom entered the process late. The Ohio LPNA apparently was there not to win an election but to drive support away from 1199OH.[5]

Fairmont, West Virginia, a small industrial city of about twenty-five thousand in 1978, is the county seat of Marion County, at the base of the state's northern panhandle about twenty miles south of Morgantown. Early twentieth-century Fairmont had flourished, based largely on a thriving glass-production industry. According to historian Ken Fones-Wolf, Fairmont employed about one-third of the state's prosperous glass bottle and container industry workforce in the mid-1920s. Major companies such as the Owens West Virginia Bottle Company (which became Owens-Illinois in 1929) and Hartford-Empire employed native West Virginians, African American migrants, and skilled glassworkers from Belgium, France, and Italy. Immigrants from Hungary, Poland, and the Slavic nations gravitated to Fairmont and its northern West Virginia environs to work in the glass, electric, and mining industries, building a diverse and lively working-class culture. Two elite West Virginia families, the Flemings and the Watsons, organized the Fairmont Coal Company in 1903 and began to organize a corporate entity that became the Consolidation Coal Company in 1909. They collaborated with the pioneering West Virginia political capitalist Johnson N. Camden, who represented Rockefeller interests in the state.

The Fairmont glass industry was not densely unionized until a production boom during World War II, when glassworkers at Owens-Illinois flocked to the Glass Bottle Blowers Association and formed the foundation of a vibrant

postwar labor movement in the city. When registered nurses, respiratory therapists, and laboratory workers at Fairmont General Hospital organized in 1978,
they enjoyed widespread support from Fairmont's steelworkers, United Mine
workers, building trades unions, firefighters, and remaining glassworkers.
Ironically, 1978 was also when Owens-Illinois began phasing out its Fairmont
works, completing its shutdown in 1982.[6]

The year 1978 was a critical one for all organized labor. A filibuster by
Republicans in the U.S. Senate destroyed an AFL-CIO labor reform bill, which
would have overturned the right-to-work provision of the Taft-Hartley law and
eliminated many other obstacles to unionization. By that time, the profound
restructuring of the nation's industrial and financial systems, which accelerated dramatically during the Reagan presidency of 1981–1989, was already un-
derway. Corporate mergers, inflated management compensation, shortsighted
investment strategies, the increased use of contingent (or contracted) labor,
"two-tiered" wage systems, the offshoring of core industries that had sustained
a decent way of life for millions of workers, and an epidemic of layoffs, job
eliminations, and plant closings destroyed the bargaining leverage that the
labor movement had built since World War II.[7]

That year of 1978 also proved significant for 1199 in West Virginia.
Immediately after the Cabell Huntington local won its election in 1975, as
referenced in chapter 5, the "West Virginia campaign" stalled following de-
feats in Charleston and Clarksburg. Then, 1199WV withdrew from elections
at Kanawha Valley Hospital and at St. Joseph's Hospital in Parkersburg rather
than endure lopsided losses. The favorable contract renewal strike at Cabell
Huntington late in 1977 encouraged the 1199WV and 1199KY faithful, especially in light of the disaster at Martins Ferry, as did a big win at Heartland
Nursing Home in Charleston early in 1978. Healthcare workers' interest in
organizing was "on the upswing," according to Dan Stewart, described by
the Associated Press as "the union's senior staff representative in the state."
Stewart also said that hospital administrators at unorganized hospitals were
concerned about the upswing and determined to weaponize their resistance
to unionization.[8]

In the fall of 1978, Fairmont General Hospital was a three hundred-bed municipal facility. The service and maintenance personnel were already organized (since 1965) into Local 550 of the Retail, Wholesale, and Department
Store Union (RWDSU), 1199's international affiliate. By terms of a contract
that settled a 1977 strike by Local 550, the local had agreed not to try to
organize any of the nonunionized employees at the hospital for the duration
of their contract. In February of 1978, the National 1199 agreed to contract

Tom Woodruff out to Local 550 to help the members with contract administration. Woodruff was already in Fairmont in response to inquiries that 1199WV had received from the professional workers at Fairmont General, including respiratory therapists, laboratory technicians, LPNs, and 160 registered nurses. He soon learned that the RNs at Fairmont General were of a militantly different mindset than the RNs at Cabell Huntington. "People were so ready to be organized," said Mary Schafer, a Fairmont State College nursing graduate who began working at the hospital in 1968. "They were so disgusted. We didn't get any overtime pay. We did not get any kind of holiday. . . . We had to work holidays. We would work stretches of thirteen to fourteen days in a row," and the hospital supervisors "were a group that was hard to deal with." Schafer remembered that "I used to tell Tom that I think a monkey could have organized us, we were so ready to be organized." To RN Beverly Charlton the tension at the hospital "was like a pressure cooker waiting to explode." [9]

Only a few years earlier, Fairmont General had shown potential for the creation of a more harmonious working environment. The RNs had taken the lead in promoting a "Personnel Policy Committee" to facilitate open communication with hospital administration. At first they were encouraged by management's apparent willingness to "openly discuss problems of mutual concern" about working conditions and patient care. This was in 1974, when hospital administrators were promoting a new "Human Resources Model" of labor-management cooperation, when collaboration was supposed to eliminate adversarial labor-management relations. "Progressive hospitals" in this new era would build a "cooperative relationship between management and employees," resulting in "more effective resource utilization results" so that the "employee and the organization" have a chance to "accomplish objectives together." As the hospital administration proved to their workers that they were "valued and respected as individuals with individual needs," the workers would develop a sense of loyalty and obligation to the organization.[10]

The cooperation-collaboration model could be useful if applied in good faith. In fact, when the RNs at Fairmont General secured their first contract, they insisted on a labor-management policy committee. Many unionists, however, particularly the organizers and members of militant unions like 1199WV, were wary of the language of cooperation and cautious of bosses who began using it. Avowedly progressive management in American industry had a long history of "personnel management" schemes that were designed to prove to workers that they did not need a union, a "third party," to represent them. In the 1930s companies created company unions or employee representation plans (ERPs) to try to co-opt workers who might be lured by the surge of industrial unionism. Labor historian Michael Yates noted in 1994 that the then current rage of employee involvement programs (EIPs), "quality circles," and "teams" were often little more than replicants of the ERPs of the Depression era. Labor educator James Rundle found that employers who used EIPs were more likely than others to use aggressive antiunion campaigns. "The rhetoric of employee involvement may be about 'voice' and 'empowerment,' " Rundle wrote, but employers who talked that talk were also most likely to send anti-union letters to workers' homes and fire union activists. Workers suspicious of the bosses' good intentions were wise to make sure that cooperation did not morph into capitulation.[11]

When Fairmont General administrator O. B. Ayers, acting for the Board of Directors, discontinued the Personnel Policy Committee in the summer of 1975, the RNs' disappointment soon changed into anger. They concluded that the hospital's initial respectful approach had been designed as a pacification program rather than one of true participation in decision making. It seems that when workers on the committee took the language of power sharing seriously, management began to see the committee idea as troublesome. One RN called the dismantling of the Policy Committee a missed opportunity for the employer. "If they had carried out and followed up on our grievances," she said when she and over two hundred of her coworkers struck for recognition in 1978, "there is a great possibility local 1199 coming into Fairmont General would never have come about."[12]

The employer devised a theory that the fraternal relationship between 550 and 1199 essentially made them one entity. Therefore Woodruff's role with 1199 was actually a stealth intervention by the RWDSU to circumvent 550's pledge not to organize nurses and other professional workers at the hospital. The hospital charged that Woodruff aggressively sought out the RNs to sign union cards; the RNs dissented, claiming that they had initiated contact with the organizer. Mary Schafer recalled that in August, when nurses began to meet with Woodruff, she was unaware of Woodruff's work for Local 550 and "didn't see him around the hospital at that time." She believed that the RNs' initial meeting with the organizer was arranged by a service employee on the obstetrics (OB) floor of the hospital, who suggested to a couple of the OB nurses that they talk to Woodruff at a house meeting; "That's how it started." Schafer did not attend the first meeting but attended a second meeting at the home of RN Tonya Boggess. Initially, Schafer was unimpressed with Woodruff:

> Okay. He looked like a bum. He had that old jacket on, that plaid jacket that he wore for, probably, thirty years. Yeah, and old shoes and then he started talking and I thought he was just a shyster. That was my first

opinion of him. I thought, "Well, this guy is shady. I don't trust him and I don't think I want to get involved with this."

So, then we started having meetings at an old restaurant. We probably had fifty, sixty people. I'm sure the hospital knew about it at that point, but we still thought it was a secret. Leon Davis and his entourage came in and talked to everybody and, I mean, that was powerful, and of course Tom, you know, the more you got to know him, the more you knew he was sincere and he was, you know, really for the working person and very self-sacrificing in his own life about what he did for the union.[13]

Schafer remarked that administrator O. B. Ayers had a paternalistic manner about him, "and he didn't even like women, you know, at all, much less women telling him they're trying to get a union." Ayers seemed stunned when the union wave swept in "out of the blue," although he acknowledged that he sometimes heard "little gripes" about work at the hospital. When RN Shirley Knisely told Ayers that "the supermarket checkout girls at Shop and Save are making more than we are. We have people's lives in our hands," his advice to her was "Well, then go work at Shop and Save."

Instead of pursuing that option, the RNs got to work building their union. Quoting labor historian Toni Gilpin, they embarked on "the tedious but indispensable tasks involved in organizing, gradually expanding their network one conversation at a time." As we have already seen, the work done by the members themselves was crucial to 1199WV's survival. Skilled union organizers, based on interactions with workers themselves, sought to identify "organic worker leaders" who could use their influence to bring coworkers into the union drive. Since a union organizer's direct access to workers at the workplace is severely limited, says Jane McAlevey, only organic leaders themselves can mobilize an effective "inside campaign," which must be able to withstand an "extremely hostile climate." Member involvement reflected 1199's historic commitment to "internal democracy." "If you ask members to work hard for their union," Moe Foner explained, "you can't easily exclude them from decisions on union policy." Mary Schafer never forgot the intensity of that work. "Shirley [Knisley] and I were on the phone, I mean, you've probably seen that movie *Norma Rae*—that was just about what it was like. It was just constant. It was a job. It was another job besides the job you had."[14]

On Wednesday, September 5, a delegation claiming to represent 85 percent of the nurses and respiratory therapists, after being refused admittance to a regular hospital directors meeting, issued a statement that "we are prepared to do whatever is necessary" to get recognition from hospital management and the beginning of "bargaining in good faith." They also submitted a petition signed by 156 nurses "affirming their desire to have Local 1199 act as their bargaining agent." The board refused and also warned that a strike for recognition would be illegal under the state's public employment statutes. That same evening, RN Joyce Lunsford and a "large delegation" of RNs, LPNs, and respiratory therapy technicians attended the Fairmont City Council meeting to announce that their newly organized union had asked for recognition from the hospital and requested the council's support. It was the first of many council meetings enlivened by the presence of Fairmont General workers and supporters from the local labor movement.[15]

On September 7, the new 1199WV local at Fairmont General Hospital (FGH) reported that it had authorized a strike if the hospital refused recognition. The secret ballot strike vote came in at 145 in favor, 9 against. The hospital declined an offer by the union to set up an "emergency care committee" for the duration of the strike and completed arrangements to close down FGH and transfer patients to other facilities. Nevertheless, the union pledged to have workers from each striking department and each shift on the picket line for emergencies. According to hospital spokespeople, when the hospital received the strike notice, the hospital census was 186. When the walkout began on Monday, September 11, the census was 4.

The employer brought in a prominent Pittsburgh lawyer named C. Richard Volk, who Mary Shafer declared "had a reputation as a union buster," to oversee its union avoidance strategy. According to one nurse who was part of the September 5 delegation to the hospital's board meeting, it was Volk who had turned them away. The usual charges against 1199WV began to appear in the *Times-West Virginian*, sowing the seeds of third-partyism in the public consciousness. Some antiunion nurses formed an ad hoc committee, akin to more formal "Nurses Against Unions" groups that often materialize during organizing or contract negotiation. The committee charged their prounion colleagues with ignoring the local *Fairmont Times-West Virginian* newspaper's warnings about the National 1199's strike history "and the problems created in other hospitals." They reminded strikers that nurses were nurses "24 hours a day, seven days a week" and accused them of putting their own desires ahead of the needs of their patients. Ayers also warned of 1199's history of "disruption" in New York. "The use of demonstrations and confrontations in organizing . . . may be useful in the big city hospitals, but they are destructive and unnecessary in Fairmont, W. Va." Ayers continued that "it would be irresponsible for me as administrator of this hospital to give in to demands made in the form of ultimatums." When he scolded the hospital's professional and technical employees for undermining his belief that they were "too responsible to let this union lead them into carrying through [strike] threats that have been made," one union member responded, "They did not organize us. We organized ourselves."[16]

Immediately as the strike began, Fairmont General petitioned the Marion County Circuit Court for a preliminary injunction based on two central premises: (1) that Local 1199WV, as an entity within the Hospital Division of RWDSU, was in fact the same union as Local 550. Therefore, organizing RNs and other professional workers violated 550's 1977 contract, and (2) that since FGH was a public hospital covered by West Virginia law, the strike and associated picketing or other concerted activity were illegal and should immediately be stopped by the court. The hospital's plea was heard by Judge J. Harper Meredith, one of the West Virginia judicial establishment's venerable eminences and a "wise man" of Fairmont. Grant Crandall, who, along with Bradley Pyles usually handled 1199WV's legal affairs in the state, believed that Meredith considered himself to be a legal and civic arbiter within the Progressive tradition of enlightened, rational government. He conveyed an aura of judicial gravitas and a commitment to civic progress, individual and corporate responsibility, and social justice, and his demeanor and evident sincerity endeared him to people in Fairmont. He therefore spoke with authority when he "adduced at hearing" that it seemed obvious to him that Tom Woodruff was representing Local 1199WV, not Local 550, in organizing Fairmont nurses. He ordered the hospital and Local 550 to submit any contractual dispute—including the status of 1199WV relative to Local 550—to arbitration. The judge agreed with the hospital that the strike was illegal but was philosophically opposed to a back-to-work order. "I'll never order anyone back to work. I don't believe in ordering people to perform labor. What kind of work would they perform if they were coerced by a judicial order?"[17]

The hospital was represented in court by two local attorneys, Alfred Lemley and Joseph Mack. Their Pittsburgh colleague, Richard Volk, had negotiated contracts between the hospital and Local 550 since 1965. According to Woodruff, Volk was familiar with Local 1199P in Pittsburgh and knew "full well that the two unions, despite their historical relationship, function completely independently of each other in organizing and collective bargaining activities." Despite his awareness of the independence of Local 1199WV, Volk dutifully embraced his client's claim that it was simply Local 550 under another name and that Local 550 had violated its contract by organizing professionals into a fictional 1199WV. The strike was into its third week when the hospital attorneys and Robert Poyourow, the lawyer for Local 550, agreed upon a Washington, D.C., arbitrator named Seymour Strongin to decide the matter. Marion Connolly of the Fairmont nurses' press committee announced that regardless of Strongin's decision on Local 550's alleged contract violation, the Fairmont General Local of 1199WV was in no way connected to the arbitration question and that arbitration "WILL NOT END THE STRIKE." Grant Crandall tried to clarify the issue for the readers of the *Times-West Virginian*. He explained that although the 1199 districts had officially been a subdivision of RWDSU in the early years of the union and still had an affiliation with its union "parent," its membership growth had outstripped that of RWDSU. In 1973 the National 1199 had become "an autonomous, independent union."[18]

Seymour Strongin's decision, announced in early 1979, confirmed Crandall's assessment. Local 550's contract prohibition against organizing professional workers at FGH "did not preclude organizing efforts by the 'National Union' [1199]. . . . It is true that the organizer of the National Union also rendered some assistance to Local 550, but it is clear that Local 550 kept its separate identity." Local 550, said Strongin, had no role in organizing the Fairmont nurses "or in the strike which grew out of these efforts." By the time Strongin handed down his judgment, however, the Fairmont workers had forced an election, voted their union in, and set out to get a contract.[19]

The Fairmont City Council minutes from September 19, 1978, make no mention of 1199WV members or supporters in attendance. Their absence might explain why the council's discussion on the "labor problems" at Fairmont General tilted toward a posture of benign nonintervention in the strike. City Manager Richard Bowen (who also served on the hospital's Board of Directors) observed, perhaps hopefully, that what seemed to be "occurring now is a little quiet diplomacy—the quieter it is at the moment, the greater the chance is for success in resolving the dispute." It could be that the city manager had been talking with R. R. Dollison, president of the hospital board, who had recently described the striking nurses as "a nice bunch of girls. Every meeting I have had with them," he said, "they have been very ladylike . . . very quiet." Council member Stanford Howes, however, warned the council they should not wish for the strike to settle itself. He had heard from members of the hospital board that the problems at FGH "were created by the hospital administration over the last year and a half. It strikes me we should not sit idly by."[20]

The quietude in the City Council chamber on September 19 was only a memory by the time the October 3 meeting adjourned. Fairmont General strikers and supporters from several unions showed up to pressure the council to force the hospital board to bargain with the union. The passions in the chamber, the *Times-West Virginian* reported, led to "an unusually stormy session." Spokesmen from the local International Union of Electrical Workers (IUE) and

UMWA Local 4060 demanded that the council expand to include prounion voices, vowing mass demonstrations if it did not immediately compel the hospital to commit to a fair contract with 1199WV. The UMWA District 31 president charged the council with being millionaires who "don't give a damn about people like us." A UMWA International Executive Board member claimed that UMWA president Arnold Miller had sent him to the meeting with a message that if the council did not take positive action, then "I can assure you the International Union will." Tom Woodruff and a delegation of RNs presented a petition with three thousand signatures asking the council to instruct the hospital board to recognize the union. If the board members refused, then the council should use its authority to appoint prounion members to the board, so as to expand the range of opinion on a governing body ostensibly managed by public servants.[21]

The City Council insisted on maintaining neutrality, but did agree to referee "informal negotiations" with the hospital board and the union. The hospital continued to insist that 1199WV was actually part of Local 550 and must abide by the impending arbitration ruling. In the event that Seymour Strongin ruled that Local 550 had indeed violated its contract by infiltrating the hospital's RNs under the guise of 1199WV (as we have seen, he ruled otherwise) the nurses and their fellow strikers would end the illegal strike and disband their ersatz union. Alternatively, the hospital proposed an immediate representation election whose results, if favorable to the union, would be nullified if the hospital won the arbitration. The 1199WV members predictably rejected both demands, still maintaining that their local was not a party to the arbitration whatever the decision.

Then, in an apparent breakthrough, board president R. R. Dollison offered on October 13 to ask the hospital board to sever 1199WV from the arbitration case if the strikers would immediately return to work. Dollison and the hospital's attorney, Joseph Mack, were troubled over the ballooning costs of maintaining a practically empty hospital. Some of the directors were worried that Fairmont General's public image would suffer irreparably if the conflict continued. Dollison's proposal was acceptable to Woodruff and the local's membership, but for reasons that are unclear, Dollison's fellow board members rejected it. This set the stage for another boisterous City Council meeting on October 17. Over two hundred strikers and supporters crammed the chamber, where Woodruff and some of the RNs spoke of their willingness to accept Dollison's proposal and their conviction that the board could not be trusted. "You can understand," one said, "why we do not go back without a union."[22]

More than forty years later, one can only imagine the combustibility of the City Council chamber that evening. Momentum appeared to be with the RNs and their fellow strikers, all but a handful of whom were women. At one point the union crowd erupted into applause, when Councilman William Boram dramatically resigned from the hospital board, declaring that in his entire professional life he had never seen the "powers of rationality and reason" face such "rejection and hostility" as in the present dispute. Boram didn't specify where his sentiments lay, but the union supporters sensed they had an ally. Whether or not Boram's gesture shocked the hospital into "rationality and reason," the October 17 council meeting probably helped bring about the end of the strike. Acceding to pressure from several directions, the hospital administration abruptly proposed an October 25 election, dropping its quid pro quo regarding the impending arbitration decision. West Virginia Department of Labor commissioner Stephen Cook assigned two of his staff members as monitors. When they counted the votes, the results showed 156 for the union and 45 opposed. The hospital resumed normal operations on October 27 after a forty-five-day strike. "Our people really stuck together because they finally got tired of years of having no say and being ignored," said Mary Schafer. "Women were held down in the past, but today they're more ready to speak out on things." Schafer sat on the first bargaining committee and on every one throughout her long career at FGH.[23]

Following tough negotiations, which began in mid-November and ended only two days before a February 13, 1979, strike deadline set by the union, Fairmont General's 160 RNs became by far the largest group of nurses ever covered by a collective bargaining agreement at a West Virginia hospital. They comprised nearly 80 percent of the 207 covered employees at the facility. Woodruff cited their "tremendous unity and strength" during the strike and subsequent contract negotiations, describing the Fairmont workers as a model for health professionals throughout the state. Their two-and-a-half-year contract, he said, came from hard, determined bargaining.[24]

The contract provided comprehensive medical coverage for members and their families. It included wage increases of from 33 percent to 40 percent over the life of the contract, sick pay, disability pay, and maternity leave covering 50 percent of one's regular wages. It included increases for "on-call" pay, for charge-nurse assignments, partial benefits for part-time workers, and enhanced vacation and holiday benefits. Shift and weekend differential pay and a uniform allowance were also included. Moreover, the bargaining committee won full reimbursement for college tuition and lost-time subsidies for attending educational conferences and seminars. And, like 1199 contracts at a growing number of locals in several other districts, the employer agreed to a fourteen-member patient-care committee including seven elected union members. The employees' hope was that this committee would exercise legitimate leverage in personnel and policy decisions at the hospital, unlike the previous sham committee of the early 1970s. At early meetings the union workers on the committee faced some obstructionism. "The management people had this look on their faces like 'What are we doing with these lowly people?' " said Mary Schafer. Eventually, however, the workers found a voice on the committee, arguing against staff cuts and for logical scheduling and work assignments, adequate orientation and training for new and transferred employees, and expanded coverage for bedside care. Any worker covered by the contract could ask to bring issues directly before the committee.[25]

After the strike ended, Fairmont General filed suit in Judge Harper Meredith's Circuit Court on grounds that since the strike was illegal and disrupted services at the hospital, 1199WV and the National Union were liable for damages. Grant Crandall and Bradley Pyles represented the union and the West Virginia AFL-CIO filed a friend of the court brief. Meredith "held that the strike did not give rise to a cause of action for damages," and the hospital appealed to the West Virginia State Supreme Court of Appeals. Woodruff and the National Union officers believed that if the court ruled in the union's favor, labor's momentum for public employee collective bargaining rights would be unstoppable. Bills guaranteeing these rights had been consistently rejected by West Virginia legislators. Now, Woodruff said, should 1199WV win the Fairmont General case, "the Legislature would virtually be forced to follow suit."[26]

The State Supreme Court decided on October 21, 1980, that the removal of patients from the hospital as the strike began was a voluntary decision by the management, that the strike was peaceful, and that it was aimed only at the employer, not the city or the patients. The hospital therefore had no right to damages, according to the decision read by Justice Thomas Burk Miller: "We conclude that where public employees who have no employment contracts with their employer [this applied during the Fairmont strike] engage in a work stoppage which is peaceful and directed only against the employer with no attempt to interfere with his customers or bar ingress to other employees there is no common law right to damages. In this context the work stoppage is not 'illegal' in the sense that it gives rise to a common law action for damages."

West Virginia AFL-CIO president Joe Powell called the decision "a step forward for public employees" and agreed with Woodruff that favorable action by the legislature was inevitable. With the court's endorsement of public employee rights to organize and strike peacefully for recognition, surely West

Virginia lawmakers would provide an orderly recognition and collective bargaining mechanism for state employees who wanted a union. Four decades after Justice Miller's opinion, that has not happened.[27]

The summer of 1979 began amidst an aura of civic enthusiasm in the small Wetzel County, West Virginia, town of New Martinsville. Located on the Ohio River just south of Wheeling and Moundsville and west of Morgantown, this county seat had once been a bustling railroad and river town with a diverse mix of industries such as a tanning mill, a brick factory, supply operations for the Burning Springs oil fields, and the works for the New Martinsville Glass Manufacturing Company, later known as Viking Glass. Much of the town's industrial base had crumbled in recent years, and the population of about seven thousand in that summer of 1979 welcomed the grand opening of the newly relocated, expanded, and modernized Wetzel County Hospital (WCH). The brand-new building—the third location for the hospital since its founding in 1920—promised some new jobs and more ready access to health services for the coal miners, chemical workers, and their families in West Virginia's northern panhandle.[28]

The opening of the new hospital was accompanied by momentum for new working conditions among many of WCH's workers. In late spring of 1979, the National Union of Hospital and Health Care Employees assigned Dan Stewart, of 1199WV, to respond to requests for union representation from WCH employees. By June 20, Stewart could report that nearly 80 percent of the hospital's full- and-part-time nonsupervisory workers (140 of 180) had signed cards designating 1199WV as their representative for the purpose of negotiating with the hospital. Accordingly, Stewart notified the hospital's Board of Trustees and its administrator, Michael Rust, of the union's willingness to verify the signatures with "any impartial third party" and to proceed to collective bargaining talks. William A. Powell, the board president, noting the municipal hospital's exemption from NLRB jurisdiction, "respectfully" denied the workers' request.

This pro forma exchange set in motion events that transformed the aura of good feelings enveloping the new hospital into bitter internecine conflict. The employer's refusal to tolerate unionization, and the union workers' commitment to "organize or die," propelled New Martinsville into a storm of recrimination that split families, coworkers, friends, and "even the churches." One hospital executive declared that the town "has never experienced anything like this before." One union member observed that "my sister and I are completely divided on this. Even when this ends, I know our relationship will never be the same again." In a contentious eight-month-long strike, the hospital mobilized an avoidance campaign including a full-court-press from the local newspaper, from a local Citizens Committee, and from a "say no to unions" crusade by the hospital's physicians and some antiunion employees. Organizers Stewart and Barry Smith were regularly attacked as outsiders, and Stewart was Red-baited by a prominent local columnist on grounds of his involvement with SDS a decade earlier. From county documents, union and hospital memos, opinion columns, letters, and reporting in the *Wetzel Chronicle*, one can glean the emotional turmoil that divided the river community as the drama played out.[29]

On four occasions in June and July, Stewart and several union members asked to be included on the Board of Trustees meeting agenda and were denied. When they attended meetings and asked to speak, the meetings were immediately adjourned. Meanwhile, prounion employees were "repeatedly interrogated in one-on-one confrontations" with their supervisors about their union work. When an existing Employee Committee, formed to create a veneer of collaboration, became a prounion forum, the trustees abolished it.[30]

This preliminary course of events led to strike preparations by the union and the hospital board. The new Wetzel County Local 1199WV elected delegates and a negotiating committee to communicate with management, formulate a public outreach agenda, approach local labor unions, and petition the Wetzel County Commission for support. The three-member commission adopted a resolution noting that the West Virginia attorney general had stated that public employees did indeed have a right to organize "and be represented by an agent of their choice." When Stewart reminded the hospital's board of these acknowledged rights and resubmitted 1199WV's request to begin negotiations, the board secretary assured the organizer that "we do not recognize your organization and do not expect to do so." Stewart informed hospital administrator Michael Rust that the membership, by secret ballot vote with close to 90 percent approval, had authorized a strike to commence at 6:00a.m. on July 31 "unless the hospital Board of Trustees recognizes the union before then." The employer ignored the local delegates' July 26 final request for a secret ballot election, and the strike began. Something that may have given Stewart and the organizing committee some concern: the 90 percent strike approval was impressive, but voter participation was not. Only 76 of 140 employees who had signed union cards, or 42 percent of the hospital's 180 nonsupervisory employees, actually cast a ballot to authorize the strike.[31]

During the runup to the strike, W. A. Powell and Michael Rust sent a letter to all Wetzel County Hospital employees. They assured the workers that "every action taken by the Board has, and will continue to be, in the best interest of all employees" and the citizens of the community. What followed was a "question and answer" script explaining the hospital's right to "change the condition of employment of public employees at any time," the illegality of a public hospital strike, the absence of collective bargaining rights for public employees, and the possible termination of employees engaged in an illegal strike. "The responsibility of a government authority is to the public as a whole," the letter stated, "not to a particular group such as a labor union." To permit a union to "speak" for employees, or for the board to "meet with employees as part of the Union, would be inconsistent with the Board's basic position." Such meetings "would be futile, and serve no useful purpose."[32]

This letter is strictly boilerplate, likely structured by the itinerant "industrial relations" expert hired by the hospital, with blanks to fill in according to the specific facility. Stewart and 1199WV lawyers Grant Crandall and Bradley Pyles (a New Martinsville native) were well acquainted with such letters, having seen them in many union drives. They estimated that the hospital eventually spent at least $200,000 ($707,000 in 2019 dollars) to beat the union. In addition to the industrial relations consultant brought in from St. Clairsville, Ohio, the employer hired Pinkerton guards for extra security, a public relations firm, and eventually brought in "scab" workers. Stewart claimed that $200,000 could have provided raises of fifty-four cents an hour for all nonsupervisory workers at the hospital.[33]

On the evening of July 31, forty-one strikers were arrested for unlawful assembly during a sit-in in Michael Rust's office. The hospital secured injunctions from the Wetzel County Circuit Court, ordering an end to the strike itself and to any picketing or strike-related activity. The court rejected the hospital's plea, however, to order the strikers back to work, calling such an action "involuntary servitude." Several times during the strike the court adjusted its order to permit limited picketing off the hospital grounds, restrictions that strikers usually ignored, risking arrest and contempt proceedings. The Wetzel County Commission, which appointed the hospital's Board of Trustees, sought to distance itself from the strike controversy but issued an early declaration of support for the hospital board and was destined to be drawn into the controversy, usually as a de facto mediator during regular Tuesday evening meetings. Carol Haught, a Wetzel County employee in 1979 who later served as county clerk, said that it was common for between thirty and one hundred spectators to attend the meetings, dominated by union supporters. The regular Tuesday meetings were often tense, reflecting profound divisions in the town, with the strike splitting many New Martinsville families. On one occasion, a county deputy was duty bound to arrest his own mother for violating the no-picketing injunction. "It was a very contentious time," she recalled, with "a lot of hard feelings."[34]

A few days into the strike, the *Wetzel Chronicle* reported that Dan Stewart had warned the County Commission that if the union were not recognized, "We will turn this town upside down." If Stewart indeed made such a threat, it was missing from the minutes of the referenced commission meeting. Whether or not Stewart said it became irrelevant, however, as it was soon adopted by the union's critics as proof of its violent nature. "Dan Stewart showed what he was in the beginning," wrote one *Chronicle* reader, "when he threatened the town would be turned upside down (or words to that effect) unless the union was recognized. He couldn't care less if he destroys your hospital and disrupts your communities or makes enemies of former good friends." Stewart and organizer Barry Smith were both arrested for physical altercations during the strike, Stewart for a tussle with a Pinkerton guard and Smith for a fistfight with County Prosecutor William Lemon during a demonstration at the prosecutor's office.[35]

Strikers and nonstriking employees exchanged numerous charges of intimidation, damage to personal property, and violent threats. After over two months on picket lines, LPN Jackie Underwood thanked local supporters and the many friends she had made but was saddened because she had "faced a hatred I never experienced before." Barbara Frame, an LPN with eighteen years' service at the hospital, said that if the administration had listened to worker complaints years ago, there would be no need for a union. The strike was an "abscess," she said, that would only get worse if not treated, but she would not return to work without a union. A union would provide the security workers needed to stand up for patients and address the hospital's problems. "The way it is now, if the hospital don't like the color of your eyes, they can fire you." [36]

About one week into the strike, the hospital notified the striking employees that if they hoped to be reinstated when the standoff ended, they must advise the hospital no later than August 11. A few did so, but most dismissed the warning, which seemed to them like a type of job blackmail to force them back to work. When Barbara Frame went on strike she initially stayed home, but the day she got this notification she immediately joined the picket line. By mid-September, the hospital began running "Help Wanted" ads for RNs and LPNs "to start immediately." W. A. Powell's term as president of the Board of Trustees ended, and he was replaced by Robert Bridgman. Hospital administrator Michael Rust left to become vice president of the West Virginia Hospital Association and was succeeded by Joe Ross, who had been serving as assistant administrator at West Virginia University Hospital. There was no discernible shift in the employer's handling of the strike with these changes.

The management mobilized a phalanx of ad hoc organizations, suggesting the touch of the union buster, to promote and defend its position. The medical staff of about a dozen physicians issued a lengthy "Statement," praising the employer's dedication not only to patient care but to financial probity. The doctors warned of inevitable union resistance to any future necessary wage cuts, layoffs, job eliminations, or "other cost-cutting procedures in the hospital." The statement recommended firing "immature, irresponsible" strikers, as well as a "selective return to work of those individuals seeking reinstatement." There could be no guarantees, however, since "their positions are already being filled by those who are willing to work." The statement praised those seventy-two workers who had refused to strike and closed with an invocation that the people of New Martinsville "seek to live in harmony with all men," an ideal apparently contingent on having a union-free hospital.

Allied with the medical staff was a special Concerned Citizens Committee, which debuted at an August 7th County Commission meeting that drew a crowd of two hundred from both sides of the strike debate. Teacher Bonnie Hawkins, who emerged as a chief spokesperson for the Citizens Committee, said she believed unions were fine in private industry but not in the public sector. Any misunderstandings at the hospital, said Hawkins, "can be settled locally and effectively without outside intercession." The Citizens Committee objected to the West Virginia Education Association's support for the strike.[37]

Organized opposition to the strike emphasized its illegality and the strikers' betrayal of patients. The union pointed to the moral hypocrisy of the employer's cloak of "Nightengalism," charging that it was used to justify unfair wages, employer disrespect, and an autocratic management style. To the strikers, the hospital's "irresponsible and arrogant" behavior amounted to a denial of basic democratic rights for the nonsupervisory employees. True, the strike might technically violate an obscure state law, one that was at that moment being challenged in the state Supreme Court by this very union. But the employer was determined to deny its workers' "speech, assembly, and associational rights," which were guaranteed them by both the West Virginia and U.S. Constitutions. To the union, the hospital's actions reflected a contempt for Americans' legal and natural rights, a far more dangerous scenario than an illegal strike. The "real violence" around the conflict, said Stewart, was the denial of workers' rights by an "arbitrary and capricious board of trustees."[38]

Ralph Montgomery wrote a regular column for the *Wetzel Chronicle*, called "First Cup of Coffee." He was not impressed by union arguments about democracy and law, especially when they came from Stewart. It turned out, you see, that "union organizer Dan Stewart was a member of the SDS" and would not apologize for it. This 1960s movement to "overthrow the government of the

United States" had no real belief in American democracy. Its members were "fed and nurtured by the most radical of leftist college professors. You can guess who their mentors were." To be fair, Montgomery wrote several thoughtful columns regarding the strike, and he was not simply a cheerleader for the hospital trustees. But this particular attack was shocking in the depth of its vitriol, a perspective, said Montgomery, learned from his experience with SDS when he was a reporter in Cleveland. The fact that he knew nothing about the Marshall SDS chapter (he learned of Stewart's membership only a few days before his column appeared, from a story in the *Wheeling Register*) apparently was irrelevant, determined as he was to expose the organizer's dangerous past to the people. He warned his readers never to forget "that there is a cadre of hardcore SDS types in the nation today, still bent on mischief." [39]

Montgomery failed to acknowledge that just a week earlier, Stewart had consented to a suggestion by state labor commissioner Stephen Cook and the county commissioners. They asked if Stewart would absent himself from proposed discussions between the union and the trustees, meaning that the board would be dealing solely with a delegation of workers. This represented a concession from the union but could possibly lead to a thaw in the negotiations. The hospital board rejected the overture. On the morning of August 28, the trustees emerged from an executive session and declared that any further talks were "unnecessary." [40]

This action, added to their observation of consistently obstructionist behavior from the trustees, prompted two members of the County Commission to issue a scathing press release. They were "extremely disappointed" that the board had "callously" and "arrogantly" refused to meet with employee representatives. The breakdown in talks was "due solely to the intransigent attitude" of the Board of Trustees. The hospital's labor-management policies were "out of the dark ages." It appeared obvious "to any knowledgeable person" that the union had not pressured the workers to organize. The board's "inept and insensitive" policies had finally caused their workers to rebel "against long-standing injustices and inequities." The commissioners also announced that they would expand the hospital's Board of Trustees by two members, something the union had been lobbying for. Given that less than a month earlier the commissioners had pledged their "complete support" to the hospital trustees, these developments lent credibility to the strikers' grievances. [41]

The union sought to build solidarity with the public and with the regional labor movement, with considerable success. Over forty-two hundred citizens signed petitions supporting the right to an election. Union members scheduled town meetings in New Martinsville and nearby Wileyville to explain their position and report on their meetings with the trustees. They educated their neighbors about work at the hospital, along with broader messages of workers' rights and the push for collective bargaining for state workers. They portrayed the hospital trustees, all of whom were from prominent families, as a hereditary elite whose concentrated economic and civic power demanded the type of countervailing authority a unionized workforce could guarantee. At least four hundred unionists from the United Steelworkers, the International Chemical Workers, and the American Flintglass Workers joined the hospital strikers and their supporters for a rally and Main Street march in mid-November. The state AFL-CIO and the Monongahela-Preston Central Labor Body supported the struggle with several large donations.[42]

As rhetoric around the strike intensified, the LPNs and service and maintenance workers at Lewis Wetzel Nursing Home, a private facility near the hospital, voted 20 to 4 to be represented by Local 1199WV. The NLRB election was held on October 11, and by late November the parties began negotiations. By February 14, 1980, the management and the union bargaining committee had agreed, without a strike, to a three-year contract. Stewart pointed to the Lewis Wetzel campaign as an example of how clearly delineated employee and management rights, respected by both sides, could lead to a stable labor-management environment. Why then, he asked, was a guaranteed right to collective bargaining still denied to West Virginia's public employees?[43]

This compendium of positive developments suggests that the union was able to sustain momentum for several months, but there were signs that the strike was breaking by Thanksgiving. A tepid attempt by the union to marshal a boycott against antiunion businesses in town faltered. The newspaper responded with the "aliens in our midst" argument again, berating union outsiders for "hoodlum behavior" and brazen extortion against the "fair-minded" merchants of New Martinsville. A boycott is "the action of bullies, trying to muscle a small business man or woman into bending to their will." The *Chronicle* urged its readers to "show the big-city bullies what a family really is." The hospital periodically offered to take employees back if they would quit the strike. Stewart claimed that the union members were determined to hold out, but administrator Joe Ross insisted that he had spoken with strikers who would return to work "after the first of the year." Finally, on February 26, 1980, about twenty-five strikers asked the County Commission to help them get reinstated at the hospital. One strike leader told the newspaper that "we tore down the picket signs, sent a group letter, and then went as individuals to apply for our jobs. We'll do whatever we're asked to do." The economic pressure of the seven-month strike, said Stewart, "was more than they could bear." A final strike-related entry in the County Commission minutes is poignantly simple:

IN RE: WETZEL COUNTY HOSPITAL

Helen Crimmel and Frances Castilow presented a letter to the County Commission signed by "Inactive Employees of Wetzel County Hospital." Letter stated that they will not request being put on the agenda at any other time. (Letter filed)[44]

Board president Robert Bridgeman announced that the fifty-five holdout strikers (the "inactive" employees") had refused to quit the strike when they "were offered their jobs back in December." The hospital would not bump any replacement workers to make a place for them, but he implied the inactive workers might be called back in the future if needed. Bridgeman also reported that the hospital would sue the union for damages, in spite of the Fairmont case then being considered by the West Virginia Supreme Court of Appeals.[45]

On April 1, 1980, the Board of Trustees voted 10 to 2 to fire the fifty-five inactive workers. The editor of the *Wetzel Chronicle* said the termination was "inevitable" and "appropriate." The workers knew they might lose their jobs "when they walked out." They "gambled that public sentiment would support a union in a hospital and they lost. . . . Too many people still believe that unions have no place in government or emergency services." [46]

Some of the strikers pledged to keep their union membership. One, Shirley Mullet, later became an organizer for 1199WV/KY. She was also one of a small group of fired workers who began a fight to expose what they identified as corruption and conflicts of interest among the Board of Trustees. They collected evidence and brought over one hundred alleged abuses by board members to a suit in the Wetzel County Circuit Court. The charges included inflated emergency room fees by three physicians at the hospital who were on the board. The same three doctors were accused of using hospital labs and supplies for their private practices, without compensating the hospital. The suit charged the board with violating competitive bidding requirements for legal and insurance services by steering bids to favored agencies. The board was also charged with violating nepotism policies at the hospital.

On June 23, the court ordered that seven of the eleven trustees be permanently removed from the board. One of those was Dr. LeMoyne Coffield, the hospital's chief of medical staff. It was Dr. Coffield who had released the "Medical Staff Policy Statement," which condemned the union drive and advised the citizens of New Martinsville to "live in harmony with all men." [47]

Chapter 8

Survival in the Time of Reagan

Beginning in 1978, 1199WV undertook an energetic organizing drive in nursing homes in West Virginia, Kentucky, and southern Ohio.[1] Over one hundred Heartland of Charleston LPNs, nurses' aides, housekeepers, laundry, dietary, and maintenance workers signed the first nursing home contract in West Virginia early in 1978. In 1980 the union returned to Beckley, where Heartland workers voted decisively to be represented by 1199WV. By 1988, Woodruff (as president of the 1199 WV/KY/OH district, southern Ohio 1199ers having merged with WV/KY in 1982) could report that the union had organized twenty nursing homes in the three states. He proclaimed that "nursing home employees are the most oppressed, overworked and underpaid group of workers in the health care field." The union drafted an ambitious organizing plan for West Virginia that targeted about forty homes in the expanding for-profit corporate chain nursing homes including Heartland (a subsidiary of Owens-Illinois, Inc.), Americare, and Care Haven. "The long-range goal," wrote Woodruff, "is to organize them all."[2] By1986, ten hospital and nursing home chapters in West Virginia had 1,220 members. Moreover, one thousand West Virginia state employees in the Department of Health were 1199 members, this in spite of the fact that state workers still had no legal right to collective bargaining. Kentucky's three nursing home and two hospital chapters totaled 725 members. And, owing to an exhaustive drive led by Dan Stewart among public service and health workers in Ohio in 1986, the Ohio membership stood at over 5,000 (See chapter 9 for more on the Ohio state employees' campaign).[3]

The Highlands Regional Medical Center (HRMC) Local of 1199WV/KY was hours away from a contract renewal strike when the hospital and the union agreed to terms on March 22, 1978. The membership had interpreted the influx of armed guards from an outfit called Storm Security and the employer's hiring of Southeastern Employers Service Corporation (SESCO) as signs that the hospital intended to force a strike in an attempt to break the union. SESCO had recently broken a union at Kearns Bakery in London, Kentucky, and, according to LPN Garnet Cox, the company was leveraging intense pressure as the expiration date approached. But a combination of effective public outreach, persistent personal contacts with some of the hospital's Board of Trustees, and a last-minute mass sit-down at the hospital administrator's office convinced hospital management that the union was not weakening. The union held, finally accepting the hospital's offer for the 220 LPNs, technicians, and service and maintenance workers at HRMC. The contract would be in effect until the spring of 1981.

Larry Daniels believed the three-year agreement was a great improvement over the original 1976 contract, which "was really just getting our feet wet, as you could say." Annual pay raises guaranteed a 22 percent wage increase over the term of the deal. Improved health and pension benefits and an expedited grievance procedure were included in the contract language. The membership ratified the contract by a 3 to 1 margin. What nobody anticipated was the calamity looming on the horizon, brought on by a perfect storm of global economic factors. The crisis erupted in 1979, described by labor lawyer Thomas Geoghegan as "that damned, horrible year." The spark that lit the kindling was the second major oil shock of the decade, when the Organization of Petroleum Exporting Countries (OPEC) tripled oil prices after the Iranian Revolution ousted the Shah, undermining U.S. leverage in the Persian Gulf. The 1979 oil crisis begat a bewildering economic phenomenon labeled stagflation, a symptom of the decline of America's post–World War II global hegemony. Stagflation referred to the combination of soaring inflation and high unemployment numbers in 1979 when, says Geoghegan, "the U.S. economy then crashed in flames." The oil crunch precipitated a brief production boom in parts of Appalachia when Jimmy Carter's President's Commission on Coal promoted a coal-based national energy policy to ease the energy crisis. West Virginia governor Jay Rockefeller predicted that Appalachian coal mines could remedy both the energy squeeze and the mountains' unemployment woes by increasing production by 100 million tons a year. Rockefeller believed, hopefully, that the social costs in terms of environmental degradation and public health could be minimized by strict enforcement of Environmental Protection Agency regulations and new clean coal technologies.[4]

Environmentalists and public health advocates warned that increasing coal production would sacrifice the people, the streams, and the mountains themselves by superheating the demand for strip-mined coal and reward an especially destructive form, mountaintop removal (MTR). The Surface Mine Control and Reclamation Act of 1978, originally conceived as a means of limiting the social and environmental costs of stripping, included loopholes as big as all outdoors. As we now know, the tree huggers were right about things. When oil prices stabilized, the coal employment boom vanished but the social costs remained. Over the years, the colossal "dragline" scoops and trucks used on MTR sites proved incomprehensively destructive, representing a new level of violence in extractive methods while displacing thousands of miners. Once again, the people of the Appalachian coalfields faced layoffs, job losses, and deep economic uncertainty as Carter gave way to Ronald Reagan in the White House.[5]

The specter of stagflation and recession, along with the long-term hollowing out of America's basic industries and consequent threats to a comfortable standard of living, wiped out the gains of the 1978 HRMC contract for 1199ers. With a cumulative inflation rate of over 35 percent between 1979 and 1981, the 22 percent wage increase over the life of the three-year contract did not nearly keep pace with the cost of living. Typical differences separating workers and management in contract negotiations—wages, seniority rights, health insurance, vacations, holiday premium pay—were exacerbated by the rapid structural changes in the American economy and the hospital industry. The workers at HRMC anticipated that hospital executives would take a hard line over operating and labor costs, but most were taken aback by the employer's "take it or leave it" posture as negotiations began early in 1981.[6]

Before long the union's twenty-member negotiating committee, working with Woodruff and organizer Barry Smith, concluded that the employer was determined to break the union. Daniels claimed that the union tried to avoid a strike "in every way possible," and during two months of negotiations before the March 25 strike deadline, the union offered not to strike and to submit the issues to binding arbitration. The administration refused. Delegate Ellis Stevens told the *Floyd County Times* that the hospital administration was slow-walking contract negotiations and that a strike appeared "unavoidable." An operating room technician and five-year employee, Stevens was paid $3.59 ($10.16) per hour. He explained how over 200 of the hospital's 280 workers were paid less than $4.00 an hour. Even with the improvements since unionization, Stevens claimed there was a "100 percent turnover rate in staff here every year, and that ought to tell you something." Assistant administrator Russell Dean said that Stevens's turnover numbers were wildly exaggerated but did not cite any figures to disprove Stevens's charge.[7]

As the deadline for the ten-day strike notice approached, the union criticized the hospital's refusal, after two months of talks, to even bargain over economic issues. The bargaining committee complained of management's redundant haggling over minor differences in contract language. The union duly issued the mandatory notice, and the members voted 201 to 1 to strike at midnight on March 24/25. The hospital proceeded to mobilize a militarized security force in preparation for a long strike. Originally the hospital retained a Tennessee firm,

Murray Guard, for security. But some of the guards reportedly developed a sympathy for the union, and Murray Guard was replaced by a particularly intimidating contingent of about forty guards from the ironically named Nuckols and Associates, a Cincinnati firm. The Nuckols guards were armed with guns, billy clubs, and blackjacks, compelling labor journalist Arnell Church to write that "the grounds had the appearance of an armed camp. Riot gear was stored in the back of vans and every move by the pickets was videotaped." In late June, ninety days into the strike, Russell Dean denied 1199WV/KY's charge of union busting but conceded that there had been no meaningful negotiations since the strike began. The strike lasted for 105 days before the two sides reached a settlement, assisted by a federal mediator. This conflict divided the community and placed a heavy burden on families already pressured by raging inflation. Many of the women workers at HRMC, constituting about 70 percent of the workforce, were their families' primary means of support and drew only $30 per week from the National Union strike fund. About one-third were married to UMWA members, who were also on strike and drew no strike pay.[8]

When the membership ratified a new contract on July 7, they had secured a 41 percent wage increase over three years, representation on the hospital's safety committee, and improved benefits and grievance handling language. But the key issue in what became a "protracted and violence-ridden strike," wrote 1199WV/KY organizer Laura Batt, "was the existence of the union at HRMC." The hospital's strategy, said Tom Woodruff, was "to starve the people out and get workers to come back with no improvements and no union." National president Leon Davis agreed, calling out the hospital for its "shocking campaign against low-paid Appalachian hospital workers striking for modest gains in Eastern Kentucky." The National Union regarded the HRMC strike as an important one for the labor movement nationally; if the union could fight back and survive there, it would set an example for all workers amidst the gathering storm of the Reagan era. Nurses' aide Lorna Branham understood the strike's significance. She and her coworkers believed they represented the vanguard of resistance to the escalating assault against labor. That responsibility "made us stronger," said Branham, "made us able to stay out longer."[9]

Violence, as Laura Batt recounted, played a more central role in this conflict than any of 1199WV/KY's many hard fights in Appalachia. This study does not presume to thoroughly deconstruct the many reasons for that violence nor definitively attribute more violence to one side than the other. As one might imagine, the many violent incidents against property and human beings that marked this strike elicited contradictory explanations from the union and the employer, although both acknowledged frequent violent behavior from all parties. The August 1981 issue of *Modern Healthcare* summarized the levels of violence in a well-balanced feature by Suzanne LaViolette, shortly after the strike was settled:

> The 15-week strike, decried by both the hospital and the union as extraordinarily violent, ended last month when the union agreed to a wage boost of about 41 percent over three years. But before the strike was over, both the union's headquarters and the hospital were riddled with bullets, security guards and union members were allegedly beaten, and taunts, death threats and "filthy language" were lobbed between the two camps. The strike turned out to be "the most vicious thing I've ever seen," according to Tom Woodruff, president of District 1199 West Virginia/Kentucky. A hospital executive agreed but placed the blame on the union.

The union accused the hospital of fomenting a violent atmosphere by flaunting the heavily armed Nuckols guards with their armored vans and SWAT team regalia. Strikers reported being followed on their drive home. Picketers came to dread the verbal abuse and bullying aura projected by the guards. A court injunction in mid-April limited the number of union picketers to five at two hospital entrances, where they were easily outnumbered by the guards. Russell Dean admitted that the presence of the Nuckols guards, outfitted with riot gear, contributed to escalating tension as the strike wore on. There were injuries on both sides of the divide but thankfully none were life threatening. Several union members, guards, and nonstriking employees faced assault charges. Some were dismissed when the strike was settled and others were settled by payment of fines.[10]

The HRMC local was able to survive the strike in great measure because of the support from the National Union and the regional labor movement. The National provided $120,000 in strike funds, launched an "adopt a striker" campaign for the Kentucky workers, and distributed literature to 1199 locals nationwide appealing for support. Members in Philadelphia, Baltimore, and New York made monthly donations to the campaign. Over fifty organizations, mostly local unions, donated over $30,000 to the Kentucky strikers. Larry Daniels was inspired by the gestures of solidarity from across the nation. "We learned," he said, "that we have brothers and sisters who care about us everywhere."[11] A support rally scheduled at Jenny Wiley State Park for July 11 turned into a victory celebration after the settlement. Speakers included Eula Hall, the legendary founder of the Mud Creek Health Clinic, and others representing UMWA Local 30, the Bluegrass Chapter of the Coalition of Labor Union

Women, the Commission on Religion in Appalachia, the Council of Southern Mountains, and the Appalachian Alliance. Ola Jean Craven, a member of the Highlands local, brought her gospel group, the Old Screech Revival, to perform along with other musicians.[12]

The Nuckols guards packed up their cameras and riot gear and left the hospital grounds on July 11. The next day patients began filling the hospital, which had operated at about 20 percent occupancy during the strike. Workers were called back as the patient census increased. Woodruff was already looking ahead. "We've moved from the Dark Ages at least to the Middle Ages," he said. "Hopefully, next time we'll move into the modern era." In a way, however, the Dark Ages were making a comeback. A few weeks after 1199WV/KY survived to fight again at Highlands Regional, the nation's Professional Air Traffic Controllers (PATCO) walked off their federal jobs. President Ronald Reagan premiered the union-busting feature of the "revolution" that bore his name, and "employers began fighting unions with a level of determination unseen since the New Deal." As neoliberal thinking and practice worked its way into the fabric of the nation's political economy, the very existence of the labor movement was threatened.[13]

During the presidential campaign of 1980, Ronald Reagan promised that his administration would work toward a "spirit of cooperation" with labor, particularly the seventeen thousand members of PATCO. A review of Reagan's appointments to the NLRB, however, forewarned that President Reagan's actions would likely not match his campaign rhetoric. The August edition of *1199 News* announced that Reagan's new chairman of the NLRB was John R. Van de Water. As a longtime management consultant, his record of advising companies how to defeat unions in over one hundred campaigns was a red flag for organized labor. To fill another board vacancy, Reagan appointed Robert P. Hunter, an aide to Senator Orrin Hatch of Utah, who had led the Republican filibuster that defeated the 1978 labor law reform bill. *Business Week* noted that "Reagan is tilting the NLRB sharply toward management."[14]

If the leadership of PATCO was aware of such worrisome appointments by the new president, they either acted too late or, worse, assumed that as federal employees the composition of the NLRB was of little concern to their union. Indeed, they had been so impressed with Reagan's preelection commitment to upgrade their outdated equipment, increase staff levels, and moderate the "unreasonable hours" worked by the controllers that the union endorsed him for president. Surely the new president would remember, wrote historian H. W. Brands, "and respond accordingly." Shortly after Reagan took office, with contract negotiations approaching, PATCO's new president Robert Poli believed the union was well positioned to secure significant contractual gains, despite the former Screen Actors Guild president's "basic antipathy for unions." [15]

Founded in 1968, PATCO had bargained over the years for generous wage and benefits packages which reflected the air traffic controllers' critical role in keeping the nation's airways safe and reliable. Americans may have envied but did not seem to resent the fact that, due to the high stress of their work, air controllers could retire at fifty with full benefits. The relative security of a federal job, however, did not make federal workers quiescent in a militant time. For example, PATCO launched a traffic slowdown at major airports in 1968, postal workers walked out in a wildcat strike in March of 1970, and PATCO staged a three-week sickout in April of 1970. The Federal District Court of Washington, D.C., then permanently enjoined federal employee strikes in 1971. Controllers at O'Hare International Airport in Chicago nonetheless staged a slowdown in 1980, a move that many industry observers believed was a dry run for a strike in 1981. Ignoring the federal injunction, President Jimmy Carter took no punitive action against the slowdown. [16]

In June of 1981 the air traffic controllers rejected, by an astounding margin, a contract negotiated by Poli and Andrew Lewis, the secretary of transportation. The major obstacle was the administration's refusal to reduce the controllers' work week from forty to thirty-two hours, but there was also union dissatisfaction over wages and management's alleged slighting of safety protocols. Negotiations broke down after the vote, and the union set a strike date of August 3, with Poli citing the main issue for the controllers as "early burnout." If the union membership believed their friend Ronald Reagan would acquiesce to an illegal strike, they were mistaken. "Dammit, the law is the law," said the Great Communicator, "and the law says they cannot strike. If they strike, they quit their jobs." On the morning of the strike, Reagan and Lewis held a press conference to announce that controllers who were not back on the job within forty-eight hours would be fired.

Poli and the union had done a poor job of educating the public about work hours and other stress-related factors and had failed to lay the foundation for a widespread show of solidarity from the labor movement. Media coverage sensationalized the union's salary and benefits demands, steadily alienating the public from controllers who were portrayed as greedy rather than as justly compensated. Burdened by stagflation and economic uncertainty, nearly 60 percent of Americans, including many union members, supported the president's hard line. On August 5, Reagan fired the more than eleven thousand air controllers who stayed out on strike and banned them from federal employment for life.

Nonstriking members, supervisors, and military controllers kept reduced flight traffic moving until replacements were trained. A massive labor Solidarity Day demonstration to protest Reagan's policies took place in Washington on September 19, as PATCO tried to keep the strike going by means of picketing, demonstrations, and marches around the country. Strikers invoked Reagan's rhetorical support for the striking workers of Poland's Solidarity movement. How could the president embrace the Polish shipyard workers striking against their government but deny that right to American workers? These tactics failed. On October 22, the Federal Labor Relations Authority, which oversaw federal labor law, decertified the union.[17]

Joseph A. McMartin, historian of the PATCO strike, cautions against identifying the strike as the cause of organized labor's crisis in the 1980s, a simplistic analysis that, he says, has taken on "mythic proportions." The PATCO episode "magnified the effects of the multiple problems" facing American labor, including the shift from an industrial to a service economy, the "reduction in job-protecting tariffs," and a "growing resistance to collective bargaining by American corporations." The strike and Reagan's response were more a catalyst than the origin of labor's decline. It was significant mostly in that it had a "dispiriting psychological effect on workers" who saw a union of highly specialized and "seemingly indispensable" workers permanently replaced. As evidenced by 1199's struggles nationally and in Appalachia, modern antiunionism had long been institutionalized. Reagan's destruction of PATCO, however, signaled employers that union busting now had support from "the highest levels of the federal government." One labor writer observed that Reagan's message would be heard and acted upon by countless employers and administrators in both the private and public sectors. Thomas Donahue of the AFL-CIO warned that bosses and city managers nationwide would "want to look like a hero" by emulating Reagan's defiance of the "civilized rules of collective bargaining."[18]

It could be that the owner of the New Martinsville Health Center, formerly the Lewis Wetzel Nursing Home, was one of the bosses who "wanted to look like a hero" in the Reagan era. You will recall that in February of 1980, management at the private for-profit facility had signed a three-year contract with 1199WV covering the service and maintenance employees. In November of 1982, owner George Crouch moved his business to a newly constructed larger facility that more than doubled the patient capacity of Lewis Wetzel to 120 and expanded the home's bargaining unit from 33 to 60. About one-half of those were new hires and still in the probationary period of the contract, which was due to expire in February of 1983. Crouch earlier had notified the chapter officers and delegates and their 1199WV/KY/OH representative, Harold Schlechtweg, that he intended not to honor the contract after the move to the new facility. All current employees would lose their seniority and "bargain with him individually for wages and benefits." They were welcome to reapply for work and go through a job interview.

Crouch apparently was planning to throw out the contract when the nursing home moved into its new building on grounds that are somewhat unclear. Perhaps the relocated facility would operate under new articles of incorporation, and the employer believed he could abrogate the contract by claiming the original business no longer existed. He may have assumed that the failed Wetzel County Hospital strike had weakened the position of 1199 in the eyes of workers at his facility. He apparently hoped that the new hires could be persuaded or bullied into rejecting the union in a new election. What this action sounds like is an attempted shortcut to decertification, and it seems plausible to assume that Crouch concluded it was worth a try in the new era, even if the tactic was a blatant violation of the legal duty to bargain in good faith. In fact, a decertification petition began circulating around the center, falsely claiming that 1199WV/KY/OH could no longer represent the workers without a new election.

Sources on this heavy-handedness are meager, but the membership, no doubt after an initial shock, implemented a systematic response. A majority of the center's workers petitioned the owner, demanding that he defend his plans in face-to-face meetings. The federal district court ordered Crouch to honor the existing contract and bargain in good faith for a renewal when it expired. The regional NLRB office in Cincinnati called the decertification petition "fraudulent," and Crouch eventually relented and agreed to negotiate a new contract. The negotiating committee consisted of Schlechtweg and six LPNs, all women. The parties signed a new contract to take effect on February 7, 1983, just one day after expiration of the original agreement. It included significant wage and benefits increases, including for part-time workers, and established a labor-management committee to handle group grievances. During the deliberations, about one-third of the entire bargaining unit showed up in force at one of the sessions. Mary Rose Yoho, one of the core members of the negotiating committee, remarked that "all those people showing up at the negotiating session helped us get it. George was very nervous when he saw all of us there."[19]

Whether the owner at the New Martinsville Health Center took such reckless actions out of ignorance or to test just how brazenly the "civilized rules of collective bargaining" could now be safely ignored cannot be determined. But if a highly skilled and professionalized union like PATCO could be busted, why not go after a union made up of practical nurses, nurses' aides, orderlies, kitchen help, laundry workers, housekeepers, and painters? Mr. Crouch may have been overzealous, but his behavior was in keeping with the ascendant corporate culture of the Reagan era.

During the Reagan years, 1199 WV/KY[/OH] intensified its program of political education so the membership would be schooled on how to confront an administration that, in the words of the National Union, was "now controlled by depraved ideologues without compassion for American workers." Phil Carter, Dan Stewart's ally from the civil rights struggle, often led workshops and discussions for delegates on civil disobedience, building community coalitions, and institutional racism. David Evans, a Vietnam veteran and double-amputee from Elkview, West Virginia, educated members about U.S. foreign policy in Central America. Evans throughout the 1980s was the director of a prosthetics program for Medical Aid for El Salvador, an organization dedicated to treating civilian victims of their country's civil war. Local 1199 members sponsored joint programs on veterans' rights, workers' rights, antiwar mobilization, Reaganomics, and campus activism with Marshall Action for Peaceful Solutions (MAPS), a student organization that identified itself as a legatee of the CIP and the SDS at Marshall.[20]

The agenda at the 1982 delegates assembly at Cedar Lakes Conference Center near Ripley, West Virginia, reflected the leadership's assessment that American unions were under siege. The Resolutions Committee, which included stalwarts Tonya Boggess from Fairmont General, Juanita Jenkins from Glen Manor Nursing Home in Cincinnati, Kay Bishop from Harrison Pavilion in Cincinnati, Judy Siders from Cabell Huntington, and Ellis Stevens from HRMC, called for a commitment from the delegates to mobilize against "Reagan's Raw Deal."[21]

The Resolutions Committee argued that the membership must join with other labor, community, and religious groups in fighting the Reagan budget's "deep slashes in human needs programs, the largest peacetime military buildup in the nation's history, and unparalleled shifts in the tax burden from the wealthy and corporations to low-and-middle-income people." Voter registration, resistance to right-to-work (referred to as "Right-to-Freeload") talk by their legislators, advocacy for nuclear disarmament, and calling out Reagan's military aid for the murderous right-wing government in El Salvador and for the murderous right-wing antigovernment Contras in Nicaragua—all must be recognized as the obligations of workers and citizens. They must call out the budget's "military overkill" at the cost of sacrificing human needs. They must fight against funding cutbacks at the NLRB, the Federal Mediation and Conciliation Service, and the Department of Labor. These cuts meant ever longer delays in elections and arbitration hearings, stacking the deck against unions. They must work to elect proworker candidates through the district's "Solidarity Fund." They must commit to organizing the fifty thousand unorganized healthcare workers in their district, 80 percent of whom are women "who have been historically discriminated against" in terms of wages, benefits, and working conditions. "Our Union has proven that through struggle and organization," healthcare workers and their patients will have a better life.[22]

Earlier, health systems personnel specialist William Rothman pointed out that hospital managers feared a unionized workforce because of "the repulsive thought that management will lose control of the operation of the institution." That fear was reinforced in the early 1980s by "inflation the likes of which people had not seen in generations." The explosion of the healthcare industry's operational costs and the pressures of competition, in the estimation of labor writer Kim Moody, "led to a growing number of hospitals to attempt cost-cutting through work reorganization." Management's ability to impose such reorganization was one of many interdependent factors in a system broadly called "lean production" or "management by stress." Critics of lean production/MBS identified a "new management-led offensive" beginning in the late 1970s and escalating in the 1980s and 1990s. "The neoliberal era had arrived," says Moody, and employers demanded concessions in wages, benefits, and working conditions. Faced with plant closings, outsourcing, and capital flight, unions' bargaining power declined and they often had to swallow the concessions. Lean production and management by stress, terms with negative connotations, were usually referred to as "synchronous production" or something like that by the "job-hopping executives" who built their careers by sowing the seeds of work reorganization at the nation's workplaces. The principles of the system were initially applied to assembly-line production but spread to such diverse industries as telecommunications and health care. Throughout the 1980s, Appalachian 1199ers encountered lean production through layoffs and job reduction (soon known as "reductions in force"), expanded record keeping, changing work rules, and creeping multitasking. Lean production in hospitals, of course, reflects an attempt to cut costs through work reorganization, says Moody. "But just as in a factory," he explains, "it usually means more output with fewer people." Flexible, "multi-functional workers," doing jobs that "can be used interchangeably," comprise the essential objective of the system. The modernized language of lean production was new, but it referred to practices that had been around for decades. To many workers, "flexibility" sounded a lot like "speedup." The 1199ers at King's Daughters, Cabell Huntington, and Fairmont General (see the next chapter) were among the millions of working-class Americans who confronted the shocks of lean production and work reorganization in the 1980s.[23]

Ashland, with a population of twenty-seven thousand in 1980, was the largest city in eastern Kentucky. Located in Boyd County on the Ohio River, the town was formed by industrialists of the Kentucky Iron, Coal and Manufacturing Company in 1854. Several feeder railroads connected Ashland to the region's iron furnace settlements and transported raw materials and finished goods for shipment on the Big Sandy and Ohio Rivers. The Chesapeake and Ohio consolidated the smaller lines in 1924 and served the thriving industrial center that included the American Rolling Mill Company (ARMCO) and Ashland Oil, a major refining operation also founded in 1924. With the downsizing of its industrial base by the 1980s, King's Daughters Hospital, which was founded in 1897, became an increasingly important employer in Ashland. The Kentucky river city was a bit player in a cast of thousands of American towns and cities confronting the realignments wrought by capital flight and deindustrialization. Within the context of accelerated global industrial restructuring, historian Lou Martin has questioned "whether any community built on industrial jobs can hope for anything approaching permanence." The new economic realities, therefore, left it up to service workers such as those at King's Daughters to protect their community's distinctive identity and define its place in the nation and the world.[24]

Service and maintenance workers at King's Daughters contacted 1199KY and began an organizing campaign early in 1980. Workers at the three-hundred-bed private-nonprofit hospital had been talking about forming a union for years but met determined management resistance, and they had lost an election with another union in 1976. In addition to low wages and "paltry benefits," basic issues of understaffing and respect motivated many of the workers. Several complained of verbal abuse toward women by one of the King's Daughters vice presidents and of favoritism shown by supervisors. Wage increases were supposedly based on a merit system but were allegedly granted arbitrarily. "No matter how well you performed," said nurses' aide Donna Holbrook, "if the head nurse didn't like you, you were denied a raise." King's Daughters employees paid for their health insurance, had no dental coverage, and there were no bonuses for working holidays. Nurses' aide Goldie Crain, who emerged as one of the union's natural leaders, got involved because she was "tired of being treated like a dog."[25]

With the new membership at King's Daughters, the West Virginia and Kentucky areas now had the required numbers to form the 1199WV/KY district, as noted in chapter 1. For seven months, leading up to the NLRB election, the employer at King's Daughters carried out a familiar union avoidance campaign. Nevertheless, with support from the local steelworkers, the Ashland Labor Council, and the Kentucky AFL-CIO, 1199WV/KY won the August 21 election by a vote of 221 to 101. As contract negotiations began in September, the hospital fired its local law firm and retained "the largest anti-union law firm in the Midwest," the Cincinnati firm of Taft, Stettinnius, and Hollister (usually referred to simply as "Taft") to handle the talks. One of the original partners was Senator Robert Taft, an icon of post–World War II Republican conservativism. The firm's labor department had helped Taft write the Taft-Hartley law in 1947. Taft died in 1953.[26]

Over two months of bargaining ended with a first contract covering 360 service and maintenance workers at the hospital. The contract guaranteed a maintenance of union membership during the two-year term and established a dues checkoff. It included hourly pay increases of $1.09–$1.96 ($3.40–$6.12) over the two-year term, vacation and holiday pay, plus company-paid health coverage and a union-elected committee to advise the administration on health, safety, staffing, and patient care. "Now that we've got this union going," said Goldie Craig, "we [can] take care of patients the way they should be cared for." The contract also included a new benefits package for retirees, who had been getting "outrageously low pensions" even after years of service. Nurses' aide Irene Howard retired in 1978 with a pension of $65 per month. When the contract took effect, her pension immediately rose to $167. She "cried for joy," said Howard, and planned to spend the money to pay bills, buy "a little bit of extra food" for her and her grandson, and maybe even some new clothes. "It certainly made Christmas a little brighter this year."[27]

Article XXV of the King's Daughters collective bargaining agreement specified that the contract would expire at midnight on November 30, 1982. The union reluctantly accepted a provision that the contract would be renegotiated annually after that. Either party could take steps to terminate the agreement within the decertification provisions of the National Labor Relations Act, provided notice of ninety days be given for any decertification effort. This is standard contract language but bears notice here because, according to King's Daughters retiree Terry Beam, the hospital management habitually formed "little decert committees" in the months before contract negotiations. Beam worked as a clerk and a psychology aide beginning in 1980 and was a union delegate for twenty-five years. Retiree Maxine Toney, who worked over thirty years at King's Daughters as a nurses' aide, a "surgical hostess," a housekeeper, and finally in the medical records office, was a delegate and served on the 1199WV/KY/OH Executive Board for years. Dealing with management at the hospital "has always been a struggle," said Toney. She remembered constantly having to warn new members that they would be pressured to "join the company team" when the "little decert committees" appeared. The human resources officers, Toney said, were particularly adept at obstructing and delaying the resolution of grievances—forgotten paperwork, important phone calls coming into the office during a hearing, emergency staff meetings—anything to frustrate the grievant and chip away at the union's credibility. When the first contract expired, a new management team at the hospital rejected union requests to negotiate a multiyear contract, so the new contract would run from December 1, 1982 to November 30, 1983. According to the union, by late summer 1983 no grievances beyond the second step had been settled since the new contract took effect.[28]

About eight months into the 1983 contract term, rumors circulated around the hospital that Timothy Maloney, the leader of the new King's Daughters management team, intended to "upgrade the services" at the hospital by "professionalizing" the labor force. To nonprofessionals, that language foreshadowed the likelihood of work reorganization, layoffs, and job cuts. On August 3, hospital vice president John L. Marks assured union delegates that the hospital had "no intention of laying off nurse aides or other employees," adding, "Employees who do their jobs are not in jeopardy." Two days later, the hospital announced that thirteen nurses' aides from the post-cardiac care wing of the hospital had been fired at the end of a midnight shift, their duties to be taken over by LPNs and RNs. Maloney declared that "in health care today, it is who has the better staff." The hospital had not given any advance warning of the firings, said Maloney, "because of anticipated problems." Maloney claimed that the hospital had "no present plans to terminate the approximately 115 remaining nurses' aides." If so, those plans soon changed, as one hundred more nurses' aides, all union workers, were fired in two rounds over the next two months. The nurses' aides job duties would be added to the workload of about sixty LPNs and RNs, none of whom were in the bargaining unit. The terminated nurses' aides eventually received letters notifying them that the firings were for "just cause," with no explanation as to the specifics of that cause. To 1199ers, Maloney was following through on a plan to bust the union, having reportedly told a group of administrators in Huntington that he did not believe in unions, that they were unnecessary, and that "I will get rid of the union at King's Daughters Hospital within a year." The firings and Maloney's rhetoric prompted 1199 organizer David Freeland to contact all the unions in Boyd and Greenup Counties to spread the word about the crisis at King's Daughters. "In these economic times of take-aways and union busting all across the country," Freeland wrote, "I am sure you will recognize some of the tactics used by hospital management against our Union."[29]

If Maloney assumed that the shock of the abrupt firings would stifle "anticipated problems," he was mistaken. The union quickly implemented a public education and mobilization campaign to counter the hospital's public relations missives. The hospital touted the avowed advancements that an all-professional nursing staff would bring, such as "more accurate, comprehensive patient assessment, care, and reporting/charting." The elimination of nurses' aides would achieve "controlled costs because of more effective utilization of nursing personnel." The union responded with a costs-benefits claim of its own, asserting that the salaries and benefits for an all-professional staff would increase costs. But the most effective arguments the union made addressed the indirect social costs of eliminating the nurses' aides. The personal care that King's Daughters' patients and their families relied on would suffer without the nurses' aides. The aides spent their time and labor on "bathing and turning patients, reporting vital signs and disconnecting intravenous units. We are the eyes for the nurse." If RNs and LPNs were forced to add these tasks to their regular duties, the increased stress would degrade the amount of time and the quality of personal contact the nurses could expend on needy patients.[30]

Union literature portrayed Maloney as cruel, inhuman, arrogant, and callous, of treating the hospital as his "personal plaything." His plans had "destroy(ed) the lives of more than 100 members of this community," some of whom feared the loss not only of their livelihood but of their homes. "With total disregard for the interests of the community, and the people who work at KDH, Mr. Maloney is experimenting with staffing at 'his' hospital." The union brought the public directly into the struggle. Fair-minded "friends and neighbors who believe in justice" were invited to walk informational picket lines and attend town meetings sponsored by the Ashland Labor Council, where citizen input could recommend "help in finding a solution to the controversy." Efforts to get the public to take ownership of the resistance were helped along by a report that the hospital's "high-priced Cincinnati lawyer" from the Taft firm had told some workers that it was "none of this town's business what happens at the hospital."[31]

The union membership made it clear they would not approve any agreement that did not provide for the return of the fired nurses' aides to union jobs at KDH. Consequently, the union negotiating committee rejected three offers from the hospital that did not promise to bring the fired workers back. On December 1, one day after the contract expired, the union formed a mass picket line and charged the hospital with not bargaining in good faith. Leading into the Christmas holidays, the Ashland Area Labor Council supported the hospital workers' call for a boycott of KDH, which was announced in a specially printed newspaper entitled the *Hospital Reporter*. On December 10 the union distributed ten thousand copies of this paper in and around Ashland, accusing KDH of "conducting an experiment [on] our families, our friends, and our community." The back page of the *Reporter* included the names, addresses, and phone numbers of the hospital's Board of Managers, all of whom resided in Ashland, calling on them to exercise their power to run the hospital as "a vital institution that serves the community, not as the private plaything of Administrator Maloney." The union prepared a "Know Your Rights" flyer for the RNs and LPNs at King's Daughters, some of whom had already declared their intention not to cross the union's picket line in the event of a strike. The flyer assured the nurses that a walkout would be an "Unfair Labor Practices Protest Strike," as opposed to an economic strike, and any employees honoring the strike could not be fired. A strike notice seemed imminent, and union workers let it be known that they "were ready to strike for our people." [32]

At last Maloney effected a tactical retreat, and KDH and 1199WV/KY/OH signed a *three-year* contract, one of the union's objectives. The agreement stipulated that although the nurses' aide jobs would not be restored, the fired workers were invited back to the hospital in other union jobs. There would be a phased hiring-in procedure for those who would accept work as housekeepers, kitchen workers, maintenance workers, and other bargaining unit classifications. "I will miss caring for patients," said former nurses' aide Joe Kemper, "but I can have just as much pride as a housekeeper or in maintenance."

On February 1, 1984, television crews and newspaper reporters, many of whom had become known to 1199WV/KY/OH workers during the six-month reinstatement struggle, documented a return-to-work ceremony on the steps of the hospital. Chapter president Ann Woods and her coworker Belle Johnson cut a yellow ribbon, and workers, "flashing victory signs and smiling, quickly ascended the steps and walked back into the hospital." Labor journalist Joe Gordon summarized how the union at King's Daughters avoided a disaster and survived in the time of Reagan: "Fueled by fury, dignity, and imagination, it was a campaign that captured the attention—and conscience—of the people of Ashland. Their united efforts, mustered amid the hardships of unemployment, succeeded in building enough community support—from clergy, union people and community leaders—to win management's agreement to a re-employment provision in the union's new three-year contract." [33]

Two months later and twenty miles east of King's Daughters, the Board of Trustees at Cabell Huntington eliminated forty-three nurses' aide jobs, including thirty-nine covered by the contract with 1199WV/KY/OH. The hospital decided "to cut down on the help so they were going to get rid of all our aides," said Judy Siders. "This was in 1984; they were going to cut the budget. They were going to take [some of] the LPNs and move them to other

units, but they were going to get rid of all our aides. Said we didn't need aides."
The announcement came on April 16, 1984, and the Cabell Huntington local
immediately began a public campaign to contest the job cuts, including mass
demonstrations at City Council meetings. On May 9, union members began
distributing leaflets protesting the firings near the hospital. On May 11, hospital vice president Walter Jacobs charged that the leafleting violated a contract
clause prohibiting "picketing or patrolling" during the life of the agreement.
Over the next three days, the management fired fourteen employees for this
alleged violation of the agreement. One of those was Judy Siders, the local's
president, who on her day off had helped organize the leafleting. "We just set
up an informational picket line, there were fourteen of us, they came out to fire
me, so they fired fourteen of us!" Siders was actually not handing out leaflets
when Walter Jacobs fired her, charging that it was Siders who "let them do
that." "I didn't let 'em do it," Siders told him. "They wanted to do it, on their
own time." Siders knew the contract as well as anyone at the hospital, and she
was confident that a peaceful informational picket was not a violation. "They
gave us our pink slips. I said, 'Good, I've been dying to go to the beach.'" She
assumed that the next step would be for Woodruff, as the district president, to
consult with the union's lawyers about how to proceed with the "picketing and
patrolling" firings. Siders went to the beach.[34]

Rather than file grievances with the hospital, the union filed a petition
directly with the West Virginia Supreme Court of Appeals, referred to in the
decision as an "original proceeding in mandamus." The petitioners claimed
that the leafleting was protected by free speech guarantees under the state
and federal constitutions. The court agreed, stating that handing out leaflets
was "unquestionably" protected speech. The opinion was issued by Justice
Darrell McGraw, a liberal judge who had been elected to the bench with the
support of organized labor in 1976. Described as "an outspoken jurist [who]
was a lightning rod for conservative critics," McGraw was also in the majority
when the court decided for 1199WV in the 1980 Fairmont General Hospital
case.[35] His opinion in the leafleting case, citing twenty precedents, pointed
out that "leafleting" and "handbilling" were not mentioned in the collective
bargaining agreement, the petitioners were not on a wildcat strike, and they
were not interfering with hospital business. "The respondents" (the hospital
officers and Board of Trustees) were ordered to reinstate the petitioners with
back pay. Judy Siders returned from the beach and went back to work. She
claims that their petition, settled in three weeks, was the "fastest case that ever
went to the [West Virginia] Supreme Court."[36]

There was a remarkable sidebar to the Cabell Huntington free speech fight
in the spring of 1984. This was near the end of Reagan's first term, a period

that some historians refer to as the "Second Cold War." A flyer that some churchgoers in Huntington found on their windshield lends credence to that appellation. It read in part:

WE THINK YOU SHOULD KNOW . . .

WOODRUFF, President of Local 1199 WV/KY/Oh (which represents half the employees at CHH) was an active SDS (Students for Democratic Society) member at Marshall University.

CONTRIBUTIONS were made by the 1199 National Union to the Angela Davis Defense Fund and the Huey Newton (leader of the Black Panthers) Fund.

DARRELL McGRAW—Supreme Court Justice who wrote the decision in the recent suit brought by the union against CHH—was a guest speaker at the Dec. 1983 District 1199 WV/KY/OH convention held in Charleston.

WE WONDER . . .

WHAT organizations does Tom Woodruff belong to now? For that matter, is Leon Davis, former National 1199 President for 50 years, really a card carrying Communist?

1199's political contributions aren't listed on their 1983 financial statements. Is that because they're even worse than the ones listed above?

IS DARRELL McGRAW as biased as he appears? If so, how could he hand down a just decision involving 1199?

IS 1199's reputation for violence the reason so many employees of CHH (both union and non-union) [are] afraid to speak out?

. . . . and why does [organizer Harold Schlechtweg] threaten to pull down the hospital if the administration doesn't accede to his wishes?[37]

When asked about Woodruff's and Stewart's reputations as student radicals, Judy Siders recalled that in the early years of the union at CHH, she had to prepare new hires to resist the Red-baiting that management used against Woodruff. "Oh, there were articles in the paper! Tom *did* join something when he was younger, over at Marshall; that's why they called him a 'communist.' And 'Tom's a communist' because he was in some kind of club when he went to Marshall. Oh, yes. They used that on us. They used that on us."[38]

Chapter 9

"Organize or Die": An Ohio Odyssey and a Big Fight in Fairmont

The Ohio area of the National 1199 (1199OH) had about five hundred members in nursing homes and hospitals when it merged with 1199WV/KY in the summer of 1982. Ohio members had voted 157 to 8 in November 1981 to join their neighboring district, which at the time had twenty-five hundred members. Laura Batt and Barry Smith were organizing in southern Ohio at the time, representing Ohio 1199ers at seven facilities: Glen Manor, Oak Pavilion (the first organized nursing home in Ohio, in 1971), Wesley Hall, and Harrison House nursing homes in Cincinnati; the Veterans Administration Medical Center in Dayton (newly organized and representing 230 RNs); and the Ohio Masonic Home in Springfield.

The membership of the newly formed 1199WV/KY/OH would more than double, from three thousand to about sixty-five hundred, within five years. This growth was largely attributable to a political shift in Ohio that led to the adoption of a public employee collective bargaining law, pushed through by a majority Democratic state legislature, in 1983. In a scramble to represent the nine thousand professional and paraprofessional workers in state healthcare facilities, 1199WV/KY/OH engaged in a competitive struggle with larger, richer unions, including the American Federation of State, County, and Municipal Employees (AFSCME) and the Service Employees International Union (SEIU). The National Union selected Dan Stewart as project director for the Ohio campaign. The expense and combative nature of the campaign contributed to a growing movement within the National Union's Executive Board to affiliate with a larger and ideologically compatible healthcare union. They concluded that, in an era of corporate mergers in the healthcare industry, 1199 could leverage more organizing and political resources by allying with a more powerful organization. A merger with the SEIU had long been promoted by Leon Davis. By the end of the 1980s that was a reality, but not before serious disruption within the National Union. The merger is the topic of the final chapter.[1]

When the workers at Oak Pavilion began to organize in 1971, said 1199er Veronica Davis, "people were ready to do it. For the [healthcare] workers in Cincinnati, it started a labor movement. For the bosses in Cincinnati, they hated it." Davis recalled that before the Ohio chapter's 1982 merger with West Virginia and Kentucky, "They were doing their thing, and we were doing ours, but neither group knew about each other. Just to be affiliated or belonging to a larger group, you know, would give us the resources and the recognition and the power to do more organizing and become like a real union. We would belong, instead of on this island, with just us five hundred members." Delores Brantley, an African American worker at Hillside/Oakside Nursing Village in Cincinnati and future district vice president, explained the importance of class solidarity in overcoming the social and cultural distance between White and Black unionists in the new district: "It was culture shock. They weren't impolite. I don't want to say that, I'm just saying you could feel the tension a little bit. They felt a little uneasy being around us and I think some of us felt a little uneasy being around some of them, because it never happened before. We were all the same. We were hard working people, looking for some dignity, and some respect. And a decent wage. That's what it all boiled down to. That's all. That's all it took." [2]

Ann Woods of King's Daughters spoke of the admiration and mutual support network that developed among workers of different backgrounds when they joined forces. She used the example of her friendship and working alliance with Juanita Jenkins, a legendary natural leader who worked at the Glen Manor Nursing Home in Cincinnati: "Juanita Jenkins, she was on the [District] Executive Board, from Cincinnati. She took me under her wing, she always called me 'Hillbilly,' because of the way I talk [laughter], and I was so country and she was from the city, you know, and she used to say, 'I'm gonna take care of you, Hillbilly, don't worry about it.' There was no way we would have ever come in contact with one another had I not been part of the union." [3]

When Ohio state employees won collective bargaining rights in 1983, 1199WV/KY/OH had been organizing state and municipal workers in West Virginia since the mid-1970s. A significant cohort of the union's public employee membership was represented at Fairmont General Hospital and Cabell Huntington Hospital. As we have established, those workers won collective bargaining contracts not on the basis of legal right but by disciplined organizing and the mobilization of public pressure. After the West Virginia Supreme Court ruled in the union's favor in the 1979 Fairmont General suit against 1199WV, optimism was high among 1199ers that state workers would finally get a collective bargaining law (see chapter 7). Since the Supreme Court had recognized public workers' right to organize and strike peacefully, surely the legislature would provide a clear, consistent legal structure for them to avoid future conflict through protected negotiations.

But it was not to be. Organized labor was never able to "move politics" sufficiently, according to Tom Woodruff. "They always play the game with you," he said. The traditionally cautious West Virginia legislature was never more than lukewarm about extending rights by government intervention. "They kind of worked it out among themselves, the conservatives ran this branch for a while and the liberals ran [the other] and you couldn't ever get through both places." The legislators justified their reticence on the collective bargaining issue based on a series of five state attorney general opinions between 1938 and 1966. A 1970 study declared that those opinions "hold that public agencies and officials *may not* enter into collective bargaining agreements with labor organizations" (italics added). That precedent had obviously been upended at Cabell Huntington and Fairmont General. But despite persistent pressure from organized labor, West Virginia lawmakers never took the next logical step by clearly establishing bargaining rights. Roy Hiteshaw, an aide at Weston State Hospital, voiced the frustration of his coworkers in the state hospital system: "Trying to make progress without collective bargaining," he said, "is like trying to play baseball without a bat." [4]

In spite of political obstacles, 1199WV/KY/OH added over eleven hundred West Virginia state hospital employees to its membership by early 1983 as a subdivision of the district. These workers turned to the union as the instrument to help them overcome some grim realities at their workplaces, including serious understaffing and underfunding and wage scales that the union portrayed as shameful. Tellingly, three-quarters of the state's hospital workers qualified for food stamps. The accelerated rate of inflation had devalued their wages to the point where, as Woodruff noted, "state hospital workers are far worse off today than in July 1981, the date of their last increase." Over one hundred West Virginia state healthcare workers attended the union's district convention in Charleston in December 1982. Joined by the new National Union president, Henry Nicholas (Davis had just retired from that post), they picketed the residence of Governor Jay Rockefeller and held a news conference to dramatize their condition. The press heard that starting monthly pay for a nurses' aide was $635 ($1,797), for a food service worker, $607 ($1718), and $4.25 an hour ($12.03) for a licensed practical nurse. Moreover, the state was proposing that its workers pay a greater proportion of their healthcare premiums, which the union claimed would force many of them to "choose groceries over insurance and do without medical care." [5]

In addition to economic survival, worker and patient safety were major concerns for state hospital employees. When the West Virginia legislature's

Health and Welfare Committee conducted on-site hearings to investigate conditions at the state facilities, the lawmakers heard directly from workers in testimony at institutions such as Lakin Hospital in West Columbia, Colin Anderson near St. Mary's, Huntington State Hospital, Weston State Hospital in Weston, and Spencer State Hospital in Roane County.[6] A *Charleston Gazette-Mail* report quoted workers at Lakin as testifying that they were forced to make adult diapers from "old rags and tape"; that their kitchen employees had to share one paring knife; and that a recreational aide "hasn't had a merit raise in 29 years." The hospital was so understaffed that employees "must work as many as ten days in a row."[7]

Data collected by union members at their workplaces revealed that understaffing led to stretch-outs, in which each employee had to work alone with "large numbers of patients," some of whom were dangerously violent to themselves and others. As a result, more than three thousand patient injuries occurred over six months in 1984, projecting to an average of three injuries a year per patient. Nearly 70 percent of workers at all state hospitals suffered injuries that year. "If you work at one of the state's 12 mental hospitals," the *Charleston Gazette-Mail* reported, "chances are 2 to 1 you'll be injured in the course of a year." Short staffing and the stretch-outs figured into mass resistance to a plan by Governor Rockefeller to close Spencer State Hospital in 1983. Closing would mean layoffs for nearly 350 employees, many of them 1199ers, and the "dumping" of three hundred patients at already overburdened facilities around the state. Rockefeller's plan prompted strong protests by 1199WV/KY/OH members at the hospital, the state AFL-CIO, and community leaders in Spencer: "Faced with such widespread support for keeping Spencer open, the Legislature in March appropriated additional funds for that purpose. A move by an obviously nettled Gov. Rockefeller to veto $1.2 million of the legislature's appropriation and reduce the hospital to a 60-bed geriatric facility was found unconstitutional by the State Supreme Court."[8]

When one of her coworkers at Spencer State Hospital began talking up 1199WV/KY/OH, laundry worker Madeline Smith "signed up in ten minutes." She started carrying union cards with her and estimated that over the next few years she recruited more than two hundred of her coworkers for 1199WV/KY/OH. She attributed Spencer State Hospital's survival until its closure in 1989 to the union members' willingness to confront the powerbrokers in the state. Spencer workers participated in the union's annual State Hospital Day at the West Virginia statehouse, where they used their growing lobbying and public relations skills to advocate for their patients and their own dignity at work. A popular feature of State Hospital Day was the presentation of the Baloney Award to an especially obstructionist legislator or state official. A proposal to cut state employee health benefits, severe budget cuts for the state hospitals, a tendency by the state Civil Service Commission to overturn legitimate employee grievances or to protect injured workers from being fired—these were the type of transgressions that would earn the offender a five-pound hunk of baloney from 1199/WV/KY/OH. The bestowing of the Baloney Award drew plenty of press, who then were instructed on the issues at hand by member lobbyists. One Wetzel County Democratic senator bolted from his office onto the statehouse lawn when he saw Teresa Ball and the baloney coming his way at the 1988 State Hospital Day. They might not have a meaningful contract, but state employees could find ways of, as Madeline Smith put it, "kickin' ass for the working class."[9]

By 1983, the politics of healthcare labor relations in Ohio were significantly different from those in West Virginia. Between 1961 and 1982, Ohio Republicans always controlled either the governorship or one of the two legislative houses. Public employees did have a right to negotiate over working conditions, but comprehensive collective bargaining bills either died in committee or were vetoed by Republican governor James Rhodes, who served from 1963 to 1971 and from 1975 to 1983. During the "turbulent 1970s," without recourse to a clearly defined negotiating structure, Ohio public employees often walked out—public schoolteachers averaged twenty-five strikes per year in the mid-1970s. When Ohio voters punished the Republicans for the state's economic depression in the election of 1982, Democrats took control of both legislative assemblies, the governor's office, and all other statewide offices. Citing a critical need for "more responsible dispute resolution," the General Assembly passed Senate Bill 133 (SB 133), the Collective Bargaining Act, in late June of 1983. The new prolabor governor, Richard Celeste, signed the bill on July 6, 1983, and it took effect on April 1, 1984. The bill included a three-person State Employment Relations Board (SERB), to be appointed by the governor. The SERB was vested with broad authority to monitor state labor relations and had "final and conclusive" power to designate bargaining units for public employees.[10]

SB 133 extended collective bargaining rights to fifty thousand state government employees and about five hundred thousand eligible municipal, county, and school board workers. Several unions had been gearing up to win the loyalty of those employees. Local 1199WV/KY/OH filed for elections among the nine thousand professionals and paraprofessionals who toiled in state-run healthcare and social service agencies. On February 6–9, 1985, eighty organizers representing all twelve autonomous districts and all six areas of the National 1199 met in Columbus. National officers, including President Nicholas, Organizing Director Muehlenkamp, Secretary-Treasurer

Jerry Brown, and President Emeritus Davis attended to dramatize the national leadership's commitment to the Ohio drive.[11]

As this study has shown, a commitment to representing public employees had long been important to 1199WV/KY/OH. The public sector had become relatively favorable terrain for the labor movement since the expansion of government services during the Great Society era, and many states and municipalities had built stable and mutually beneficial labor relations with their employees. Nationwide, about 35 percent of public sector workers had union representation in 1985 while private-sector union density had declined to about 19 percent from a high of 35 percent in the mid-1950s. Some scholars claim that the major difference between public- and private-sector unions "comes down to the levels at which the employer opposes the union." Thomas Geoghegan wrote that "the public sector is the only place where unions can organize without being maimed," implying a climate of labor-management harmony at public worksites. Workers at Cabell Huntington, Fairmont General, Wetzel County Hospital, and the West Virginia state hospitals, however, might have taken exception to Geoghegan's comment.[12]

Given the experience 1199WV/KY/OH had with public sector organizing, the union expected to do well in the elections approaching in Ohio. But its competitors also had wide experience in the public sector and, by virtue of their size and financial resources, considerable clout to devote to Ohio. The SEIU, for example, had about 350,000 healthcare workers in its total membership of around 800,000. AFSCME, which had been organizing public workers since the early 1930s, had over a million members. The National 1199, on the other hand, was in the midst of a hangover emanating from bitter infighting between the leadership of the National Union and the original New York Local 1199. The result was the severing of the New York District from the National Union that it had founded in 1969. This separation, which was finalized on July 1, 1984, instantly reduced the total membership of the National Union by about half, down to seventy-two thousand. At the same time, the National Union finally broke with the RWDSU when that international union revealed a plan to dismantle the NU and absorb its membership. This "Great Separation," a development that is more completely summarized in the concluding chapter, came with a consequent shock to organizing, strike, and arbitration funds.[13]

The financial squeeze was critical, as such resources proved to be a significant factor in the Ohio campaign. The 1199/WV/KY/OH drive would rely as usual on its commitment to person-to-person mobilization but could not match their competitors' finely tuned "techniques that have proved effective in national political campaigns—from slick television ads and opinion polling to computer-targeted direct mail and satellite-fed news conferences." The

Washington Post estimated that AFSCME spent $6 million, more than the other competing unions combined, to pay for satellite transmissions and a staff of one hundred. Traditional door knocking, leafleting, and worker-to-worker dialogue were being squeezed by the newer methodologies as the unions in Ohio scrambled "to sign up the younger, predominantly female legions of office workers and service employees who make up the fastest-growing sectors of the nation's work force." At one point in the campaign, AFL-CIO president Lane Kirkland ordered 1199WV/KY/OH to abandon its contacts with some mental health workers who were already claimed by AFSCME. This is called "raiding," and before long 1199WV/KY/OH complained that AFSCME was raiding its state hospital locals in West Virginia. The *Post* reported that organizers in Ohio met a range of responses "from strong support to indifference and hostility," often having to explain some basic principles to workers unfamiliar with unions. One AFSCME organizer commented that many had no concept of what collective bargaining was, initially having assumed that when the law took effect on April 1, 1984, "they would get an automatic pay raise. But now they realize there's a lot more involved." [14]

The voting in the fall of 1985 brought mixed results. Some thirty-three hundred of the nine thousand professionals and paraprofessionals throughout Ohio voted to go with 1199/WV/KY/OH, the biggest win ever for the district but well short of aspirations. The thirty-three hundred votes were widely dispersed among fourteen agencies throughout the state at about 250 workplaces, or an average of thirteen workers at each site. The new 1199ers included folks with job titles like technical typist, clerical specialist, programming aide, corrections offer, parole or probation officer, child and family social worker, research assistant, and community health worker. Their annual pay averaged about $18,000 ($43,000), which was 10 percent less than the national average for state employees in 1985. Wages were an issue with these workers, but they were also concerned about job security, pay equity (most were women), career development, job stress, and "having a voice in decision making." [15]

On January 24, 1986, Tom Woodruff mailed a letter to the relevant health and social service agencies, confirming that the State Employment Relations Board had certified 1199WV/KY/OH as the exclusive representative in Ohio for its thirty-three hundred new members. The union was looking forward to meeting with the agencies' representatives within ninety days to negotiate a collective bargaining agreement for those members. Woodruff, Lisa Watson, and Bob Callahan headed up a member-elected sixty-five person negotiating committee, which began a regimen of sixteen bargaining sessions in Columbus with the state's representatives in March. A commissioner from the Federal Mediation and Conciliation Service sat in on the sessions, which concluded with a tentative agreement on April 29. Over 250 new union members from around the state, most of them using a vacation or personal day, attended the April 23 session as a demonstration of resolve. They represented tangible support for the union's central negotiating themes: that other states had outperformed Ohio in their treatment of public employees, and stress on the job was a persistent problem in health and social services work. "After that," said Woodruff, "things started to move." The contract called for pay raises of 30 percent compounded over two years, improved benefits, and an impartial grievance procedure. Twelve regional information meetings with staff and members of the negotiating committee drew over eight hundred members and over half of the new membership participated in the ratification vote in late May. The vote to ratify the contract was 1,680 to 77. "We didn't solve every problem," said Woodruff, "but we made a big start." [16]

Between 1986 and 1988, 1199WV/KY/OH's mantra of "organize or die" served the union pretty well during a hard time for organized labor. The union staff and the organic leaders within the membership continued to use training and education in the process of "internal organizing" so that members would be able to represent themselves without relying overmuch on staff. Woodruff also urged the various locals to dedicate increased resources to external organizing, bringing new work sites and members into the organization. [17] Organizers David Mott, Teresa Ball, and David Freeland, to name a few, were especially effective in organizing new members at private for-profit nursing homes, including several owned by the Owens-Illinois Corporation. Ball had a particular affinity for nursing home workers, with many of whom she had common life experiences. "Little nursing home workers that make minimum wage," she said, "have no benefits, no rights, and it was mostly uneducated, single head of household females much like I [had been] and just struggling to survive. I worked in West Virginia and Kentucky." She continued, "The workers are mistreated no matter what state you're in and the nursing home industry is the worst I've ever seen. They make millions of dollars in profit and never share it with the workers or provide adequate care for the patients." [18]

The union was also organizing privately owned community health centers in Sutton and Richwood, West Virginia, and Hindman and Hazard, Kentucky. A report issued by1199/WV/KY/OH cited victories in nineteen elections covering fourteen hundred members (not including the Ohio state employee numbers) in 1986–1988, including "seven nursing homes, seven community health facilities, two mental retardation [sic]/developmentally disabled facilities, two health departments and one independent social agency's employee union." In the same period, the union lost five elections and "negotiated 24 contracts covering 5,850 members. Seven were initial contracts and 17 were renewals. We had only one strike." [19]

That strike began at Fairmont General Hospital in the fall of 1987, after the union had been established there for nearly a decade. It differed from other conflicts that 1199WV/KY/OH had gone through in three significant ways: (1) the strike occurred near the end of the second year of a three-year contract, based on a "reopening clause," rather than at the end of the contract; (2) the hospital changed ownership one year into the contract, becoming a private nonprofit owned by a corporation rather than a municipal hospital owned by the city of Fairmont; and (3) the strike ended only after a remarkable intervention by a Marion County Municipal Court judge. It served as one of many object lessons for the National Union, and for District 1199WV/KY/OH, that survival as a small union in a merger-driven industry faced long odds.

One feature of the Fairmont local's first contract in 1979, like that at many other 1199 locals, was the formation of a fourteen-member patient-care committee. Four permanent and three rotating members represented the union, but any worker could bring an issue to put before the committee. By the time the union's third contract negotiation came up in 1985, the union members on the fourteen-member committee had learned some important lessons in reconfiguring the traditional (and patriarchal) power arrangements at the hospital. The management's first reaction to an employee concern brought to the committee was often to trivialize or deflect the matter, to raise their voices, or to call an issue groundless. Sometimes an issue *could* be groundless, of course, so part of the committee's learning curve included training themselves and other workers to gather evidence and always be prepared to present it to management in a logical, professional way. At first, said RN Joyce Lunsford, "they very definitely tried to break us up from working together like a group. We had to get over that boss-worker thing. It wasn't easy because of the way you're trained as a nurse." By 1985, to cite a few examples, the 1199ers on the committee could point to successes in reversing some planned staff cuts at the hospital, upgrading the size and composition of bedside nursing teams, and establishing a thorough training and orientation period for workers transferred into new jobs. As for new hires, veteran members made sure to educate them about the benefits of the union. "Anti-union managers do their job at orienting new RNs," said Lunsford. "So we developed a new member packet. It informs them of what RNs had before the union, and what they have gained since." [20]

Systemic factors in the healthcare industry, some of which have been summarized in previous chapters, provide the larger context for the events surrounding the 1987 strike at Fairmont General. Developments described by Fink and

Greenberg as "ominous" affected the hospital industry in the 1980s. Many if not most public hospitals faced regular fiscal crises because of shrinking resources. This was due in part to Reaganomics' ideological devotion to supply-side economics and neoliberals' messianic belief in the inefficiency of government at any level. Moreover, in large and small communities nationwide, hospitals and nursing homes were being swallowed or driven out of business by corporate consolidation. As noted in chapter 4, Raleigh General, a small proprietary hospital in Beckley, was purchased by the newly formed Hospital Corporation of America (HCA), the country's first investor-owned chain, in 1969. The HCA model rapidly spread throughout the healthcare system (HCA was taken over by Columbia Healthcare Corporation in 1994), commodifying health care so that, according to one CEO, the industry was "not any different than an airline industry or a ball bearing industry."

Commodification unleashed a "wave of mergers," wrote Fink and Greenberg, which "placed a growing proportion of the nation's health care— and healthcare workers—under the management of a few large chain operations virtually untouched by unionization." Nonprofit institutions, competing with the for-profit corporate chains, "were themselves bending before the stiff winds of cost containment and general market pressures." In the newly "fiercely competitive market," said financial historian Maggie Mahar, "the differences between for-profit and not-for-profit hospitals have all but melted away." Survival, she wrote, "depends on revenues." A hospital might have an established history of fulfilling vital needs in a community, but under the new corporate healthcare "business plan" there was no room for unprofitable hospitals.[21]

These crosscurrents buffeted Fairmont General Hospital. On September 17, 1985, the Fairmont City Council, concerned with the hospital's "declining market share," approved an ordinance authorizing the transfer of the city-owned hospital to a private association called the Fairmont Building Commission. By June 1986, the city of Fairmont had completely divested from operation of Fairmont General, which now was incorporated by the state of West Virginia as Fairmont General Hospital, Inc. As a "private, non-stock, not for profit corporation" rather than a municipal hospital, Fairmont General was free to generate revenue through "independent business enterprises," which would enable the hospital to "compete in the market place." The new bylaws, continuing the hospital's established practice, provided for the new corporation's Board of Directors to be appointed by the City Council.[22]

The contract renewal negotiated between the hospital and 1199/WV/KY/OH in 1985 remained intact under the new ownership scheme. The agreement was for three years, meaning it would expire in the late summer of 1988. The contract included a "reopener clause," which provided that negotiations over wages or other issues could be held while the contract was still in force. For example, in a typical three-year contract a reopener might allow for the re-negotiation of a wage freeze if economic conditions for the employer improve during the first two years. There is no legal obligation for the employer to raise wages during a reopener, but both parties must bargain in good faith. Should the renegotiation collapse, the reopening clause at FGH left open the possibility of a strike before the 1988 expiration date. And that is what happened.[23]

In August of 1987, registered nurses Shirley Knisely and Vickie Tennant, president of the Fairmont chapter of 1199WV/KY/OH, told the City Council that the professional employees represented by the union had accepted a wage freeze in 1985 because of the hospital's tenuous financial position. Hospital revenues improved in 1986, and the management at FGH consented to activate the reopening clause to renegotiate wages and other economic issues. The hospital's nonunion employees, the hospital management, and the service and maintenance workers of Local 550 had all recently gotten wage increases. The 1199ers expected their request for cost-of-living increases would be acceptable to the employer.

When reopener talks began, however, the hospital proposed a cut in insurance benefits and a "flexible Retirement Plan" that would have undermined the current defined benefit pension. The hospital referred to these proposals as "alternative benefit measures." Union workers called them givebacks. The hospital was also asking the 1199ers to wait until November 1989 for any wage increases and floated proposals to institute half-shifts and to eliminate the rollover of sick days from year to year. To 1199WV/KY/OH, putting such conditions forward amounted to bad-faith bargaining, therefore the union had set a strike deadline of August 28. Shirley Knisely was asking the City Council to use its influence to compel the hospital to approve a fair wage agreement before that date.[24]

The employer insisted, however, that they were obliged only to implement pay increases to employees "whose salaries were determined to be non-competitive. Our united position for the economic reopener is that we cannot increase costs and in fact must find ways to reduce costs." The hospital argued that the RNs at FGH were paid better than at other area hospitals, which did not really negate the argument for cost-of-living increases or justify denying them for two more years. The RNs did not deny that their current wages outpaced the regional market, a fact that merely confirmed Joyce Lunsford's point that unionization improved workers' lives significantly. The union pointed out that the hospital had made over $800,000 in revenues in 1986, was top-heavy with administrators who overstated the FGH professionals' wages, that hospital administrator Robert Ptomey was drawing $78,000 ($176,604), and that administrators and supervisors had gotten 5 percent raises in 1986. "We agreed to a wage freeze last year to help the hospital," a union statement read. "We were promised good faith negotiations this year on wage increases." [25]

The union charged that the hospital's wage freeze on the professional workers violated an order from the state's Health Care Cost Review Authority. The HCCRA had authorized patient rate increases at FGH based in part on the need to increase nonsupervisory wages. The approval from the HCCRA included a directive for the hospital to "use these allowed revenues *only for non-supervisory wages, salaries, and benefits*" (italics added). The daily rate for inpatients had increased from just under $600 per day in 1985 to $700 per day in 1987, and no nonsupervisory workers in 1199WV/KY/OH had gotten a wage increase. Responding to a union complaint, the HCCRA announced an investigation, as the reopening talks stalled. As Knisely told the City Council, two months of sporadic talks led to an impasse, which finally broke off on August 27. The hospital immediately carried out patient transfers to other regional facilities and vowed to keep FGH open throughout the impending strike, albeit with reduced services. Ptomey, who began a long career at the hospital in 1954, said that about sixty nurse supervisors would provide for the thirty-seven patients who remained at the hospital, which had a capacity of 267 beds. The day before the strike began on August 31, seventy service workers were laid off. [26]

About two hundred 1199ers, adopting the slogan "Whatever it takes for as long as it takes," set up picket lines at three locations near hospital entrances, the most visible at the main Locust Avenue approach. Robert Ptomey immediately announced that the hospital had begun hiring permanent replacement nurses to fill vacancies caused by the strike, a provocation that continued throughout the strike. Ptomey warned that "some of those strikers may find themselves displaced by the new nurses once the walkout ends." When strikers charged FGH with union busting, Ptomey responded that "I call it people not wanting to work." On the picket line, organizer David Mott told the *Fairmont Times-West Virginian* that the strikers were prepared for "a long haul" if that was necessary. He spoke with reporter Sue Morgan over the steady blaring of horns from passing motorists. "It's been like this all day," Mott said. "The public support has been incredible." [27]

Dave Mott began his work in the labor movement in the northeast in the 1970s. He organized newspaper workers in New York for the Graphics Communication International Union before going to work for the National 1199 on a 1981 campaign in Springfield, Vermont, a declining industrial town in the shadow of the Green Mountains. Rick Fantasia documented the intricacies of the Springfield campaign in a lengthy chapter in *Cultures of Solidarity*.

The union drive at Springfield Hospital, a private-sector facility, mobilized workers facing "the tide of specialization and mechanization" that hospital employees were dealing with everywhere. At Springfield, Mott deepened his understanding of the role of an organizer in identifying "member leaders" who can form an effective organizing committee and then, by training new leadership, sustain a progressive, active institutional union. Mott agreed with Fantasia that this was the most important step in transmitting critical union education to the membership and to help convince workers of "the power of collective interest and organization." Since the members of the union "had to do the work," said Mott, some may apply the necessary skills of building a strong local to a broader analysis of social justice. This integration of pragmatic organization building with a democratic vision is why Mott "fell in love with 1199." [28]

The Springfield campaign also educated Mott about the consulting firm Modern Management Methods (3M), the premier union-busting firm in the country (as discussed in chapter 5). The prounion LPNs and technical workers at Springfield faced down the 3M bear and won the election. The National Union later sent Mott to West Virginia "to work with this guy Woodruff," where he joined the 1199/WV/KY/OH organizing staff. As noted earlier, he helped organize nursing home and state hospital workers throughout the district. A committed believer in the inspirational and mobilizing power of music, Mott, accompanied by his acoustic guitar, often led the singing of labor songs at rallies, meetings, and on picket lines. By 1987 he was in Fairmont for what transpired as, in his words, "my strike." [29]

On Labor Day, September 8, over two hundred FGH strikers and supporters rallied near the hospital to sing union songs led by Dave Mott and hear messages of support by representatives from local unions. "Mott's strike" was entering its fourth week when the employer filed a petition on September 24 with the Marion County Circuit Court, claiming intimidation of working employees by strikers and alleging damage to some vehicles. Circuit judge Fred Fox refused a request from the hospital to order strikers back to work and would not limit the number of pickets at designated areas. He did grant an injunction forbidding "threatening, intimidating, or committing acts of violence" by either party. As the strike transpired, each side filed petitions, with testimony, against the other for numerous alleged violations of the injunction. On November 3, for example, one of the hospital's local attorneys filed forty-nine charges of contempt against union picketers. The claims included damage to vehicles, egg-throwing (Mott was arrested on an egg-throwing charge), intimidation of nonstriking workers, and threatening language. Two days later the union filed its own charges, accusing nonstriking workers with reckless driving near picketers, harassing phone calls, and photographing and video recording strikers. Union members (and probably just about everyone else) were particularly outraged that union leader and RN Joyce Lunsford was receiving threatening phone calls at her home in Grafton. Lunsford, although she had appeared on the picket line a few times, had been unable to work since being diagnosed with terminal brain cancer in May.[30]

When the strike began, Reverend Richard Bowyer was in his twenty-fifth year as director of the United Methodist campus ministry at Fairmont State College. In 1971 he was a local coordinator of Senator Ted Kennedy's Health Care Crisis in America hearings, which were conducted at twenty-one sites around the country, sponsored by the AFL-CIO.[31] He also served on the Board of Directors at the Fairmont Clinic, a private nonprofit facility subsidized in part by the United Mine Workers of America. His father was a union member for nearly a half century. Reverend Bowyer was named to the Fairmont General Hospital Board of Directors by the City Council in 1978 and was one of only two current members who were on the board during the 1978 1199WV organizing drive. In the summer of 1987, Bowyer wrestled with a challenge to his conscience. As a possible strike approached, Bowyer sensed that his strong prounion position annoyed some of his colleagues on the board and the physicians on the hospital staff. Early in the strike, Bowyer concluded that his longstanding effort to serve as a moderating voice on the board was doomed and that the hospital administration as a whole was "totally against having a union, even after ten years. The good old boys wanted to get rid of it."[32]

Bowyer struggled to reconcile his work at the rigorously prounion Fairmont Clinic, his family history, and his personal convictions about organized labor with the antiunion sentiments of his colleagues on the hospital board. He discerned "strong opposition on the board to even deal with the union." He and one other board member, Frank Polis, formed a minority of two who believed the board's refusal even to meet with nurse representatives in informal discussions was unreasonable and puzzling, especially given that the union had been established at the hospital for almost a decade. Bowyer began meeting with small delegations of nurses himself, promising to take their concerns to the directors. When the hospital administration began to bring in permanent "scabs" and installed surveillance cameras on the hospital rooftop to watch picketing employees, he had had enough. The cameras were for security reasons, the administration claimed, but to Bowyer's thinking the act was one of pure intimidation. The administrators "were adamant in not giving in, and stalling on the negotiations as long as they could," said Bowyer. "They began to do some aggressive things, I felt, to irritate and agitate the union and stir up the situation." Finally, he concluded that he was being "made party to something that ran against my character" and against "the social principles of the United Methodist Church," which endorsed the right of collective bargaining. Rev. Bowyer resigned from the Board of Directors during the third week of what became a three-month strike. He told the *Times-West Virginian* that "I have long seen my community role as that of an agent of mediation and reconciliation." He volunteered to serve as a mediator between the employer and the union. The Fairmont Labor Council also recommended him for that role, but the Board of Directors rejected the idea. "The board was happy to see me go," Bowyer told me. "They weren't going to accept me as a mediator." [33]

As the strike wore on, the hospital's continued recruitment of replacement workers emerged as the major obstacle to a settlement. Mott claimed that the steady hiring of replacements was an indication that the hospital had no intention of settling and proved that the administration was union busting. Robert Ptomey insisted that bringing in replacements, who were hired with the understanding that they would have permanent jobs if they so desired, was "the only way the hospital can survive, to get back into operation." Ptomey inflamed the situation by announcing that when the strike was settled, new nurses would have priority over strikers in terms of getting the permanent nursing staff back to prestrike numbers. The union protested this action as an attack on seniority, which it defined as a necessary protection in any legitimate contract. The administration, conversely, claimed it had a "moral obligation" to favor the replacements over strikers, regardless of how long they had been at the hospital, when the walkout ended. Woodruff, who joined Mott in Fairmont partway through the strike, contended that the union could accept keeping the replacements on if "there is work available" but could not tolerate threats to workers' seniority rights. [34]

A significant turning point in the strike occurred on Tuesday, November 10, when Marion County Circuit Court judge Fred Fox injected his court directly into the stalled negotiations. In the midst of a long lull in any substantive talks, Fox summoned union and hospital negotiators to the grand jury room of the Marion County Courthouse and ordered them to resume regular meetings until the strike was settled. According to the *Fairmont Times-West Virginian*, Fox wished the two sides "Good luck and Godspeed," shut the jury room door, and the adversaries started talking at 1:00 p.m. Hospital attorney Steve Brooks said that for the moment his client would negotiate but questioned whether the judge had the legal right to issue such an order. Fox responded that he believed he had the authority to force the negotiations "or I wouldn't have done it," but of course the order could be appealed to the State Supreme Court. Brooks called the judge's order "unprecedented." David Mott agreed that Fox's order was "new territory" but welcomed it as "real healthy." [35]

While the hospital lawyers pondered an appeal to the judge's order (they decided against it), the replacement worker dilemma still blocked a resolution. Annoyed at the lack of progress, Fox warned the employer that if he saw fit, he would issue a court order upholding employees' seniority rights. In the arena of wages, union members published an offer they had made to the hospital for a "no-cost contract." Union members would pay for their wage increases through adjustments to their pension and sick leave benefits—therefore agreeing in part to a proposal the hospital itself had made earlier. But the hospital's offer, you will recall, did not include any pay raises. The employer was not willing to offset benefits cuts with wage increases, and the union's proposal was quickly dismissed. Again Judge Fox intervened, with a plan designed to address both the hospital's demand for cost savings and the union's demand for cost-of-living raises: in order to bring all the strikers back to work, FGH and 1199WV/KY/OH would come up with a formula for savings through benefits cuts, with 50 percent of the savings going to hospital revenue and 50 percent going to wage increases. The *Times-West Virginian* related that the proposal was "reportedly acceptable to the union" but was rejected by the hospital, which again claimed that Judge Fox was overstepping the Circuit Court's authority. This response tried the patience of the editor of the newspaper. Charges of union busting are typical in strike settings, the paper said, but in this case "one has to wonder if this rhetoric might have some validity." [36]

David Mott confirmed that the union was amenable to Judge Fox's recommendation. The judge's formula was a step backward from what the union wanted, he said, but "we made the decision to accept it." When the hospital rejected Fox's formula, Mott concluded that the hospital did not want to settle the strike but was more determined than ever to get rid of the union. "They avoid settling at every turn; they just put up new roadblocks." Mott voiced a rumor that was spreading around that the hospital wanted to break the union or "sell the place," or maybe both. Perhaps a for-profit corporation like Humana or Hospital Corporation of America had designs on incorporating Fairmont General into their growing healthcare empire. Hospital spokesman Richard Graham said the hospital board had no intention of soliciting or listening to offers from the big for-profit chains. "I don't believe Humana has any interest in West Virginia hospitals," he added. The rumor about selling FGH may have had no merit, but it was not illogical in the era of the industry's consolidation. David Lindorff wrote in 1993 that the for-profit healthcare industry as a whole had a strong antiunion record and "studiously avoided acquisitions of hospitals that had labor pacts." If the hospital's owners had wanted to divest, the hospital's market attractiveness would be enhanced if unions were not in the picture. Regardless of the credibility of this rumor, it is instructive in uncovering the depth of suspicion that permeated the labor relations environment at FGH in 1987.[37]

Judge Fox ignored the hospital's recurrent claim that his court was exceeding its authority. On November 25, with talks continuing but no settlement imminent, Fox declared that the "continuing work stoppage constitutes a threat to the public health and safety." The court had every right and power to protect and promote public safety "and good order." Therefore, he ordered the hospital to resume operations effective December 1, at 80 percent of the normal work week. Assuming a quick return to full patient capacity, all replacement workers could continue at the hospital if they wanted, and striking workers must be called back "in the order of seniority" within six weeks. All pickets and strike materials would be removed from the hospital's property by December 1. The hospital and 1199WV/KY/OH would continue negotiations, with the court ordering binding arbitration if a settlement was not reached by March 4. The court's order would remain in force until the issue was settled by negotiation or arbitration. The hospital challenged the conditions of the judge's order to the State Supreme Court, where their petition was rejected by a 3 to 2 vote, without comment. Larry Harless, now a graduate of the West Virginia University law school, represented 1199WV/KY/OH at the hearing. Ultimately, the strike was settled in early December along the lines of Judge Fox's order.[38]

Contrary to the well-worn homily that "no one wins a strike," the fact is that one side mostly wins a strike and the other side mostly loses. But in the case of the Fairmont General strike in 1987, there was no clear winner, except in the sense that the Fairmont local survived. Whatever the employer's ultimate objective at FGH in 1987, the pattern of obstructionism and provocation faced by 1199WV/KY/OH forewarned that the hard fights of the past would continue in the future. As the union closed out its first two decades in Appalachia, the realities of the healthcare industry and upheaval in the National Union were about to bring dramatic changes for 1199WV/KY/OH. Mary Schafer's observation about Fairmont General suggests the motive for those changes. Speaking nearly thirty years after she helped bring 1199WV to FGH in 1978, her union still faced a struggle. The hospital bosses "have fought it ever since then. From the beginning till now. Till right now. They want rid of it."[39]

Chapter 10

"A Howling Voice in the Wilderness": Separation and Merger

Leon Davis had long dreamed of the formation of "one big hospital union." To Davis, it was imperative by the late 1970s that 1199 join forces with the large and powerful Service Employees International Union if it were to survive the relentless consolidation of the industry and the growing sophistication of management resistance. Consequently, negotiators from 1199 and SEIU's hospital division entered into merger talks in 1979. The merger would create a new international healthcare division and enjoyed widespread rank-and-file support throughout the 1199 districts and locals. It was scheduled to take effect conditional to a concurrent merger between the broader SEIU international and 1199's international "parent," the RWDSU. Negotiators understood that the RWDSU constitution mandated the union board's approval for any merger, but the principals considered this a formality.[1]

By late 1980, debilitated by two strokes and believing that the merger was imminent, Davis prepared to step down from the presidency of both the National Union and the New York district. Davis wanted Doris Turner to succeed him as president of the New York district. Turner, a Florida native and former dietary clerk at Lenox Hill Hospital, began her union career as a rank-and-file leader in 1956. She was a fierce advocate for the district's autonomy and the "union power, soul power" tradition. Turner, as vice president of the New York district, was the highest-ranking woman in the union. As for the National Union, Davis anticipated that his successor would be Henry Nicholas, a Mississippi sharecroppers' son who migrated to New York after a stint in the navy. Nicholas was an orderly at Mt. Sinai Hospital during the 1959 strike who, as we have seen, became a leading organizer and executive for both the National Union and for 1199C in Philadelphia.[2]

Ironically, Doris Turner was instrumental in the collapse of Davis's planned merger with the SEIU. In the summer of 1980, President Al Heaps of the RWDSU, who had initially supported merger talks, launched a whispering campaign to sabotage the process. Heaps apparently had grown skittish about losing out in the reshuffling of power that would follow a merger between two international unions, his own and the SEIU. Similarly, Turner suspected that her local might ultimately be marginalized as part of the massive SEIU. Capitalizing on her popularity and influence with the rank and file, Turner lined up opposition to the merger throughout the New York district. In a bizarre twist, at a crucial moment in December 1980, Heaps was injured by a letter-bomb explosion in the RWDSU office. The crime, never solved, effectively killed the merger, even though talks did not completely break down until the spring of 1981. Davis, now privately alienated from Turner and no longer the energetic fighter he had been, feared an open conflict with Turner could destroy New York's original Local 1199. Reluctantly, he followed through on recommending that Turner succeed him as president of the New York district. And as expected, Henry Nicholas was elected president of the National Union.[3]

In the aftermath of the merger collapse and the 1982 departure of Davis, Al Heaps then ran a power play. Although he enjoyed an alliance with Turner and the New York local, Heaps suspected that Nicholas might attempt a unilateral merger between the National Union and SEIU. Heaps invoked the constitutional prohibition against a formal National Union disaffiliation from the RWDSU without the parent union's consent. Moreover, Heaps accused the National of financial mismanagement and, beginning in the fall of 1983, tried to break it and absorb its members into the RWDSU.[4]

For over six months the RWDSU, District 1199NY, and the National Union fought a "complicated series of legal and internal union battles" that greatly weakened the National's financial health. The final settlement advanced the National Union's movement toward greater independence but cost it over one-half of its membership by effecting the secession of the New York district from the National. As part of the "historic 'Separation Agreement,' " signed by Heaps, Turner, Nicholas, and U.S. District Court judge Leonard B. Sand, the National Union would itself finally completely break from the RWDSU and seek its own international charter from the AFL-CIO. Fink and Greenberg summarize the core of the agreement: "With the tacit approval of the AFL-CIO, the RWDSU agreed in early May to allow the national to disaffiliate and establish its own international charter, within the labor federation. At the same time District 1199 in New York was permitted to detach itself from the national *it had itself created*, returning as of July 1, 1984, to its old status as Local 1199 of the RWDSU" (italics added).[5]

The agreement separating the New York district from the National Union slashed the National's membership from about 140,000 to about 70,000 in eighteen districts. The national leadership of the union feared being "a howling voice in the wilderness," representing only about 1 percent of the country's healthcare workers. In 1987 Tom Woodruff, still the president of 1199WV/KY/OH but becoming an increasingly influential figure in the National Union, warned that the movement to join with the SEIU must be resurrected, "in order to carry out our mission to unite healthcare workers in a militant, progressive Union." If anything had been proved since the separation agreement, Woodruff said, "it is that we need a merger more. The industry is more concentrated, politically and socially this country is much meaner." Small districts such as 1199WV/KY/OH, which coveted its history of self-directed social activism and leadership development, might not survive without a powerful ally. The membership in West Virginia, eastern Kentucky, and the southern Appalachian counties of Ohio (later named Region I) at the time of the 1989 merger vote totaled about four thousand. The membership in northern Ohio, later named Region II, also totaled about four thousand.[6]

Woodruff's sentiment reflected a consensus among the National Union's Executive Board to unify healthcare workers nationwide. Accordingly, the board appointed a "Unity Committee" at the union's national convention in December 1987. The committee was directed to deliberate with other healthcare unions to talk about creating "the largest, most autonomous and democratic organization of health care workers possible." Unfortunately, the Unity Committee faced disunity within the National Union's leadership structure, with one faction favoring merger with AFSCME and another with SEIU. Woodruff, along with Jerry Brown of 1199E (New England) and Robert Muehlenkamp, spoke forcefully for the SEIU faction of the committee. National president Henry Nicholas was the chief advocate for AFSCME, especially for its record of organizing public workers. The SEIU faction described it as a "more natural fit for 1199," based on the unions' similar models for organizing service workers and long history of progressive values and politics. Numbers were important also, said Woodruff, noting that SEIU had 850,000 total members, including 300,000 healthcare workers, which would translate into greater resources and political power for the 1199 districts. Nicholas, however, was convinced that AFSCME would be most effective in terms of "greater political clout" at the state and federal levels.[7]

A merger promised greater power and protection for the 1199 districts, but the AFSCME/SEIU debate provoked internal divisiveness, as witnessed by several contentious Executive Board dustups. Nicholas accused the SEIU faction of having a "hidden agenda" to carry out a hostile takeover of the National Union. The pro–SEIU faction accused the Nicholas group of intimidation and disruption at Unity Committee meetings. The pro–AFSCME hinted vaguely that key leaders of the pro–SEIU cohort were tinged with racism and sexism. All-out fratricide may have been avoided early in 1989 when the AFL-CIO, responding to pressure from rank-and-file members of several 1199 districts, devised a formula. The National Union would forgo a winner-take-all vote in favor of each district membership deciding with which union to affiliate. When the votes were cast in May of 1989, following an intense campaign by the AFSCME and SEIU factions to secure the loyalty of each district, thirteen of the eighteen districts voted to go with the SEIU, with five, including Nicholas's 1199C in Philadelphia, selecting AFSCME. As for 1199WV/KY/OH, the vote was 3,794 for SEIU and 234 for AFSCME. The SEIU districts totaled about fifty thousand members, the AFSCME districts about twenty-five thousand.[8]

The delegates at the 1199WV/KY/OH district meeting in April of 1988 had endorsed the SEIU merger. The delegates were influenced by the pro–SEIU position of Woodruff and Bob Callahan, both of whom were National Union vice presidents who had been with them through many hard fights. Teresa Ball pointed out, however, that the district membership had some concerns, which reflected those of 1199ers in other districts:

> The merger was a ten-year dream of Leon Davis. Leon wanted to do it for years because he realized that we weren't powerful enough by our-selves, 1199 wasn't, to be able to really make a difference, and he chose SEIU because of their philosophy, their organizing attitude.
>
> We were all a little apprehensive. Were we going to lose our identity if we went with SEIU? We were proud of 1199. We liked what we stood for. We didn't want to change that and [we had questions].
>
> "What's this mean? Is our name going to change? Are we still going to be the union that we've always been, what they say, kicking ass for the working class, in your face kind of union," and that's what a lot of people were proud of. They felt like we really fought for workers and they didn't see that with other unions and we didn't know anything about SEIU, but the real problem was that Henry Nicholas, who was the president, wanted to merge with AFSCME. So, when it came down to the vote, the workers had the choice of whether they wanted no merger, SEIU, or AFSCME.
>
> It was not a difficult campaign for us. Our workers trusted us [organizers] and trusted the staff and trusted Tom, so our local was in good shape as far as the vote goes, so a lot of us were sent into other locals. I worked in Baltimore for two months. I had to go up and live in Baltimore and work that campaign for two months, and we did win Baltimore and the SEIU and they were really worried about that one, but we won. There were some locals in Henry's camp, but the majority of 1199 locals voted to merge with SEIU.[9]

It stands to reason that some members in the small locals of 1199 in Appalachia would be wary of relinquishing the familial relationship that had evolved with the National Union in favor of joining the massive SEIU. Dissonance between regional working-class cultures in several industries, notably textiles and pottery, had historically fractured small locals' commitment to the parent organization. Recognizing that many district members feared the loss of local control of their union, the pro–SEIU advocates had sought to reassure them in the months leading up to the vote. The membership could rest assured that the 1199 identity would be preserved. The National Union would become a National Local within the SEIU, keep its present constitution and Executive Board, and no district could be "trusteed," or have its financial or organizational framework taken over by SEIU. Only the National 1199 would be able to trustee one of its districts. With a merger, the National Union's organizing budget would expand from $1.75 million in 1990 to $3.25 million in 1996. There was also a three-year "window" through which, by membership vote, the districts within the National 1199 could dissolve the merger.[10]

SEIU advocates anticipated an immediate burst of organizing energy after the merger. New NLRB rules were to be in effect by late 1989, identifying seven defined bargaining units for healthcare workers. The SEIU reasoned that the new designations would reduce the likelihood of workers with little in common, "such as clerical workers and janitors," being incorporated into the same unit. Essentially, the more clearly defined units would include workers with an obvious "community of interest," and the SEIU could put together an energetic healthcare organizing agenda. Among the early postmerger successes for the SEIU was a campaign at Jackson Memorial Hospital in Miami, Florida, which brought fifteen hundred RNs into the union. That drive was overseen by the new SEIU healthcare division organizing director, Dan Stewart. A few years later, in 1994, Stewart was working on an ambitious SEIU campaign organizing home healthcare workers in Los Angeles. Then, president Bob Wages recruited him as organizing director for the Oil, Chemical, and Atomic Workers Union.[11]

Led by President John Sweeney and Organizing Director Andy Stern, SEIU expanded its national staff from twenty to over two hundred during the 1980s, recruiting both from within its own locals and among campus activists. By the time of the 1989 merger with 1199 districts, the union enjoyed the reputation of leading the way to labor's renaissance by means of "massive efforts to organize the unorganized—a combination of organizing, affiliations, and mergers made SEIU the fastest-growing union in the country, with membership more than doubling during a period when most unions experienced substantial declines."[12]

In 1996, Sweeney left the SEIU to become president of the AFL-CIO. Sweeney hoped to convince the federation's member unions to commit additional resources to organizing the masses of workers in the "Wal-Mart economy," now that the union power built during the "General Motors" economy was debilitated. Sweeney was unable, however, to effect the changes he wanted. Most of the member unions in the AFL-CIO still prioritized "business unionism," or contract administration first and organizing a distant second. Within the AFL-CIO federation, the SEIU grew steadily, but nationally the overall decline in union density continued.[13]

When he moved to the AFL-CIO post, Sweeney was succeeded at SEIU by Andrew (Andy) Stern, formerly the union's organizing director. Tom Woodruff left SEIU District 1199WV/KY/OH to join the national SEIU staff as director of organizing in 1996. Dave Mott went to SEIU shortly thereafter. Stern became something of a darling to prominent political liberals because of his record as a progressive and his dedication to creating a "modern, pro-growth, dynamic, progressive, problem-solving labor movement." Stern was particularly feted for his willingness to establish political and corporate "partnerships." The U.S. Chamber of Commerce and the *Wall Street Journal* praised Stern as a new kind of labor leader, one "that business could work with."[14]

Stern's critics accused him of pursuing growth at any price, of relying too much on "back-room deals with employers" and "tactical partnerships with corporate America that made other unionists uneasy." A key SEIU tactic during the Stern years, one adopted by some other unions as well, was the use of "employer neutrality" agreements, in which management would accept unionization on a "cooperative" basis without resistance. To many unionists, the cooperation model all too often benefited the boss more than the workers, eliciting a charge that Stern was turning SEIU into a "company union." "If gaining the voluntary assent of an employer to union recognition meant a less than perfect bargain," said labor historian Melvyn Dubofsky, "Stern took it, never subjecting such agreements to the vote of members." Like the UMWA's autocratic John L. Lewis, Dubofsky continued, "Stern believed that union power was more important than union democracy." Stern's own words reveal an impatience with the language of democracy and class conflict that had mobilized so many workers in the past. Although the "accepted vocabulary" of a union, he said, "is that of a militant venture," a union is (and should be, at local, regional, and national levels) "a business enterprise all through." In an era of corporate mergers, Stern remarked, "smaller-scale union bodies, no matter how participatory, are simply anachronistic." This last observation, you will recall, echoes the arguments Tom Woodruff made in promoting the 1199/SEIU merger in 1988: to avoid being a "howling voice in the wilderness," in order to "organize the unorganized," and "to have a real presence in Washington, DC and all state capitals," he told the membership, "we need the clout that comes from merger."[15]

The SEIU decisively applied that clout in the 2008 political campaign to elect Barack Obama. SEIU was the largest contributor to a multiunion pro-Obama coalition, and in appreciation President Obama praised Stern as the "voice of ordinary working Americans." But Stern's dismissiveness toward input from local leadership challenged that contention and contributed to some major battles between Stern and dissident leaders from some of the larger locals. Stern's heavy-handed tendency to trustee dissident locals or merge them with more "loyal" locals in SEIU earned him enemies within the labor movement, even as his skillful leveraging of SEIU's political clout with state legislatures (for example, winning expanded rights for public and home health-care workers) won him praise. Labor relations scholar Kate Bronfenbrenner concluded that Stern's administration lost sight of the membership's need to have a significant voice in policy for the union. Unions succeed, she said, by combining "top-down leverage with bottom-up organizing. . . . In recent years [SEIU] started to back off from the bottom-up approach." For all the SEIU's aggressiveness during the Stern era, when he abruptly left the union in 2010 it represented only 10 percent of the nation's hospital workers and 11 percent of its nursing home employees.[16]

Stern's most audacious move during his presidency was a controversial decision to take the SEIU (with its nearly 2 million members) and six other unions out of the AFL-CIO and form a new labor federation called Change to Win, or CTW, in 2005. Change to Win grew from the 2003 "New Unity Partnership," a John Sweeney–led effort to reform the AFL-CIO by means of dramatically expanding the organizing of unorganized workers. The SEIU Executive Board designated Woodruff, who had been the "chief architect" of SEIU growth under Stern, to direct CTW's Center for Strategic Organizing, with a goal to guarantee that the "nine out of ten American workers not yet in a union have the opportunity to benefit from a 21st century, global economy." The CTW's loyalists believed the new federation would revitalize a battered labor movement much as the CIO had in the 1930s; its critics accused Stern of weakening an already faltering labor movement. Steve Early referred to CTW as "more mirage than real, and hardly the second coming of the CIO." Within a few years, three of the CTW federation's original members had abandoned the rebellion and rejoined the AFL-CIO. By 2009, Stern had also orchestrated a disastrous internecine conflict with SEIU's largest local, the California-based United Healthcare Workers (UHW), and launched a raid on UNITE-HERE, a four hundred thousand-plus member progressive union of textile and hospitality workers.[17]

Stern's hostile takeover of some UNITE-HERE locals into SEIU (UNITE-HERE launched some raids of SEIU locals in retaliation) not only diverted millions of dollars from SEIU financial resources but contributed to the exodus of the aforementioned CTW unions. The poaching enraged many of SEIU's progressive allies and, according to UNITE-HERE leader John Wilhelm, one of the founders of the CTW federation, undermined the support of key Democrats in Congress for the Employee Free Choice Act. The EFCA, which would have amended several key provisions of the NLRA to the benefit of labor, failed in 2009. The fallout from the raid on UNITE-HERE also contributed to Tom Woodruff's maneuvering to stop Andy Stern's favored successor from taking office.[18]

Woodruff's four decades-plus trek through the ranks of organized labor tracks with what Melvyn Dubofsky described as "a perpetual dilemma in labor history: the evolution of labor leaders from rebels to union administrators." Jane McAlevey, a Woodruff critic, attacked the SEIU's penchant for "neutrality agreements" as a willingness by its national leaders to sacrifice workers' voices in service to "growth metrics." This poses a fair question as to whether the postmerger 1199 districts would be able keep faith with the union's dedication to autonomy and democracy or simply be water carriers for the international machine. McAlevey chastised the SEIU bureaucracy for abandoning the militant "CIO language" of organizing in favor of the language of Wall Street. "Semantics matter," she wrote.[19]

It should be noted, however, that the language of Wall Street did not have absolute sway in Woodruff's rhetoric. The "bare knuckles" climate of upper-level SEIU politics during the Stern tenure called on the deep reservoir of political toughness that Woodruff had developed over decades. Leftist organizer Wade Rathke, who was critical of SEIU's Stern-era philosophy of centralized top-down mass organizing, nevertheless admired Woodruff's survival and navigation of the tumult of those years. Woodruff, he wrote, was "indisputably second to none as an internal organizer." Rathke declared "with total admiration" that Woodruff had a "sixth sense for maneuvering behind the scenes and emerging on the winning side of internal conflict." As for semantics, labor journalist Mark Brenner notes that Woodruff's matriculation among labor's powerbrokers did not diminish his connections with rank-and-file members. When he spoke at the 2008 leadership assembly of SEIU District 1199WV/KY/OH in Fort Mitchell, Kentucky, delegates roared their approval when he attacked CEOs who were "getting richer by sticking it to the working class." "Woodruff's old school, kick the bosses' ass style," Brenner wrote in 2008, "was well-suited to talking about the vultures that dominate today's economy." Brenner might just as well have been describing Leon Davis, who, paraphrasing Dubofsky, managed to hold on to some of the fire of being a "rebel" while becoming a hardball administrator. Davis, said his onetime protegé Doris Turner, had a sincere commitment to rank-and-file leadership at the local level, but he, Moe Foner, and a third National Union leader named Jesse Olson "ran the union driving home in the car to Queens each night." [20]

Rathke explains how Woodruff, along with three other SEIU executive vice presidents, played "kingmaker" by blocking Stern's handpicked successor, Anna Burger, from the SEIU presidency when he retired in April of 2010. The EVPs announced that their candidate was Mary Kay Henry, who had been with SEIU in several capacities since 1980 and was well respected throughout the union's network. Stern, claimed a top-level SEIU staffer, "left pretty much without a friend in the labor movement." Henry promised to mend fences with the rest of the union movement and progressive allies in the civil rights, environmental, and immigrant rights movements. Vowing to lead by consensus "rather than demands," Henry soon won the support of local unions representing 60 percent of the SEIU's 1.9 million members. Many local union leaders charged Burger with being too close to "the authoritarian Stern" but were encouraged by Henry's declaration that the "local unions and divisions should drive our national priorities, not the other way around." If this were true, Henry would be committed to pursuing the balance between "top-down leverage with bottom-up organizing" recommended by Kate Bronfenbrenner. Henry was elected by the SEIU Executive Board on May 8, 2010. After finishing the final two years of Stern's term, she was elected to her own term at the union's national convention. Henry still serves (spring 2021) as SEIU president. [21]

Epilogue

Way back in 1971, Don West warned the hippie printers from the Appalachian Movement Press that they should not, like the "bourgeois radicals" he disparaged, expect to change anything overnight. The long project undertaken by Local 1199 in Appalachia has been a work in progress for over a half century. The youngest of the original 1199WV members would today be approaching seventy. To some, 1199 was a transient thing, being part of their lives only during losing campaigns or the closing of their facilities. Some became immersed in union work and culture, like Penny Burchett, Mary Schafer, and Larry Daniels. Daniels, who died in 2016, often told unorganized workers that "to be unorganized is like the boss having your hands tied behind you. To be organized is having your hands untied and it is a true statement." They helped their union grow, mature, and survive many hard fights for them and difficult times for the labor movement. Region I, the southern Appalachian district that is the major focus of this study, now has about nine thousand members and is part of an international union of more than 2 million. Local 1199 in Region I represents workers at over fifty hospitals, nursing homes, community health centers, councils on aging, Head Start sites, mental health agencies, and Red Cross centers.[1] A mother-daughter team from Huntington, representing only one example among many of multigenerational 1199ers, has labored for hospital and healthcare workers out of the same local for nearly all of that half century.

When I interviewed Anna Jenkins in 2008, she had recently retired after forty-four years at Cabell Huntington Hospital. A few days later I interviewed her daughter, Joyce Gibson, who was and still is the division director of Region I. While she was growing up, her household was immersed in union culture. Her father was in a United Steelworkers local in Huntington, and her grandfather had been a trucker in the International Brotherhood of Teamsters. Joyce remembered that when she about seven years old, she marched on the picket line with her mother during the 1977 strike. When she graduated from Vinson High School in 1987, she moved briefly to Savannah, Georgia, where her brother lived. After a while she came home and got a job in Food Services at

Cabell Huntington. She knew going in that this was one service job that could provide her with a decent standard of living. Starting out at nineteen, she was paid $2.00 an hour above minimum wage and had full health benefits, courtesy of the union contract.

"My mom had a legacy," Joyce said, "as a delegate, contract negotiator, activist, a leader," and Joyce quite naturally moved into union work. "I knew that my mom's struggles were what put food on the table," and she became a delegate and negotiator, sometimes serving on the same bargaining committee with her mother. Gibson's union work started just as the merger with SEIU was taking shape, and she remembered that here was "a change that we weren't sure of. We were apprehensive." She and her coworkers understood that the merger would integrate them into a powerful international union. But they also worried that the local, whose members thought of the union as family, might lose its distinctiveness, as Teresa Ball articulated earlier.

Gibson believes that once the membership realized that resources for organizing, education, and support for arbitrations would increase, their fears were somewhat assuaged. They were also probably reassured by the "escape clause" in the merger documents, a provision that Steve Early advised all smaller unions to insist upon, in the event that "separate 'union cultures' just did not mesh."[2]

After the merger was finalized, her mother encouraged Gibson to take advantage of specialized training in contract administration, grievance handling, and bargaining, all of which had been enhanced with added resources from the SEIU. Her mentor in these first trainings was Al Bacon, the local's training and education director. She later was recruited for field organizing internships with other 1199 districts by Teresa Ball, who was her local's administrative organizer.[3] She participated in many of these internships, doing organizing in the field with seasoned union representatives from many SEIU locals. All of this education was through the SEIU's paid union leave program.

Her union leave assignments took her to work on campaigns in California, Florida, Nevada, and other ports of call. She told members nationwide about her union's pioneering committee structure, formed in 1994 to release 1199 staff from getting "bogged down in grievances." "We train workers not to be dependent on a union administrator," said Gibson. Each chapter has a grievance chair who handles all three-step grievances and meticulously documents the proceedings to determine whether a grievance has merit to go to arbitration, at which point Joyce will step in. Depending on the facility, "sometimes you don't even have to file. That depends on the relationship of management to labor." One place may have no problems, whereas another "violates the contract every day." Many of the Appalachian chapters have developed their own permanent organizing committee and maintained continuing education in political action, health and safety, labor solidarity, and civil rights. Gibson discovered that wherever she goes in the SEIU network, workers know about 1199WV/KY/OH. She has learned that her union's history of militancy, aggressiveness, and leadership transcends the district's boundaries. "When we went to California," she said, "they knew us."[4]

Her shops get a lot of new employees who come in and "know nothing about a union. Their education begins on day one." New hires are first taught about the job security and benefits a union contract protects, and then they learn how those benefits came to be. Citing Cabell Huntington as an example, Gibson explained that many new employees "truly believe, they just believe that they walk in, the highest paid [hospital] workers in the Tri-State, with 100 percent paid health care, and with all these benefits, that the hospital just gives them that. They have no idea of the years and years of bargaining, blood, sweat, and tears, the fights, that that's why they're reaping those benefits." The new workers learn the contract and soon understand that at bargaining sessions between the union and the bosses, "we're there trying to get something, they are there trying to take something away. We teach them that everything they have can be taken away in a day. The strongest leadership is from someone who has had something done to them."[5]

Of the four major hospitals featured in this study, one is now closed and the others are privately owned not-for-profit corporations. In 2019, Highlands Regional Medical Center was acquired by Appalachian Regional Healthcare, the system originally developed by the United Mine Workers of America and later owned by Presbyterian Church USA. Cabell Huntington became a private nonprofit in 1988, owned by Cabell Huntington Hospital, Inc. In 2018, after four years of negotiations, the corporation finalized its acquisition of St. Mary's Hospital, the city's largest with 393 beds, and formed a new entity called the Mountain Health Network. King's Daughters Medical Center is owned by the Ashland Hospital Corporation. Kristie Whitlach, president and CEO of KDMC, recently assured the Ashland community that "we are not for sale."[6]

Whitlach may have sensed that the citizens of Ashland were nervous about ongoing developments in Fairmont. In 2014, Fairmont General Hospital was purchased by a California-based chain called Alecto and renamed Fairmont Regional Medical Center. Alecto was created in 2012 and, according to CEO Lex Reddy, was "not only in the business of providing care, but also of breathing new life into hospitals. We often seek out communities that are underserved, where its healthcare services are considered essential." Alecto also acquired the

Ohio Valley Medical Center in Wheeling, and the East Ohio Medical Center in Martins Ferry, where Local 1199OH had lost its union election in 1976. Reddy had founded Alecto shortly after his hasty resignation from Prime Healthcare, Inc., in the midst of a federal investigation into allegations that "its hospitals had been billing Medicare for exotic but pricey medical conditions." Reddy hired several of his former Prime associates to manage his new company.[7]

With that business history, it may not have been much of a surprise on February 18, 2020, when Alecto announced that the Fairmont Regional Medical Center would be closing its doors in two months due to "financial losses." Fairmont and the surrounding communities were still absorbing that shock when Alecto moved the shutdown date to March 19, just one month after the closure announcement. The company also shut down the Wheeling and Martins Ferry facilities. Just as the coronavirus outbreak was beginning, these small towns were losing a total of 530 hospital beds. "We've now got a hospital that existed for over one hundred years," said Fairmont businessman Jonathan Board, "that now, in the middle of a pandemic, sits empty." More than eighteen hundred workers at the three hospitals lost their jobs, six hundred at the Fairmont Center.[8]

Working in league with West Virginia attorney general Patrick Morrisey and Governor Jim Justice, SEIU District 1199WV/KY/OH negotiated settlements from Alecto of over $1 million in earned benefits and 401K payments for its membership (registered nurses and other professionals). Alecto also forfeited over $240,000 for 120 service and maintenance workers still represented by Local 550 of RWDSU. Those settlements are significant but will not go far in today's economy. Some of those workers in and around Fairmont will hopefully be able to resume their work with patients in the future. West Virginia University Medicine has announced plans to build a new one hundred-bed hospital close to the now vacant Fairmont Regional Medical Center by the spring of 2022, with about five hundred employees.[9]

As we have seen, as part of the 1977 1199WV contract settlement at Cabell Huntington Hospital, which ended a twenty-one-day strike, the hospital's registered nurses left the union. LPN Judy Siders, one of the union's key activists, was adamant that letting the RNs leave was a major mistake, both for the union and for the RNs. Over the ensuing decades, whenever the Cabell Huntington RNs voiced their concerns about short staffing and mandatory overtime, they were not satisfied with the management's reluctance or refusal to act. Finally, in October 2019 they notified the employer that they intended to organize with SEIU District 1199/WV/KY/OH. On December 9, the registered nurses voted for the union. After more than forty years, the RNs are back in 1199. Judy Siders is probably happy about that.

Joyce Gibson e-mailed me with that news the day after the vote: "We won the election at Cabell, 1,000 RNs just joined our Union!! Very exciting. I'm bargaining their first contract in January." In West Virginia, which is now a right-to-work state, this is a significant achievement for organized labor. Gibson also wrote that SEIU 1199WV/KY/OH could bring twenty-five hundred more new members into Region I, from Huntington's St. Mary's. She told me that "Tom Woodruff worked with me this past summer on organizing efforts at St. Mary's Medical Center. Cabell Huntington now owns them, too. We are currently in an organizing drive there. Tom is supposed to be retired. But we know how that goes."[10]

Notes

INTRODUCTION

1. Hennen, "Toil, Trouble, Transformation," 234–236; Kelley, *Race, Class, and Power*, 4–7 (direct quotations are found on page 5), outlines the "new labor history." Brody, "The Old Labor History," 1–27, synthesizes the development of the "new labor history."

CHAPTER I

1. Before the formation of the district in 1980, West Virginia was an "area" of the National 1199 (known as 1199WV); Kentucky was an area identified as 1199K or 1199KY. Ohio was 1199H, or sometimes 1199OH, before merging with 1199WV /KY in 1982, to form 1199WV/KY/OH. Woodruff and Stewart petitioned to form a district from the two areas in a letter to Leon Davis, May 10, 1979.
2. Huntington *Herald-Dispatch*, March 2, 1980. The swearing-in photo was published in the National Union's magazine, *1199 News* 15:9, September 1980, 22. The new bylaws were detailed in Proposed District 1199 WV/KY By-Laws, Article I, Name and Affiliation, 1980. For Davis, refer to Fink and Greenberg, *Upheaval*, 19–21. Davis's date of birth has been reported as 1906, 1907, and 1908 in different sources. Fink and Greenberg attest to 1906. Some details from "Leon J. Davis, Founder of 1199, 1907–1992," a memorial pamphlet produced by the staff of *1199 News*.
3. Hennen, "Struggle for Recognition," 127–147.
4. Tom Woodruff interview, April 5, 2008. Davis quoted in *1199 News*, 15:9, 22.
5. Lorence, *A Hard Journey*, 19–36.
6. Whitehead, "Don West," 821.
7. The Appalachian Movement Press has been briefly acknowledged in many articles about the region in the past quarter century. The press has now found its historian in Shaun Slifer, who published "So Much to Be Angry About," 132–173. Slifer's book on the AMP was published by West Virginia University Press in the spring of 2021.
8. "Alternative unionism" includes the "dual union" movement of the American Communist Party in the late 1920s and 1930s. A related yet broader application of the term is covered in Lynd, *"We Are All Leaders."*
9. King used this and similar expressions regularly. His thinking was powerfully encapsulated in his speech, "A Time to Break Silence," delivered at New York's Riverside Church on April 4, 1967. It is often referred to as King's "Beyond Vietnam" speech.

10. Fink and Greenberg, *Upheaval*, 19.

11. Fink and Greenberg, *Upheaval*, 19–21; Spector, "Pinsk," vol. 5, 276–279.

12. Foner and North, "Celebrating the Life," 3–4. Author interview with Seymour (Sy) Slavin, July 19, 2011. Slavin, born in 1921, was a welder at a General Motors plant in Cleveland in the early 1950s. He was active in the United Auto Workers, but later turned to academics, earning two graduate degrees at Case Western Reserve University. He became a social worker on the staff of Cleveland mayor Carl Stokes and later taught social work at the University of Louisville for thirty years. In 2010, at age eighty-nine, he cofounded the Kentucky Labor Institute, in order to facilitate working alliances between educators, community activists, and organized labor.

13. Rosswurm, *CIO's Left-Led Unions*, ix; Fink and Greenberg, *Upheaval*, 20–23.

14. The early 1980s witnessed internecine conflict within the various districts of 1199, which had become the National Union of Hospital and Health Care Employees in 1973. This conflict catalyzed the dissolution of the RSDWU connection. It is summarized in the closing chapter.

15. Fink and Greenberg, *Upheaval*, 20–23; Rosswurm, *CIO's Left-Led Unions*, 22–24.

16. The questions over legislative protection for the various classes of hospital and healthcare workers is a recurring theme in this work. These issues played significant roles in 1199's Appalachian story and are addressed in the context of several union campaigns. Foner and North, *Not for Bread Alone*, 36–38. As they point out, "The Wagner Act wasn't amended to include voluntary hospitals and nursing homes until July 11, 1974. By that time, however, ten states had extended union rights under state law to all hospital workers." West Virginia and Kentucky were not among these ten, nor are public employees in those two states guaranteed collective bargaining rights today.

17. *1199 News* 11:9 (September 1976), 35.

18. Foner and North, *Not for Bread Alone*, 25–32; Fink and Greenberg, 5–6; 19–21; Ossie Davis, *1199 News* 17:3 (March 1982), 3. Ossie Davis and his wife, Ruby Dee, were devout supporters of 1199 and often performed in benefits for the union.

19. Foner and North, "Celebrating the Life," 5–11; *1199 News* 14:12 (December 1979), 18; Fink and Greenberg, *Upheaval*, 28–43.

20. Lorence, *Hard Journey*, chapter 1; Inscoe, "Race and Racism in Appalachia," 112–113.

21. Lorence, *Hard Journey*, 14–15.

22. Lorence, *Hard Journey*, 19–23. The anecdote about the murder of Barney Graham and West preaching his funeral is from an interview with West that Tom Woodruff and Michael Kipnik recorded on December 3, 1970, at Pipestem. It was published in the January 1971 edition of *Mountain Life and Work*, the magazine of the Council on the Southern Mountains, pages 6–13. The Wilder strike, in which Myles Horton also participated, began in July 1932. Graham was actually murdered on April 29, 1933. Graham's killers reportedly beat him brutally and shot him ten times. One was acquitted of murder and the other was never tried. Graham's assassination also ended the strike. A reproduction of the Knoxville *Times Sentinel* on Graham's murder, plus a synopsis of the case, can be seen at http://cdm16945.contentdm .oclc.org/cdm/ref/collection/p16945coll1/id/17, accessed June 2, 2019.

23. Baker et al., "Highlander Research and Education Center," 317–318.

24. Hudson's long and storied career was chronicled by Nell Irvin Painter in *The Narrative of Hosea Hudson: His Life as a Negro Communist in the South* (Harvard,

1981), rereleased in 1993 as *The Narrative of Hosea Hudson: The Life and Times of a Black Radical* (Norton).

25. Whitehead, "Don West," 821; Naison, "Herndon Case," 307.
26. Lorence, *Hard Journey*, 63–65; Buhle, Buhle, and Georkas, *Encyclopedia of the American Left*, 201.
27. Lorence, *Hard Journey*, 65.
28. Piven and Cloward, "Unemployed Workers' Movement."
29. Lorence, *Hard Journey*, 69–72.
30. Biggers, "Fugitive," 164; Lorence, *Hard Journey*, 23–24. *Crab-Grass* was printed in Nashville by the Art Print Shop.
31. Biggers, "Fugitive," 164; Lorence, *Hard Journey*, 47.
32. Biggers, "Fugitive," 164–169; Cary Nelson, *Revolutionary Memory*, 144.
33. Lorence, *Hard Journey*, 124–125; Biggers, "Fugitive," 164–169. Also refer to the fine analysis of West's writing and activist career in David C. Duke, *Writers and Miners*, especially chapter 2, "Two Appalachians: Don West and Denise Giardina," 46–66.
34. Lorence, *Hard Journey*, 125–129. For James Dombrowski's exemplary life, read Adams, *James Dombrowski*.
35. Lorence, *Hard Journey*, 129–136. Lorence concludes that "although West consistently denied that he was a 'card-carrying member' of the Communist Party from 1940 on, it is difficult to determine conclusively whether his assertion is accurate. What is certain is that he never abandoned his belief in Marxism and that he frequently took positions consistent with those of the Party on issues of great importance. The post-1940 membership issue is debatable, but anecdotal accounts strongly suggest that West retained his CP ties and stubbornly held to his political beliefs" (251, n1).
36. Lorence, *Hard Journey*, 169–177; Biggers, "Fugitive," 172.
37. Lorence, *Hard Journey*, 198, 200, 204–205; Slifer, "So Much to Be Angry About."
38. Slifer, "So Much to Be Angry About," 149.
39. Woodruff interview, April 5, 2008.

CHAPTER 2

1. *Marshall University Official History* accessed at http://www.marshall.edu /muhistory/ accessed June 6, 2019.
2. James E. Casto, "Huntington," in *E-WV: the West Virginia Encyclopedia*, https:// www.wvencyclopedia.org/articles/751, accessed on June 6, 2019. The print citation for the encyclopedia is Ken Sullivan, *The West Virginia Encyclopedia* (Charleston, West Virginia: The West Virginia Humanities Council), 2006. The hollowing out of American manufacturing in the 1980s hit Huntington as it did other industrial towns; the 2019 population is just above 47,000, according to the World Population Review at http://worldpopulationreview.com/us-cities/huntington-wv -population/, accessed on June 6, 2019.
3. The student population figure is an estimate based on a 1965 figure of 7,000 in the 1966 *West Virginia Blue Book* (Charleston, WV: compiled and edited by J. Howard Myers, Clerk of the Senate), 429. I have the receipt for my spring 1970 tuition costs at Marshall: fifteen hours of course work at the in-state rate cost $129, equivalent to $839 in 2018 dollars.

4. Author interviews with Phil Carter, July 6, 1999; Frank Helvey, July 9, 1999; Roger Adkins, July 17, 1999.

5. Stewart's high school offices and club activities are documented in Barboursville High School's newspaper, the *Pirateer,* and yearbook, the *Treasure Chest,* 1960–1962. At Marshall his offices were documented in the campus newspaper, the *Parthenon.* Specific issues of the *Parthenon* will be cited later in this chapter.

6. Phil Carter, Frank Helvey, and Roger Adkins interviews. Author interview with Bob Wages, June 29, 1999.

7. The *Parthenon*, November 20, 1963; March 29, 1963; December 20, 1963.

8. Braden, *The Wall Between*, 86; Roger Adkins interview, July 17, 1999.

9. Chafe, *Unfinished Journey*, 159–160; "Greensboro Sit-In," at https://www.history .com/topics/black-history/the-greensboro-sit-in, May 21, 2020.

10. Zinn, *A People's History*, 443–445; "Sit-in Movement," at http://www.ushistory.org /us/54d.asp, accessed June 8, 2019; Martin Luther King, Jr., "A Creative Protest," 447.

11. The *Parthenon*, March 8, 1963. Tom Woodruff used the precise term "cultural shift" in an interview with the author on April 5, 1986. Thompson, "Appeal for Racial Justice."

12. Fain, "Into the Crucible," 43. The University of Illinois Press published Dr. Fain's book entitled *Black Huntington: An Appalachian Story* in 2019. The job descriptions of railroad laborers are enumerated and described in Nelson, *Steel Drivin' Man*, 26–28, 39–40, 69–77.

13. Lewis, "From Peasant to Proletarian," 81; Fain, "Black Response," 2.

14. Fain, "Black Response," 1. Ancella Bickley's estimate is from her March 15, 1996, interview with Reger, *Integration and Athletics*, 7. The population of Huntington in 2019, reflecting the hollowing out of the city's manufacturing base since the 1970s, was 48,638, of whom 4,202 were African American. See worldpopulationreview .com and suburbanstats.org.

15. Fain, "Black Response," 12–14; Spurlock, *Survey of Cabell County*, 20.

16. Fain, *Black Response*, 7–18. Frederick Douglass Junior High and High School was built in 1924 on a corner lot at Tenth Avenue and Bruce Street, west of Sixteenth Street. Between 1893 and 1924 the original Douglass on the corner of Eighth Avenue and Sixteenth Street schooled grades 1–12. When the new Douglass was built, the elementary school, renamed Barnett after an early Black Huntington minister, remained in the original building. Historian Carter G. Woodson, the second African American (after W. E. B. DuBois) and first descendant of slaves to earn a PhD from Harvard, graduated from the original Douglass in 1896 and later served as its principal from 1900 to 1903. See Ancella Bickley's entries on the Douglass schools and Dr. Woodson at https://www.wvencyclopedia.org/, accessed June 12, 2019.

17. Phil Carter interview with author, July 6, 1999.

18. Carter interview with author, July 6, 1999; Kelley, *Race, Class, and Power*, 101; Reger, "Integration and Athletics," citing interviews with Ancella Bickley, March 15, 1996, and Jim Venable, March 20, 1996, 47. Historian Henry Louis Gates spoke of the loss of pride, and Douglass High School graduate Nancy Smith Robinson spoke of "closeness." Thomas, *West Virginia and the Perils*, 104.

19. Dr. Bickley, who has researched and written widely on West Virginia's African American history and culture, lectured on "Black Education in West Virginia,

1861–1871" at Shepherd College on April 8, 2003. She is cited in Thomas, *Reawakening*, 104. Carter interview with author, July 6, 1999.

20. Carter interview with author, July 6, 1999.
21. Carter interview with author, July 6, 1999.
22. The *Parthenon*, April 19, 1963, and November 22, 1963.
23. Carter interview with author, July 6, 1999.
24. The *Parthenon*, May 1, 1963. Gustavus (Gus) Cleckley, a Huntington native, was the president of the local NAACP in addition to being a Marshall student and CIP leader. Hicks and Tucker were Carter's teammates on the basketball team, and Austin, as we have seen, was one of the founders of the CIP.
25. The *Parthenon*, May 22, 1963.
26. *Herald-Advertiser* (Huntington's Sunday paper), August 4, 11, 1963; *Herald-Dispatch* (the morning paper), August 9, 13, 15, 16, 1963.
27. Miller, *Herald-Advertiser*, September 8, 1963.
28. Miller, *Herald-Advertiser*, September 8, 1963.
29. Carter interview with author, July 6, 1999. Quesenberry might have felt exonerated when West Virginia's governor William Wallace Barron, a conservative Democrat, reneged on a promised clause in an executive order mandating that any business licensed by the state must "serve all persons without distinction." Barron made this commitment when cornered by CIP members at the Southern Governors Conference at White Sulphur Springs but did not deliver. The *Parthenon*, October 4 and October 23, 1963.
30. Thomas, *Reawakening*, 117–118; Thompson, *An Appeal for Racial Justice*. Isaac McKown also documented the White Pantry episode in a handout distributed by the Carter Woodson Center at Marshall. Helvey interview with author, July 9, 1999.
31. Helvey interview with author, July 9, 1999.
32. Carter interview with author, July 6, 1999.
33. Carter interview with author, July 6, 1999.
34. Judt, *Ill Fares the Land*, 88–90.
35. Fink and Greenberg, *Upheaval* (2009 edition), 184–186.
36. For an early history of the SDS, see Sale, *SDS*; see also early SDS activist, Gitlin, *The Sixties*; and Burroughs, *Days of Rage*. Burroughs includes material on SDS factionalism and collapse into the violent Weathermen.
37. Levy, *New Left and Labor*, 34–37.
38. Allen, "Between Students and Workers."
39. Levy, *New Left and Labor*, 20–23.
40. Kahlenberg and Marvit, *Why Labor Organizing*, 1–14; Horowitz, *"Negro and White, Unite and Fight!"*, 206–207; Foner and North, *Not for Bread Alone*, 36; Fink and Greenberg, *Upheaval*, 102–103; King, *All Labor Has Dignity*, 31–33, 39–40.
41. Levy, *New Left and Labor*, 14–15, 41, 55; Morgan, *What Really Happened*, 45–46. The ILWU (International Longshoremen's Workers Union) and UE (United Electrical, Radio, and Machine Workers Union) also aided SNCC. They were two of the eleven unions expelled by the CIO during labor's anticommunist purge of 1949–1950. They survived as independent unions and today are the only two of the eleven surviving. Rosswurm, *CIO's Left-Led Unions*, 1–19.

42. The material on the TAA at Wisconsin is from Levy, *New Left and Labor*, 159–160.

43. Levy, *New Left and Labor*, 6–25; Helen Garvy to Frank Helvey and Phil Carter, March 8, 1965.

44. The *Parthenon*, October 10, 1965. Much of the material in the SDS battle at Marshall is from Hennen, "A Struggle for Recognition," 127–147. The source notes for the article are cited in this chapter's endnotes.

45. The *Parthenon*, October 20, 1965.

46. Flynn, *The Draft*, 233. Stewart would have been in his fourth year at Marshall when he was inducted on February 21, 1966—so he either was out of school, did not have a student deferment, or his had lapsed. Stewart married Jeanine Caywood in 1965, but if the marriage happened after midnight on August 26, marriage deferments were no longer available, having been canceled by an executive order by Lyndon Johnson. It is possible that Stewart had decided that it was not right for a college student to be exempt from the draft.

47. "Report of Transfer," 463. Emily Stewart's life's work has been for the labor movement. At this writing, she is the organizing director for the SEIU's Midwest Initiative. https://www.linkedin.com/in/emily-stewart-b32a08a/, accessed May 23, 2020.

48. Moffat, *Marshall University*, 207–208. The *Herald-Dispatch* featured the various student groups on February 8, 1969. Phil Carter mentioned that Richard Diehl, who was one of the most outspoken SDS supporters, had earlier been a member of the YAF. Perlstein, *The Bridge*, 238, 306, 309, 406, 413, 451–452, 640, 742. Perlstein writes on the importance of the YAF to the Republican Party in this, the third volume in his multivolume history of modern American conservatism.

49. Constitution of the Marshall SDS, submitted with a petition for recognition as a recognized student organization, December 12, 1968, Roland H. Nelson papers, Special Collections at Marshall University Library.

50. Nelson's description of the Metroversity and SDS comments from the Marshall SDS newspaper, the *Free Forum*, December 2, 1968, SDS file, Special Collections at Marshall University.

51. Burroughs, *Days of Rage*, 66–67.

52. Burroughs, *Days of Rage*, 56; Young, *Dissent in America*, 386–387; author interview with Keith Peters, February 28, 1986.

53. The *Parthenon*, February 4, 1969; *Huntington Advertiser* (the city's afternoon paper), February 3 and 6, 1969. Tom Woodruff described Mrs. Payne as a "nice person" and was perplexed by the extremism of her political views. "I can't explain why she was, what she was." Commenting on Rev. Warren's oratorical power, Woodruff recalled that at a large meeting where Warren was mercilessly Red-baiting the SDS, the reverend was so persuasive that "he almost had me reaching for my wallet." Author interview with Woodruff, April 5, 1986.

54. Warren, "Activism on Marshall's Campus."

55. The *Parthenon*, February 18, 1969; author interview with Woodruff, April 5, 1986.

56. Author interview with Woodruff, April 5, 1986; *Huntington Advertiser*, February 17, 1969; the *Parthenon*, January 16 and February 18, 1969.

57. Nelson papers: Nelson to Mrs. E. Wyatt Payne, March 11, 1969; Nelson to Harry Sands, March 19, 1969.

58. Nelson papers: Roland Nelson to Donald Dedmon, "Possible Letter to Alumni," March 24, 1969. Nelson left Marshall for the presidency at University of North

Carolina at Charlotte not long after the town-gown fight. Dedmon became interim university president and was serving in that post when seventy-five Marshall football players, coaches, supporters, and the plane's crew perished while approaching the Tri-State Airport on November 14, 1970. Dr. Dedmon endeared himself to Marshall and Huntington with the compassion and leadership he displayed in the wake of the tragedy. He later became president of Radford University in Virginia.

59. Godoff, "Organizing Report."
60. Niebuhr, *Irony of American History*, 62–63.
61. Woodruff and Kipnick, Don West interview, 6–13; Lorence, *Hard Journey*, 200; Nelson, Barrett, and Ruck, *Steve Nelson, American Radical*, 76.

CHAPTER 3

1. Operation Dixie was a Southern campaign by the CIO during which about four hundred organizers sought to organize industrial workers, especially in key cities in states where right-to-work laws (protected by the 1947 Taft-Hartley Act) were imminent. After a wave of early successes, particularly in textiles, timber, and tobacco operations, the movement stalled and finally collapsed. Southern Democrats were under the influence of business leaders who wanted no increase in labor costs, and the idea of unionizing African Americans alienated civic powerbrokers and many workers themselves. Murray, *The Lexicon of Labor*, 130–131; also see Elizabeth and Ken Fones-Wolf, *Struggle for the Soul*, a recent full-length scholarly study of the CIO campaign.
2. Fink and Greenberg, *Upheaval*, 129–131; Foner and North, *Not for Bread Alone*, 67–80; Hoffus, "Charleston Hospital Workers' Strike," 245.
    For the Charleston, South Carolina, and Pittsburgh campaigns in this chapter, I rely largely on Fink and Greenberg, *Upheaval*, chapter 7, "Stayed on Freedom: A Labor Crusade behind the Magnolia Curtain," 129–158; and chapter 8, "High Expectations and Harsh Realities: Confronting a Changing Health Care System in the 1970s," 159–180.
3. Foner and North, *Not for Bread Alone*, 71.
4. Fink and Greenberg, *Upheaval*, 158; *1199 News* 17:3 (March 1982), 11.
5. Foner and North, *Not for Bread Alone*, 71.
6. Hoffus, "Charleston Hospital," 247.
7. Fink and Greenberg, *Upheaval*, 156.
8. The background on Kay Tillow is taken from an interview by the author on June 20, 2011; and from an interview by historian David Cline for the civil rights Oral History Project of the Museum of African American History and Culture, the Smithsonian, and the Library of Congress, August 14, 2013, accessed on June 21, 2019, at https://www.loc.gov/item/afc2010039_crhp0099/.
9. Cline interview with Kay Tillow, August 14, 2013.
10. David Cline interview with Walter Tillow, June 21, 2013, accessed on June 21, 2019, at https://www.loc.gov/item/afc2010039_crhp0092/, for the MAAHC, the Smithsonian, and the LOC. By the late 1960s, Walter Tillow had become the western Pennsylvania district organizer for the CPUSA. He later was an editor of *People's World*, a journal of leftist thought and practice that is a continuation of the party's old *Daily World*. Cline interview with Walter Tillow; "Birthday Greetings to Walter Tillow," *Marxism-Leninism Today* (a digital journal of Marxist-Leninist

thought), January 23, 2020, at https://mltoday.com/birthday-greetings-to-walter -tillow-roll-in/.

11. Cline interview with Kay Tillow; author interview with Kay Tillow; Fink and Greenberg, *Upheaval*, 161–163; email from Kay Tillow to author, December 24, 2019. A good article on the Appalachian Committee for Full Employment is by Black, "The Roving Picket Movement," 110–127.

12. Author interview with Kay Tillow, June 20, 2011.

13. Fink and Greenberg, *Upheaval*, 160, and 322n10; Author interview with Kay Tillow, June 20, 2011.

14. Fink and Greenberg, *Upheaval*, 160–162, and 322n13.

15. Author interview with Kay Tillow, June 20, 2011.

16. Fink and Greenberg, *Upheaval*, 165.

17. Kendi, *Stamped from the Beginning*, 4. Nearly all of the 1199 WV/KY/OH members and every one of the organizers with whom I spoke emphasized the common tactic of hospital management using the "race card." Examples follow in subsequent chapters.

18. W. E. B. DuBois, cited in Goldfield, "Race and the CIO," 2; Yates, *Why Unions Matter*, 146–147.

19. Hennen, "Toil, Trouble, Transformation," 257. A full story of Local 236 can be found in Gilpin, *The Long Deep Grudge*; see "Part Three: The FE Against the Grain," 141–226. Local 236 was one of four left-progressive locals in Louisville known collectively as the Seventh Street Unions. They "shared a militant perspective, a weekly newspaper, and a bustling union hall on Seventh Street." They were FE Local 236, city bus drivers in the Transport Workers Union of America, sanitation workers in the United Public Workers, and a local of the United Furniture Workers. Fosl, *Subversive Southerner*, 92.

20. Braden, *The Wall Between*, 48.

21. Fink and Greenberg, *Upheaval*, 165–166; Fantasia, *Cultures of Solidarity*, 129; author interviews with Teresa Ball, Penny Burchett, David Cormier, Larry Daniels, Joyce Gibson, Anna May Jenkins, David Mott, Mary Schafer, Judy Siders, and Tom Woodruff; agenda for 1199 Organizer's Conference in Columbus, Ohio, February 6–9, 1985; email to author from Gabe Kramer, SEIU/District 1199 director for staff development, April 16, 2008.

22. The law, Public Employee Relations Act 195, took effect as of July 20, 1970. It includes public employees in nonprofit institutions and establishes an arbitration procedure for any collective bargaining impasses. Email from Kay Tillow to author, December 24, 2019.

23. Author interview with Kay Tillow. Joseph (Jock) Yablonski was a longtime UMWA official who ran an insurgent campaign for president of the union against W. A. Tony Boyle in 1969. Boyle won the election and then arranged for Yablonski's murder. Yablonski, his wife, and their adult daughter Charlotte were shot to death as they slept on New Year's Eve, 1969. The Department of Labor overturned Boyle's election after a fraud investigation, and Boyle was defeated by Arnold Miller in 1972. Miller ran as the candidate of Miners for Democracy, which had formed in the UMWA after Yablonski's murder. Boyle was later convicted of hiring the hit men who carried out the killings. See Clark, *Miners' Fight for Democracy*.

    See "Union at Lewistown," a report on 1199P's victory at the Lewistown hospital, 119.

    1199P also won an important victory at Butler Hospital in 1974, despite what organizer Anthony Ross described as management's "vicious anti-union" drive with "many racial overtones." The vote among the 280 service employees was 127–102. The Butler chapter was the target of decertification drives by the hospital in 1974, 1978, and 1979, succeeding in pushing the union out in 1979. *1199 News* 9:3 (March 1974), 21.

24. Moody, "Beating the Union," 186–187; Balliet, *Survey of Labor Relations*, 143; Harris, "Politicians, Bureaucrats," 443–444; Murray, *Lexicon of Labor*, 157–158, 172–73.
    Union activity was further regulated by the Landrum-Griffin Act (1959), officially called the Labor Management Reporting and Disclosure Act.

25. Drake, *History of Appalachia*, 201–202; Mulcahy, "United Mine Workers," 1670–1671. The full history of the fund is in Mulcahy, *Social Contract for the Coal Fields*. The official name was changed to the UMWA Health and Retirement Funds during a restructuring in 1974. Also see Smoot, "Miners Memorial," 1659–1660. In 1986 the company changed its name to Appalachian Regional Healthcare. The ARH and the United Steelworkers signed their latest three-year contract in 2016; see http://www.arh.org/Articles/arh-employees-represented-by usw-approve-three-year -labor-contract-agreement, accessed July 8, 2018.

26. Following the American Civil War, a cadre of "local color" writers produced a body of literature that cemented an essentialist *mentalité* of Appalachia in the minds of urban readers. These universalist assumptions about the region survived in popular culture and academic studies. For an impressive recent analysis of the emergence and durability of local color tropes, see Satterwhite, *Dear Appalachia*. It is one of many valuable researches into the "idea of Appalachia."
    Fisher, "Grass Roots Speak Back," 206–207; Wilkerson, *To Live Here*, 3, 11, 15; Clark, *Miners' Fight for Democracy*, 24–26.
    The Charleston *Daily Mail*, May 26, 1980, included just one of many stories the Charleston papers published on local Vietnam veterans in the early 1980s. Some 711 West Virginians, or 85 out of every 100,000 males in the state, were killed in Vietnam, more per capita than any other state. Sumrock, Giles, and Mitchell-Bateman, "Public Health Legacy," 196.

27. The structural economic changes and the resulting damage done to communities suggested in these few paragraphs have been well documented. For three excellent works on post–World War II Appalachia, see Kiffmeyer, *Reformers to Radicals*; Eller, *Uneven Ground*; and Thomas, *An Appalachian Reawakening*.

28. *1199 News* 5:11, November 1970, 27. The National Labor Relations Board is an independent federal agency created within the National Labor Relations Act (Wagner Act) in 1935. The main function of the NLRB is to oversee and enforce provisions of the act. It supervises union certification (representation) and decertification elections, hears and decides on unfair labor practice charges, and conducts research. The board originally had three members and was expanded to five by the Taft-Hartley Act of 1947. The members are appointed to five-year terms by the U.S. president, subject to approval by the Senate. Murray, *Lexicon of Labor*, 125. The NLRB headquarters are in Washington, D.C., and now it has twenty-six regional offices, as opposed to thirty-four in 1988. Schwartz, *Legal Rights*. A current NLRB regional map is available at https://www.nlrb.gov/about-nlrb /who-we-are/regional-offices, accessed July 25, 2019.

29. *1199 News* 5:12, December 1970, 20. A few years later, in 1974, the twenty-two clerical workers at Doctors Memorial NLRB secured an election and voted for the

union 16–1, joining the 150 service and maintenance workers. Drake and Harless credited LPN Dot Ross and X-ray technician Floyd Baker with signing up the clericals to ask for the election.

30. "AGREEMENT entered into between Madison General Hospital" and "Local 1199 W. Va., hereinafter referred to as the Union," October 26, 1970, Collection 5525 Box 76 file folder 1, "West Virginia-General" in National Union of Hospital and Health Care Employees collection at Kheel Labor Archives, Cornell University.

31. Gillenwater, "Welch," 755–756; Myers, "McDowell County," 465–466.

32. Author interview with David Cormier, June 2, 2008; Bacon, "History of SEIU," 5; *1199 News* 6:3, March 1971, 22; *1199 News* 6:5, May 1971, 19.

33. *1199 News* 6:5, May 1971, 19.; *West Virginia AFL-CIO Observer* (n.d., but probably September 1971), 2; Wendell Drake to Merle Charney, June 11, 1975; Anne Shore to Donald Frazier, Doctor's Memorial administrator, April 9, 1975; William Taylor of the national 1199 to John W. Bross, October 3, 1977. All three of these letters are related to pension deliberations and follow-up. Collection 5525, Box 76, file folder 1, 1199 papers at Kheel Archives, Cornell University. The *Observer* article is also Collection 5525, box 8.

34. "Constitution of the National Union," 5–6; "Proposed District 1199 By-Laws," 5.

35. Local 1199 used the term "delegate" rather than steward. Fink and Greenberg claim the reason is that it was "a less industrial-sounding term than shop steward." This may have been a linguistic device to appeal to professionals within the jurisdiction of the union. Fink and Greenberg, *Upheaval*, 190.

36. Greenberg, *Upheaval*, 190. The SEIU District Local 1199 WV/KY/OH now has a grievance chair in each department/bargaining unit, written into the contract, who participates along with the delegate at the third step. The chair determines whether a grievance unresolved at the third step has merit to advance to arbitration and submits a report to the district representative, Joyce Gibson, who handles arbitrations. Author interview with Joyce Gibson, February 11, 2008.

  1199 Hotline, March 1978. The capitalization of "National Hospital Union" in this passage is significant. Although the original New York Local 1199 established a "national" office in 1969, the National Union of Hospital and Health Care Employees AFL-CIO was not formally established until 1973.

  There are many publications that offer a valuable education in the role of union stewards, including Prosten, *Union Steward's Complete Guide*, and Schwartz, *Legal Rights of Union Stewards*.

37. Foner and North, *Not for Bread Alone*, 34–35.

38. *1199 News* 6:11, November 1971, 19; Robert Muehlenkamp to Elliott Godoff, September 13, 1971, Call number 5525, Box 76 file folder 1, "West Virginia-General" in National Union of Hospital and Health Care Employees collection at Kheel ILR Archives, Cornell University; Fantasia, *Cultures of Solidarity*, 132–133.

CHAPTER 4

1. Stafford, "Beckley"; Mahar, *Money-Driven Medicine*, 83. The rise of the for-profit hospital chains, established to capitalize on revenues from Medicare and employer-based health insurance, is the focus of Mahar's chapter 3, entitled "For-Profit Hospitals," 80–138. These developments had significant implications for the small for-profits that Harless was organizing and for healthcare employees nationwide. Later chapters in this book return to these issues.

2. Stafford, "Beckley," 48–49; *Beckley Post-Herald*, February 25, 1971.
3. *Raleigh Register*, August 12, 1971; *Beckley Post-Herald*, February 25 and 26, 1971.
4. Moody, "Beating the Union," 186–189.
5. *1199 News* 6:5, May 1971, 13–15; *Beckley Post-Herald*, February 23, 1971. (The August 13 *Post-Herald* claimed that the NLRB petition was filed on February 15.)
6. *Beckley Post-Herald*, February 25, 1971. McCulloch would have been correct about permanent replacements only if the NLRB eventually denied union charges of unfair labor practices by the hospital and declared the walkout an economic strike. That decision could take years, and once 1199 lost the election in August 1971, it appears it abandoned pursuing unfair labor practice charges.
7. *1199 News* 6:5, May 1971, 13–15.
8. *1199 News* 6:8, August 1971, 19; *1199 News* 6:5, May 1971, 15.
9. *1199 News* 6:5, May 1971, 15, 19; *Raleigh Register*, February 23, 1971; *Beckley Post-Herald*, February 25, 1971, and August 13, 1971.
10. Stafford, "Hulett C. Smith," 662–663.
11. West Virginia AFL-CIO press release, May 14, 1971; Miles Stanley to Elliott Godoff, May 17, 1971; Local 1199 papers, call number 5525, Box 76, file folder 1, West Virginia-General; ILR Kheel Library Center, Cornell University. As president of the West Virginia State Labor Federation, Stanley directed the AFL-CIO's progressive civil rights agenda in the state. For details, see Colin Fones-Wolf, "A Union Voice," 111–128.
12. *1199 News* 6:6, June 1971, 13; *Beckley Post-Herald*, August 13, 1971; *Raleigh Register*, August 12, 1971.
13. *Beckley Post-Herald*, February 25, 1971.
14. *Beckley Post-Herald*, August 12, 13, 1971.
15. *Beckley Post-Herald*, August 13, 1971.
16. *1199 News* 15:4, April 1980, 7.
17. *1199 News* 9:6, June 1974, 21.
18. Flanery, "Review."
19. *Richlands News-Press*, February 28, 1973; "History of Richlands and Tazewell County," at https://visittazewellcounty.org/richlands/, accessed on July 9, 2019.
20. Census of Population and Housing, 1970–1990, https://www.census.gov/prod/www/decennial.html, accessed on December 13, 2020.
21. The hospital assigned nurses to work with the clinic's doctors, and an assignment to the clinic was, according to the NLRB, considered more desirable than an assignment to the hospital. When the nurses struck, the clinic doctors accused them of "nonprofessional conduct" and vowed never to work with them again. National Labor Relations Board, *Clinch Valley Clinic Hospital* v. *NLRB*.
22. *Richlands News-Press*, February 7, 1973.
23. "Unions and Jobs," 11. Job classifications in the two bargaining units included nurses' aides, orderlies, housekeeping and maintenance workers, ward clerks, and LPNs. The vote numbers were reported in *Hospitals* 46:21, November 1, 1972, 129.
24. *Richlands News-Press*, February 7, 1973, *Mountain Life and Work*, February 1973, 13.
25. *Richlands News-Press*, February 14, 1973, *Mountain Life and Work*, February 1973, 13.
26. *Richlands News-Press*, February 14, 1973; Judge Sexton's order: Case # 6107, File #28, Civil Records in Tazewell County Courthouse, *Mountain Life and Work*, April 1973, 15.

27. *Mountain Life and Work*, February 1973, 12, 14, and 49:4, April 1973, 16; *United Mine Workers Journal* (UMWJ) 84:4, March 15, 1973, 4.

28. Arnold Miller to Dan Stewart, July 9, 1976, call number 5651, box 7, file folder 8, ILR Kheel Library Center, Cornell University. The five thousand number is widely reported, including by Elliott Godoff. The miners' walkout ended with an injunction. Godoff, "Organizing Report," 5; Nyden, "Contours of Class Struggle," 15; *Richlands News-Press*, March 7, 1973.

29. *Richlands New-Press*, March 7, 1973.

30. Wilkerson, *To Live Here*, 9.

31. Under a union shop contract, all new hires are required to join their union after a specified time and retain that membership as a condition of employment. Murray, *The Lexicon of Labor*, 180.

32. Author interview with Teresa Ball, December 30, 1998.

33. *1199 News* 13:10, November 1978, 21; *Fairmont Times-West Virginian*, September 8, 1978. The Fairmont General story is covered in chapters 5 and 6. Author interview with Anna May Jenkins, January 29, 2008; Loretta Williams cited in *Mountain Life and Work* (July/August 1984), 3.

34. Berry, *What Are People For?*; Berry, "About Civil Disobedience"; Thoreau, "Civil Disobedience," 463.

35. *Richlands News-Press*, February 28 and March 8, 1973.

36. Mahar, *Money-Driven Medicine*, 83; Fantasia, *Cultures of Solidarity*, 244–245.

37. Between 1969 and November 1973, the union's official name was the National Union of Hospital and Nursing Employees. At the union's constitutional convention in November 1973, it became the National Union of Hospital and Health Care Employees. Hereafter in this study I will refer to it as the National Union. Article I of the Constitution states that the "Districts or other forms of organizational sub-divisions established by the National Union may be designated by the prefix or suffix "1199" followed by an alphabetical letter as the President shall determine." This form of a district's identification had been practiced since 1969. "Constitution of the National Union," 6.

38. Tazewell County Circuit Court, *Contempt Proceedings of March 16, 1973*, 2, 36–65, Case 6107, File 28, Tazewell County Courthouse. Incidentally, Weinstock was a close friend of one Alfred Knobler, a New Yorker with business interests in Huntington. Knobler supported many progressive social justice issues and lent moral and financial support to the Appalachian Movement Press. Author interview with Tom Woodruff, April 5, 2008.

39. Tazewell County Circuit Court, *Contempt Proceedings*, 4–11 (Weinstock statement); and 11–13 (Hudgins's statement). Decisions by the appeals courts are found in Case 6107, File 28, Civil Records, Tazewell County Courthouse.

40. Tazewell County Circuit Court *Contempt Proceedings*, 69–71; Order of the Supreme Court of the United States to the Supreme Court of Virginia, No. 73–1252, April 1, 1974. Case 6107, File 28, Civil Records, Tazewell County Courthouse.

41. Larry Harless to Elliott Godoff, July 21, 1973, Call number 5651, box 7, file folder 8. ILR Kheel Library Center, Cornell University.

42. Fink and Greenberg, *Upheaval*, 188.

43. Leon Davis to Larry Harless, August 7, 1973, Call number 5651, box 7, file folder 8. ILR Kheel Library Center, Cornell University.

44. Weaver, "Remembering Larry Harless."

45. Yates, *Power on the Job*, 107.

46. Author interview with Tom Woodruff, April 5, 2008; National Labor Relations Board, *Clinch Valley Clinic Hospital* v. *NL RB,* No. 74–2149, case 516 F.2d 996 (1975), at https://www.leagle.com/decision/19751512516f2d99611349, accessed July 14, 2019.

CHAPTER 5

1. Sherman Act summary found at https://www.ourdocuments.gov/doc.php?flash =false&doc=51, July 24, 2019. Philip Dray addressed the antilabor shift of the Sherman Act in *There Is Power in a Union*, 214–215. Dray cites the precedent set in *United States v. Workingmen's Amalgamated Council of New Orleans*, Eastern District Court of Louisiana, 54 Fed. 724, 744–745 (1893), cited in Berman, *Labor and the Sherman Act*, 7.
2. Becker and Rakich, "Hospital Union Activity," 59–66; Rothman, *Strikes in Health Care Organizations*, 75; Davis, "Report from the President," 23.
3. Greenhouse, *The Big Squeeze*, 249.
4. Harris, "Politicians, Bureaucrats," 439.
5. Lynd, *"We Are All Leaders,"* 6–7.
6. Rothman, *Strikes in Health Care Organizations*, 74–77.
7. "Officers' Report," 37.
8. Rothman, *Strikes in Health Care Organizations*, 74–77; Kruger and Metzger, *When Health Care Employees Strike*, 3–16.
   Public Law 93-360 also established guidelines for five (later, in 1991, expanded to eight) designated bargaining units for the "private health care field": units of registered nurses; units of other professional employees; units of technical employees (including licensed practical nurses and nurses' aides); units of service and maintenance employees; and units of clerical employees. *Fortieth Annual Report*, 58–65.
9. Mulcahy, "Hill-Burton Hospital," 1652–1653. The 90 percent figure for the Fairmont General expansion was posted at https://www.fghi.com in 2010. Mulcahy notes that communities raised start-up capital for the projects, and "once a specific threshold was reached, Hill-Burton funds were awarded on a dollar-per-dollar basis, covering half of all costs." That formula could indicate that the 90 percent posting was overstated. In 2011 the hospital declared bankruptcy and was purchased by Alecto Healthcare. Local 1199WV represented three bargaining units at FGH from 1978 until the 1989 merger with SEIU. ALECTO, a chain hospital that acquired the hospital in 2014, closed it in the spring of 2020. Chapter 10 briefly addresses these developments.
10. Starr, *Social Transformation*, 429, 335; Moody, *In Solidarity*, 254.
11. Rakich, "Hospital Unionization," 7–10; Melosh, *"The Physician's Hand,"* 215; Fantasia, *Cultures of Solidarity*, 152.
12. Vaccaro and Saletsky, "How to Preserve," 5–7; Wilkerson, *To Live Here*, 14–15.
13. Rakich, "Hospital Unionization," 7–10; Rothman, *Strikes in Health Care Organizations*, 63.
14. Lichtenstein et al., *Who Built America*, 577–578; Moody, *In Solidarity*, 183–184. The 1959 steel strike and the significance of unionization for American families following World War II are covered in Jack Metzgar's brilliant memoir, *Striking Steel*.
15. Moody specifies Mike Davis, *Prisoners of the American Dream* (London: Verso), 1986; Michael Goldfield, *The Decline of Organized Labor in the United States*

(Chicago: University of Chicago Press), 1987; Metzgar, *Striking Steel*, 2000; and Nelson Lichtenstein, *The State of the Union: A Century of American Labor* (Princeton, NJ: Princeton University Press), 2002.

16. Moody, *In Solidarity*, 184; Logan, "Union Avoidance Industry," 651–653.
17. Levitt and Conroy, *Confessions of a Union Buster*, 72–73.
18. *Hospital Topics* 53:5 (September/October 1975), 27–31, 54; *Hospital Topics* 54:2 (March/April 1976), 53–58; *Hospital Topics* 60:5 (September/October 1982), 13, 22; *Hospital and Health Services Administration* 29:6 (November/December 1984), 68–78; *Hospital and Health Services Administration* 28:1 (January/February 1983), 24–29; *Hospital Topics* 60:1 (January/February 1982), 5–7. The forward to Yeiser's primer is reproduced in "Pressures in Today's Workplace," 121.
19. Kistler, "Pressures in Today's Workplace," 41, 53; Muhlenkamp statement, 158–172, 189.
20. Roel, "Labor-Management Consultants," 15–20.
21. *1199 News* 14:5 (May 1979), 9. Kay Tillow interview, June 20, 2011.
22. Author interview with Larry Daniels, July 29, 1998.
23. This is a composite (and partial) list, extracted from several sources: Greenberg, *Union Avoidance in Hospitals*, 24–29; Vaccaro and Saletsky, "How to Preserve," 5–7; Robbins and Rakich," Hospital and Personal Management," 18–33; Rutkowski and Rutkowski, *Labor Relations in Hospitals*, 3, 5, 35, 41. In 1984, management at Cabell Huntington distributed a flyer linking both Davis and Woodruff to disloyal "organizations" and suggested the National Union was violent. Judy Siders collection.
24. Author interview with Tom Woodruff, April 5, 2008.
25. Author interview with Anna Jenkins, January 29, 2008.
26. Jenkins interview.
27. Jenkins interview, January 29, 2008. In its heyday, ACF had 1,600 employees and a payroll of $30 million. By the time it finally shut down in 2010, it employed three security guards and a janitor. Developers had plans to demolish the plant and build a modern baseball park, hotel, and retail center, but the empty plant still stands. James E. Casto in the May 22 *Herald-Dispatch*, accessed on August 13, 2019, at https://www.herald-dispatch.com/business/acf-plant-dates-to-city-s-earliest -years/article_78400a5e-9209-53fa-81ee-d1a9bebac6c7.html.
28. Woodruff interview, April 5, 2008; Huntington *Herald-Dispatch*, October 15, 1974.
29. Cabell Huntington Hospital Board of Trustees Minutes, October 21, 1974, 3; *Herald-Dispatch*, October 20 and 22, 1974; Muehlenkamp, "Organizing Never Stops," 4; Huntington *Advertiser*, January 1, 1975. The *Herald-Dispatch* was Huntington's morning paper; the *Advertiser* was the evening paper. On Sundays the paper was published jointly as the *Herald-Advertiser*.
30. Huntington *Advertiser*, October 26, 1974.
31. Huntington *Herald-Dispatch*, November 15, 1974. The organizing committee number was documented in *1199 News* 10:5 (May 1975), 5. Anna May Jenkins estimated that the nurses' aides had seventeen seats on the committee. Jenkins interview, January 29, 2008.
32. Resolution by the Huntington Ministerial Association, undated but about November 7–13, 1974, in the Judy Siders collection; figures for West Virginia union membership were viewed on December 29, 2020, at https://www.npr.org /sections/money/2015/02/23/385843576/50-years-of-shrinking-union

-membership-in-one-map; local union support noted in *1199 News* 10:5 (May 1975), 5; Huntington locals found in R. L. Polk's 1975 and 1981 *Huntington City Directories*, 143, 145; Huntington *Herald-Advertiser*, November 17, 1974.

33. Woodruff interview, April 5, 2008.

34. McAlevey, *No Shortcuts*, 58–59; Huntington *Herald-Advertiser,* November 19, 1974; Cabell Huntington Hospital Board of Trustees Executive Committee Minutes, November 27, 1974.

35. Frankel reference, Huntington *Herald-Dispatch*, December 10, 1974. Frankel had become a consistent advocate for an election, as evidenced by his remarks at Board of Trustee meetings on November 25, December 30, and January 27, 1975. Broadside paid for by the Cabell-Huntington Hospital Organizing Committee, National Hospital Union (*sic*), Ann Wookey, treasurer. This and several other documents referred to in this chapter were donated by Anna May Jenkins and Judy Siders.

36. Wood claimed substantial employee opposition to the union at the November 27, 1974, meeting of the Board of Trustees Executive Committee meeting, according to the Minutes; *1199 News* 10:5 (May 1975), 5.

37. Although public workers in West Virginia had no protected right to collective bargaining, some, as we have seen, did belong to unions. In the event of a union election the public hospitals usually used the NLRB guidelines as a model for determining bargaining units. But as we saw earlier, the practice was flexible, and in this case the Cabell Huntington trustees devised their own sweeping terms for voting eligibility. Their arguments are clearly recounted in the Board of Trustee Minutes of January 27, 1975. It could be that some of the trustees believed the union would lose, but they would be off the hook by approving an election.

38. Author interview with Judy Siders, March 13, 2008.

39. Siders interview, March 13, 2008. Leon Davis's correspondence and that of other national officers suggest close scrutiny of the locals' expenditures. Each year the National Union published a financial report of all the locals in the *1199 News*.

40. The question and answer document from employer to workers, with nine "question and answer" summaries, some quite detailed, of the hospital's position. The exact date is uncertain, probably between February 29 and March 7, 1975. A response from "Cabell Huntington Hospital Union Employees" is dated March 13. Found in the Judy Siders collection.

41. Woodruff interview, April 8, 2008; letter to Kenneth Wood from "Cabell Huntington Hospital Union Employees," March 13, 1975, found in the Judy Siders collection. The hospital did use an outside consultant during contract negotiations *after* the 1975 election. On September 15, 1977, with a possible strike approaching, Kenneth Wood asked the Board of Trustees to approve hiring an outside consultant to advise the administration. The minutes report that Wood reminded the board that "the consultant was very beneficial during the last contract" (1975).

42. *1199 News* 10:5 (May 1975), 5; *WV AFL-CIO Observer* 8:8 (April 15, 1975), 1; Woodruff interview, April 8, 2008; Siders interview, March 13, 2008.

43. "Public Statement by the Cabell-Huntington Negotiating Committee," July 23, 1975, from the Judy Siders collection; Woodruff interview, April 8, 2008; *Mountain Life and Work* 53:9 (October 1977), 6; opening remarks by Woodruff to the 1980 delegates' convention, Judy Siders collection.

44. "Organizing Report to the National Executive Board."
45. "You organize or you die" was the union's constant cry. Fink and Greenberg, *Upheaval*, 186. Practically every member I interviewed repeated the phrase "organize or die" at some point.

CHAPTER 6

1. Morris, "Prestonsburg," 739; *Floyd County Times*, August 27, 1975.
2. Robert Muhlenkamp to Jo Anna Martins (*sic*), July 30, 1975.
3. Author interview with Jo Anna Martin Risner, September 5, 1998. Following quotes are from this interview.
4. Risner interview, September 5, 1998.
5. Author interview with Larry Daniels, July 29, 1998. Portions of the material on the HRMC campaign were published in Hennen, "Putting the 'You' in Union." I am including source citations directly from the article.
6. Daniels interview, July 29, 1998; Hennen, "Putting the 'You' in Union."
7. Risner interview, September 5, 1998; Daniels interview, July 29, 1998.
8. Author interview with Penny Burchett, August 15, 1998.
9. Other active "worker leaders" included Rebecca Wells, Cheryl Whittaker, Irene Dale, Linda May, Earleth Meade, Debbie Wheeler, Martha Robinson, and Ora Lee Hills. *1199 News* 10:12 (December 1975), 11; Risner interview, September 5, 1975.
10. *Floyd County Times*, August 27, 1975; *Paintsville Herald*, August 27, 1975.
11. *1199 News* 10:11 (November 1975), 12; Burchett interview, August 15, 1998; Daniels interview, July 29, 1998. SESCO was also brought in by HRMC in 1978 during contract renegotiations. *1199 Hotline*, April–May 1978. This was a newsletter published by the 1199 locals in West Virginia, Kentucky, and Ohio. *1199 News* 13:5 (May 1978), 21.
12. Burchett interview, August 15, 1998; Risner interview, September 5, 1998; Daniels interview, July 29, 1998. Risner heard, from several sources, that HRMC spent at least $60,000 on its union avoidance strategy. Daniels said the hospital spent "hundreds of dollars a day to pay a union-busting firm and couldn't give us a raise or a pension plan or any other kinds of benefits."
13. *Paintsville Herald*, November 5, 1975, one week before the election at HRMC; *Floyd County Times*, September 10, 1975. Penny Burchett joyously recounted the story of Stewart's bail hearing in her August 15, 1998, interview.
14. *1199 News* 10:12 (December 1975), 11; Risner interview, September 5, 1998.
15. *Floyd County Times*, November 5, 1975; Fink and Greenberg, *Upheaval*, 173.
16. *Floyd County Times*, November 5 and 12, 1975; Yates, *Power on the Job*, 116–117.
17. *1199 News* 10:12 (December 1975), 11; Risner interview, September 5, 1998.
18. *Paintsville Herald*, March 10, 1976; *Floyd County Times*, March 24, 1976; Murray, *Lexicon of Labor*, 12, 39, 180, 111; Yates, *Power on the Job*, 119. In terms of favorability to the union, the order of union security would be the closed shop (now outlawed except in building trades), union shop, agency shop, maintenance of membership, and open shop (in which a union does not exist or may be a presence, but no employee can be required to join or pay dues; this is the objective of right-to-work laws).
19. *Paintsville Herald*, November 12, 1975, March 17 and 24, 1976; *Floyd County Times*, March 10 and 24 1976; *1199 News* 11:5 (May 1976), n.p.; Burchett

interview, August 15, 1975. Burchett and Daniels estimated that Gene Divine was administrator for less than a year all told.

20. Risner interview, September 5, 1998; *1199 News* 11:5 (May 1976), n.p.

21. Tom Woodruff to Leon Davis, April 22, 1976, call number 5651, Box 25, file folder "West Virginia 1974–1975," ILR Kheel Library Center, Cornell University.

22. "Agenda," National Union of Hospital and Health Care, 1199 W.Va., RWDSU AFL-CIO, July 17, 1976, call number 5651, Box 7, file folder 8, ILR Kheel Library Center, Cornell University; Delegate Assembly Registration and July 9, 1976 Press Release, retrieved from storage at the 1199WV/KY/OH Huntington office, fall 2008; Fleming, "Ken Hechler," 327.

23. Observations by Marshall Dubin, call number 5651, Box 7, file folder 8, ILR Kheel Library Center, Cornell University.

24. Siders interview, March 13, 2008.

25. *1199 News* 12:11, November 1977; *1199 Hotline*, January 1978.

26. Minutes of the Cabell Huntington Board of Trustees "Special Board Meeting," September 15, 1977, 1–2; Trustees minutes, reconvened meeting of September 29, 1977, 2. The two members from the Huntington AFL-CIO were Wilbert Ward and Charles Spurlock. Spurlock was listed as attending this meeting, but Ward was absent.

27. Trustee Robert Trocin advised that the mobilization of extra security "should not be done as a flagrant thing which might cause problems for negotiations." Trustees minutes, September 15, 1977, 2; Woodruff interview, April 5, 2008; *Herald-Dispatch*, September 28–October 2, 1977; *Mountain Life and Work* 53:9 (October 1977), 6–9.

28. Civil Action No. 77-2061 in the Circuit Court of Cabell County, October 7, 1977. This "Decision Order" recounted the facts of Judge Conaty's injunction decision and documented his decision from the bench to remove himself from the case. Found in Cabell County Circuit Court Division I Order Book number 34, page 517. *Herald-Dispatch* October 7, 1977.

29. *Herald-Dispatch* October 2–4, 1977.

30. Ehrenreich and Ehrenreich, *The American Health Empire*, 30–31; Fink and Greenberg, *Upheaval*, 117, 120.

31. Kruger and Metzgar, *When Health Care Employees Strike*, 46–49; Melosh, *The Physician's Hand*, 3–10; *Herald-Dispatch*, September 30, 1977; Ducey, *Never Good Enough*, 1–21.

32. Risner interview, September 5, 1998; *Herald-Dispatch*, October 6, 1977; trustees' minutes, "Reconvened Board Meeting," October 7, 1977, 4.

33. Melosh, *Physician's Hand*, 201–202; *Labor Agreement between Cabell Huntington Hospital and the National Union of Hospital and Health Care Employees, 1199 W.Va., AFL-CIO, Effective October 22, 1979 through October 21, 1981*, 76–77.

34. *Herald-Dispatch*, October 2, 1977, as recounted in Hennen, "1199 Comes to Appalachia," 229–230.

35. Lindorff, *Marketplace Medicine*, 12–13; Melosh, *Physicians Hand*, 23; trustees minutes, "Reconvened Board Meeting," October 7, 1977, 3.

36. Barocci, *Non-Profit Hospitals*, 150. Kruger and Metzgar, *When Health Care Employees Strike*, 46–47, describe Nightingalism as "an antediluvian image of angels of mercy" which still exits; Melosh, *Physician's Hand*, 3–23; Wilkerson, *To Live Here*, 14–15.

37. Nash, "Interview with Leon Davis," 99; Wilkerson, *To Live Here*, 14–15.

38. *Herald-Dispatch*, October 5, 10, and 12; *1199 News* 12:11, November 1977, 7. The

cited court documents on the trespassing charges are found in Order Book number 34, pages 603, 607, and 663, for October 21 and 31, 1977 (Civil Action no. 77-2061 in the Cabell County Circuit Court); *Mountain Life and Work* 53:9 (October 1977), 6–9.

39. *Herald-Dispatch*, October 10 and 14, 1977; Jenkins interview, January 29, 2008.
40. Trustees minutes October 7, 1977, 3–4; September 30, 1977 reconvened meeting, 1–2; and October 7, 1977 reconvened meeting, 3.
41. *Herald-Dispatch*, October 22 and 23, 1977; *1199 News* 12:11 (November 1977), 5; *West Virginia AFL-CIO Observer* 12:3 (November 1977); *Labor Agreement between Cabell-Huntington Hospital and the National Union of Hospital and Health Care Employees 1199 W.Va., AFL-CIO,* effective October 22, 1977–October 21, 1979, 3–6; Siders interview, March 13, 2008; Trustees minutes, September 29, 1977, 1.

   Judy Siders's wish finally came true. On December 10, 2019, the nearly one thousand registered nurses at Cabell Huntington voted to join the Service Employees International Union District 1199WV/KY/OH. Tom Woodruff came out of retirement to assist a major campaign to organize the RNs at Cabell Huntington and at St. Mary's. District press release, December 10, 2019; email from Joyce Gibson to author, December 10, 2019.
42. *1199 News* 12:11 (November 1977), 7.
43. These figures are found at https://www.cnn.com/interactive/2019/business /us-minimum-wage-by-year/index.html and https://www.usinflationcalculator .com/, accessed June 20, 2019. *1199 Hotline,* January 1978; Foner and North, *Not for Bread Alone*, passim, especially chapter 6, "Bread and Roses: Working People Deserve the Best," 84–102.

CHAPTER 7

1. Woodruff to Berman, January 28, 1988; Bacon, "History of SEIU," 1996; Foner and North, *Not for Bread Alone*, 33.
2. *1199 News* 13:9, October 1978, "Letters" page on inside cover.
3. *1199 News* 12:7, July 1977, 21; Woodruff interview, April 5, 2008.
4. *1199 News* 12:7, July 1977, 21–22. Davis testified before the Congressional Committee on Labor and Education (the Hartley Committee) of the House of Representatives, where he was questioned by Charles Kersten of Wisconsin and John F. Kennedy of Massachusetts. Fink and Greenberg, *Upheaval*, 23.

   Angela Davis was a charismatic African American radical activist and academic, involved with SNCC, SDS, the Black Panther Party, and the Communist Party. In 1970 Davis was charged with providing a weapon to seventeen-year-old Jonathon Jackson. In August of 1970 Jackson was at the center of a courthouse kidnapping and shootout resulting in his death and that of three others. Jackson's motive was to negotiate the release from Soledad Prison in California of his brother, George, with whom Davis was involved. Davis was tried for murder, kidnapping, and conspiracy, touching off an international protest campaign organized by the National United Committee to Free Angela Davis. The National 1199 contributed to the campaign's defense fund. Davis was acquitted in 1972. As of 2020, she is still active in revolutionary politics, especially focused on mass incarceration and prison issues. Kendi, *Stamped from the Beginning*, 410–420; Georgakas, "Angela Davis," 182–183.
5. *Times-Leader*, October 29, November 18, 1976. The *Times-Leader* had offices in

Martins Ferry and Bellaire, with circulation in Belmont, Harrison, Jefferson, and Monroe counties. *1199 News* 12:7, July 1977, 22–23.

6. Koon, "Fairmont," 227; Cook, "Consolidation Coal," 262–263; Venham, "Owens-Illinois Glass Company," 551; *1199 News* 20:1 (January 1979), 12–13; Fones-Wolf, *Glass Towns*, 186–188.

7. Cowie, *Stayin' Alive*, 288–296. There is a vast and growing literature on the restructuring of the American economy and its effects on industrial communities. Two early (and good) ones are Hoerr, *And the Wolf Finally Came*, and Harrison and Bluestone, *The Great U-Turn*.

8. Huntington *Herald-Dispatch*, October 15, 1978.

9. *1199 News* 14:4 (April 1979), 26–27; affidavit of Tom Woodruff, Civil Action no. 78-C-633 in the Circuit Court of Marion County, West Virginia, January 23, 1979; *Fairmont Times-West Virginian*, September 20, 1978; author interview with Mary Schafer, August 11, 2004.

10. Robbins and Rakich, "Hospital Personnel Management," 24.

11. Yates, *Power on the Job*, 80–81; Juravich and Bronfenbrenner, *Ravenswood*, 15; Rundle, "Winning Hearts and Minds."

12. *Fairmont Times-West Virginian*, September 20, 1978.

13. Shafer interview, August 11, 2004.

14. *Fairmont Times-West Virginian*, September 17, 1978; Shafer interview August 11, 2004; Gilpin, *The Long Deep Grudge*, 74; McAlevey, *No Shortcuts*, 30–34; Foner and North, *Not for Bread Alone*, 34–35.

15. Woodruff affidavit, January 23, 1979; *Fairmont Times-West Virginian*, September 6, 1978; Supreme Court of Appeals of West Virginia 166 W.Va. I; 283 S.E.2d 589, Case no. CC911, accessed on January 22, 2020, at http://web.lexis-nexis.com/universe 660 (hereafter Fairmont General Hospital SCA W.Va. CC911,) 3; Fairmont City Council Minutes, Journal 35, 488, September 5, 1978, Fairmont City Clerk's Office.
    IUE Local 627 from the Fairmont Westinghouse plant was represented at several City Council meetings. Eugene Schafer, Mary's husband, was the local's president. UMW District 31, UMW Locals 4047 and 4060, and the Marion County Federation of Labor Unions were among the local supporters. Fairmont City Council Minutes, Journal 36, 19–20, October 3, 1978.

16. Fairmont General Hospital SCA W.Va. CC911, 3; *Fairmont Times-West Virginian*, September 6, 7, and 8 and October 17, 1978; Western Union Mailgram from Woodruff to O. B. Ayers, September 7, 1978. Woodruff described Volk as "a pretty standard union buster." Woodruff interview, April 5, 2008; Schafer interview, August 11, 2004.

17. Civil Action No. 78-C-633 in the Circuit Court of Marion County, West Virginia, September 11, 1978. Comments on Judge Meredith by Mary Shafer on August 11, 2004, and Grant Crandall on March 7, 2008; *Fairmont Times-West Virginian* September 15, 1978.

18. Woodruff affidavit, January 23, 1979; *Fairmont Times-West Virginian*, September 15 and 28, 1978.

19. Woodruff affidavit, January 23, 1979; *Fairmont Times-West Virginian*, October 26, 1978.

20. Fairmont City Council Minutes, Journal 36, 3, September 19, 1978; *Fairmont Times-West Virginian*, September 13 and 17, 1978.

21. *Fairmont Times-West Virginian*, October 4, 1978.

22. *Fairmont Times-West Virginian*, October 18, 1978; Fairmont City Council Minutes, Journal 36, October 17, 1978, 33–37.

23. *Fairmont Times-West Virginian*, October 23–27; *1199 News* 13:11 (December 1978), 26; Schafer interview, August 11, 2008.

24. *1199 News* 14:4 (April 1979), 26.

25. *1199 News* 13:11 (December 1978), 26; *1199 News* 20:1 (January 1985), 12–13.

26. Fairmont General Hospital SCA W.Va. CC911, 2–3; *1199 News* 14:10 (October 1979), 12. Robert Poyourow, who represented Local 550, joined Pyles and Crandall on the case. He was the third partner in their law firm.

27. Fairmont General Hospital SCA W.Va. CC911, 7; *1199 News* 15:12, 29.

28. Myer, "New Martinsville," 527–528; *New York Times*, December 2, 1979; "Wetzel County Hospital," accessed November 2, 2019, at http://wetzelcountyhospital.com/.

29. Affidavit of Dan Stewart, Civil Action No. 79-C-121-W, Circuit Court of Wetzel County, September 24, 1979, 1; Western Union Mailgram from Dan Stewart to W. A. Powell Jr., June 20, 1979; W. A. Powell to Stewart, June 22, 1979; *New York Times*, December 2, 1979. Stewart's June 20 Mailgram informed Powell, president of the hospital's Board of Trustees, that the cards were signed by "Registered Nurses, LPNs, Nurses Aides, Orderlies, Work Clerks, Laboratory and Radiology Technicians, Business Office Clerical, Departmental Secretaries, Dietary, Housekeeping/Laundry, and Maintenance Personnel."

30. Stewart affidavit, Civil Action No. 79-C-121-W, August 30, 1979; *Mountain Life and Work* 56:3 (March 1980), 28.

31. Resolution of the Wetzel County Commission, Glen W. Riggenbach, president. The date of Stewart's second communication to the hospital board was undated but before July 3, 1979. The board's second rejection of the union's request was sent in a Mailgram to Stewart from James E. Fauber on July 9, 1979. Stewart confirmed the strike date to Rust in a Mailgram dated July 25, 1979. Letter signed by Wetzel County Hospital Grievance Committee, 1199, to Michael Rust, July 26, 1979. The Grievance Committee included seven female and one male employees. The letter included an attachment with a synopsis of union requests signed by eight delegates. Vote figures from *Wetzel Chronicle*, July 26, 1979.

32. W. A. Powell, Michael Rust, and the Board of Trustees to Wetzel County Employees, undated but probably between July 9 and July 31.

33. This letter is roughly analogous to the legislative templates drafted today by the right-wing American Legislative Exchange Council (ALEC) for use by conservative state legislators to promote free-market and socially conservative laws. For more on ALEC, visit the home page of the Center for Media and Democracy. Figures for the hospital's avoidance campaign are from the *West Virginia AFL-CIO Observer* 14:5 (February 1980), 2; and the Wetzel County Commissioner's Order Book 29, page 272, October 31, 1979. *Mountain Life and Work* 56:3 (March 1980), 26–29, reported that the Pinkertons cost $58,000; the St. Clairsville consultant, $17,000 for six months; strikebreaker wages, $65,000; public relations, $44,000.

34. *Wetzel Chronicle*, August 2 and 9, 1979; statement on the injunction orders by Judge Steven D. Narick, in the Circuit Court of Wetzel County re. Civil Action 79-C-121-W, August 6, 1979; author interview with Carol Haught, May 30, 2008.

35. *Wetzel Chronicle*, August 9, 1979; Wetzel County Commissioner's Order Book 29, 187–188, August 7, 1979; *Wetzel Chronicle*, October 18 and 25, 1979.

36. Allegations of violent and intimidating actions by both sides are documented in many court filings, including that of August 6, 1979, in which the hospital requested

its second injunction and the union offered its counternarrative challenging the injunction. In the Circuit Court of Wetzel County, Civil Action 79-C-121-W, August 6, 1979, 1–7. The union further presents its case in "Defendants' Memorandum Regarding Criminal Contempt and in Support of Motion to Dismiss," submitted by Grant Crandall, Bradley Pyles, and Robert Poyourow, Counsel for Defendants, Civil Action 79-C-121-W, September 24, 1979. *Wetzel Chronicle,* October 11, 1979 (Jackie Underwood), and August 16, 1979 (Barbara Frame).

37. *Wetzel Chronicle,* September 20, September 13, August 16, October 18, September 23, November 8, 1979; Wetzel County Commissioner's Order Book 29, page 200, August 13, 1979.

38. Western Union Mailgram, Dan Stewart to Michael Rust, July 12, 1979; defendants' [1199] response to the hospital's complaint of August 6, in the Circuit Court of Wetzel County Civil Action No. 79-C-121-W, September 4, 1979, 4; and defendant's memorandum in the same case, September 24, 1979, 1; *Wetzel Chronicle,* October 11, 1979.

39. *Wetzel Chronicle,* September 6, 1979.

40. Stewart affidavit of September 24, 1979.

41. Wetzel County Commission Order Book 29, August 28, 1979, 213; *Wetzel Chronicle,* August 30, 1979. The two commissioners were James Shepherd and Anthony Estep. The third member, President Glen Riggenbach, was away on county business. *Wetzel Chronicle,* August 2, 1979.

42. *Wetzel Chronicle,* September 30 and November 15, 1979; *Mountain Life and Work* 56:3 (March 1980), 26–29.

43. *Wetzel Chronicle,* November 22, February 14, and October 11; *West Virginia AFL-CIO Observer* 14:6 (March 1980), 3.

44. *Wetzel Chronicle,* November 22, 1979; Wetzel County Commission Order Book 29, February 29, 1980, 483.

45. *Wetzel Chronicle,* February 28, 1980.

46. *Wetzel Chronicle,* April 3, 1980.

47. *1199 News* 16:9 (September 1981), 31; *Wetzel Chronicle, Sept. 13, 1979.*

CHAPTER 8

1. Before the formation of the district in 1980, West Virginia was an "area" of the National 1199 (known as 1199WV); Kentucky was an area identified as 1199K or 1199KY. Ohio was 1199H, or sometimes 1199OH, before merging with 1199WV/KY in 1982, to form 1199WV/KY/OH.

2. "Organizing West Virginia Nursing Homes," October 1, 1987, found in Drawer #4, Columbus Union Hall Miscellaneous Papers, labeled "Organizing Plan Prior to 1992"; *WV AFL-CIO Observer* 12:6 (February 1978), 3; *1199 Hotline* [WV District newsletter], January 1978.

3. Muehlenkamp, "Affidavit of Dan Stewart"; author interview with Robert Wages, June 29, 1999; author interview with Wayne Horman, July 12, 1999; *1199 News* 17:4, April 1982, 14; Tom Woodruff to Netta Berman, "Membership Profile," January 28, 1988; Tom Woodruff to Andy Stern, December 8, 1988. The letters were found in Tom Woodruff's correspondence, District 1199 WV/KY/OH office, Columbus office. The Woodruff papers were contained in several folders in two file cabinets when I was given access in 2008.

4. *1199 News* 13:5 (May 1978), 21; *1199 Hotline* (April–May 1978), 1–2; Daniels

interview, July 29, 1998; Geoghegan, *Which Side Are You On?*, 223; Eller, *Uneven Ground*, 196–197.

5. There has been considerable writing on the social costs of conventional strip mining and MTR. I recommend Shirley Stewart Burns, *Bringing Down the Mountains: The Impact of Mountaintop Removal Surface Mining on Southern West Virginia Communities* (Morgantown: WVU Press), 2011; and Erik Reece, *Lost Mountain: A Year in the Vanishing Wilderness: Radical Strip Mining and the Devastation of Appalachia* (New York: Riverhead Books), 2006.

6. *Mountain Life and Work* 57:6 (June 1981), 12–13; Historical Inflation Rate from 1913 to the present, accessed March 27, 2020, at https://inflationdata.com /Inflation/Inflation_Rate/HistoricalInflation.aspx.

7. *Floyd County Times*, March 25, 1981; *1199 News* 16:5 (May 1981), 18.

8. *Floyd County Times*, March 18, 1981; *UMWA Journal* 92:7 (August 1981), 21; *Mountain Life and Work* 57:8 (September 1981), 3.

9. *Paintsville Herald*, July 15, 1981; *Floyd County Times*, July 8, 1981; *UMWA Journal* 92:7 (August 1981), 21; *1199 News* 16:8 (August 1981), 18.

10. Suzanne LaViolette in *Modern Healthcare* (August 1981), n.p. This article was reprinted in a scrapbook compiled and distributed by the hospital after the strike. The scrapbook is editorially heavily weighted against the union but is a valuable resource, including regional newspaper clippings and strike photographs. Its foreword explains that "we hope to provide motivation and encouragement for all health care professionals living with or facing the threat of unionization." The Louisville *Courier-Journal*, July 2, 1981, noted that the guards outnumbered the picketers.

    Civil Action File No. 81-210, United States District Court for the Eastern District of Kentucky (based in Pikeville), documents some of the assault and harassment charges, October 8 and November 19, 1981.

11. *1199 News* 16:8 (August 1981), 18.

12. *Mountain Life and Work* 57:8 (September 1981), 4–6.

13. *1199 News* (16:8) August 1981, 18; *Paintsville Herald*, July 8, 1981; McMartin, *Collision Course*, 9–10.

14. *1199 News* 16:8 (August 1981), 8; *1199 News* 16:12 (December 1981), 10.

15. Dray, *There Is Power in a Union*, 621–636; Brands, *American Dreams*, 233–234. Exit polls suggested that Reagan won nearly 50 percent of the vote in union households in both 1980 and 1984. Edison Media Research, "Union Household Support in Presidential Elections, 1976–2016," accessed November 29, 2019, at https://www.washingtonpost.com/news/the-fix/wp/2016/11/10/donald-trump -got-reagan-like-support-from-union-households/.

16. *New York Times*, April 14, 1970, at https://www.nytimes.com/1970/04/14 /archives/air-traffic-protest-appears-near-end-air-traffic-controller-protest.html; *Christian Science Monitor*, September 2, 1980, at https://www.csmonitor.com /1980/0902/090232.html; Dray, *There Is Power in a Union*, 625–626. The Taft-Hartley Act of 1947 and the Civil Service Reform Act each outlawed strikes by federal workers. The legal argument against federal workers striking as of 1981 can be found in Federal Labor Relations Authority 10, accessed on January 29, 2020, at https://www.flra.gov/decisions/v07/07–010.html.

17. Dray, *There Is Power in a Union*, 625–627; 633–636. The vote rejecting the government's offer was 13,495 to 616. McMartin, *Collision Course*, 300–320.

McMartin's book is a thorough analysis of PATCO's history, the strike, and the effects of the Reagan years on organized labor.

18. McMartin, *Collision Course*, 361; Bronfenbrenner et. al., *Organizing to Win*, 4–5; Hennen, "1199 Comes to Appalachia," 241–242; Dray, *There Is Power in a Union*, quoting A. R. Raskin and Thomas Donahue, 637.

19. *1199 News* 18:4 (August 1983), 21.

20. Woodruff to Phil Carter, November 2, 1987, Woodruff correspondence, Columbus; Carter interview, July 6, 1999; author interviews with Dave Evans, February 24, 1985, and September 13, 2017; author telephone interview with David McGee, December 16, 2019.

21. Officer's Report to the Seventh Convention of the National Union of Hospital and Health Care Employees, December 9–12, 1987, 3.

22. Resolutions 7, 2, 5, 4, 1, and "Human Rights in Central America," *1199 WV/KY/OH Delegates Assembly*, April 16–17, 1982.

23. Rothman, *Strikes in Health Care Organizations*, 63; Moody, *In Solidarity*, 255–257; Parker and Slaughter, *Working Smart*, 67–68, 80–81. Many of the elements of lean production/MBS are reminiscent of scientific management, or "Taylorism," a system of standardized work rules designed to maximize efficiency. Taylor's early twentieth-century theories in turn incorporated some ideas that had been around since the first American industrial revolution. *The Lexicon of Labor* defines speedup as "a condition imposed by an employer in which employees are required to produce more or increase their performance without a compensating increase in pay." Murray, *Lexicon of Labor*, 167.

    For a valuable case study of the effects of globalization, corporate restructuring, and lean production on an Appalachian community, see Juravich and Bronfenbrenner, *Ravenswood*.

24. Powers, "Ashland," 36–37; Martin, *Smokestacks in the Hills*, 184.

25. *1199 News* 15:10 (October 1980), 7. Longtime 1199 leaders and District Executive Board members Maxine Toney and Terry Beam especially mentioned Goldie Craig, nurses' aide Ann Woods, and a married couple, Ernestine and Roy McKenzie, as natural leaders at Kings Daughters. Author interview with Maxine Toney and Terry Beam, May 27, 2008.

26. *1199 News* 15:10 (October 1980), 6–7, and 15:12 (December 1980), 28. Robert Taft (1889–1953) was the son of President William H. Taft. He was known as "Mr. Republican." For a quick summary of Taft's career, see https://www.senate.gov /artandhistory/history/common/generic/People_Leaders_Taft.htm, accessed December 1, 2019.

27. Collective Bargaining Agreement between King's Daughters and District 1199 WV/ KY, December 1, 1980, 32; *1199 News* 16:1 (January 1981), 19. Irene Howard's daughter, Mary Martin, was a dietary worker at the hospital and a member of the union's negotiating committee. The mother-and-daughter team was featured in a leaflet entitled "Introducing District 1199 WV/KY." Maintenance of membership means that no worker is forced to join the union, but those who do join may not leave the union during the term of the contract, barring a change in employment status. Murray, *Lexicon of Labor*.

28. Collective Bargaining Agreement, effective December 1, 1980, 32; author interview with Terry Beam, May 27, 2008; author interview with Maxine Toney, May 27, 2008; letter from District 1199 WV/KY/OH to all Greenup and Boyd county

unions, August 16, 1983. (Terry Beam succeeded Maxine Toney on the District Executive Council when Toney retired.)

29. *Ashland Daily Independent*, August 8, 1983; *1199 News* 19:3 (March 1983), 15. Human Resources vice president Marks circulated a "Fact Sheet" dated August 24 that specified the hospital's position on employee concerns. Nurses' aide Peggy Benton told of the "just cause" letter in the August 12, 1983, *Ashland Daily Independent*. "Affidavit" of Nita Gae Sparks, August 15, 1983. Sparks's testimony is notarized, but is on plain paper with no court, lawyer, or agency identified. It is probably safe to assume that the union was collecting testimony for later use. The notary was in Lawrence County, Ohio, which indicates the statement was likely recorded in Huntington, just across the river from Lawrence County.

  David Freeland's August 16, 1983, letter opened with the greeting "Dear Brother and/or Sister." He then summarized actions taken by the hospital management since September 1982, culminating in the first-wave firing of the thirteen nurses' aides (he used the term "attendants") on August 5. Freeland, David Mott, and Teresa Ball dedicated much of their organizing to 1199's nursing home and State Hospital campaigns, which deserve more attention than I am able to give them in this study. Harold Schlechtweg worked alongside Freeland at King's Daughters, as did Patty Freeland, who divided her time between office management and organizing. Maxine Toney and Terry Beam recalled that Schlechtweg was so well versed in law and contract administration that members assumed he was an attorney.

30. "Fact Sheet" from John L. Marks, August 24, 1983; informational picket produced by KDH Hospital Employees, Local 1199.

31. Pamphlet distributed by "King's Daughters' Hospital Employees" with opening headline, "I never dreamed a hospital could be so cruel"; handout "To Our Friends and Neighbors" inviting citizens to protest the firings on Thursday, December 1, one day after the contract expiration. These and other important union-generated materials were provided by Terry Beam and Maxine Toney. Some union- and hospital-produced documents used for analysis of the King's Daughters fight were generously provided by the 1199 staff at the Huntington office. The King's Daughters files were labeled "Big Battle."

32. Press release from District 1199 WV/KY/OH, December 7, 1983; the *Hospital Reporter*, December 15, 1983; "RNS and LPNS, *Know Your* Rights," issued by District 1199WV/KY/OH, n.d.; *1199 News* 19:3 (March 1984), 17.

33. *1199 News* 19:3 (March 1984), 14–17.

34. Supreme Court of Appeals of West Virginia, No. 16313, "Prepared Order [Unpublished Opinion]," May 30, 1984, 1–3; Judy Siders interview, March 13, 2008.

35. "Darrell McGraw," 467. McGraw was defeated in 1988 when he ran for a second term on the court but was later elected to five consecutive four-year terms as state attorney general (1992–2002).

36. McGraw's opinion in Prepared Order No. 16313; Judy Siders interview, March 13, 2008. I was unable to determine if all of the nurses' aides who were laid off were called back. The job category was not eliminated, however, and still exists at the hospital under various names such as nurses' aide and nurses' assistant.

37. Carol Fink entitled a chapter "The Second Cold War, 1981–1985" in the 2017 edition of her book, *Cold War: An International History* (Boulder: Westview Press), 200–223; undated flyer with no author cited, found on windshields of cars in church parking lots, according to Judy Siders.

38. Judy Siders interview, March 13, 2008.

CHAPTER 9

1. *1199 News* 16:11 (November 1981), 12; *1199 News* 20:3 (March 1985), 8.
2. Veronica Davis and Delores Brantley, in *Give Us Twenty-Five Years and We'll Build You a Union*, 1199/SEIU 25th Anniversary Video (SEIU District 1199 WV/KY/OH), 1995, produced by Judith Helford and Beverly Peterson, 17 minutes, in author's possession.
3. Ann Woods, interviewed for *Give Us Twenty-Five Years*.
4. Tom Woodruff interview, April 8, 2008; Williams and Hall, "Legal Status," 1, 7; *1199 News* 18:1 (January 1983), 11.
    The West Virginia legislature passed a right-to-work law in 2016. It was overturned twice by Judge Jennifer Bailey of the Kanawha County Circuit Court, but her decisions were stayed by the State Supreme Court. The law is in place and is being challenged by the West Virginia AFL-CIO. It does not apply to public workers, but the *Janus v. AFSCME* decision by the U.S. Supreme Court in 2018, which prevents union security clauses for public employees, could have a chilling effect on any progress for West Virginia public worker bargaining rights. Accessed on September 18, 2019, at https://www.wvnews.com/news/wvnews/right-to -work-lawsuit.
5. *1199 News* 18:1 (January 1983), 7–8.
6. Lakin Hospital is a long-term nursing facility operated by the State Division of Health and Human Services. It is near the site of the Lakin State Hospital for the Colored, which operated from 1926 until the mid-1970s. Lakin State Hospital, Huntington State, and Spencer were three of the facilities where Dr. William Freeman conducted lobotomies during his "West Virginia Tour" in 1950. He performed over two hundred of these operations at the three facilities. For a book-length treatment of this "father of American lobotomies," see David Shutts, *Lobotomy: Resort to the Knife* (New York and Cincinnati: Von Nostrand Reinhold), 1982.
7. *1199 News* 20:2 (February 1985), 11–14, citing *Charleston Gazette-Mail* report from January 6, 1985.
8. *1199 News* 20:4 (April 1985), 23; *Charleston Gazette-Mail*, January 6, 1985.
9. *1199 News* 23:3, March 1988, 23; Madeline Smith interview from *Give Us Twenty-Five Years*.
10. "Bargaining's Last Overhaul in 1983," the *Toledo Blade*, February 18, 2011, at https://www.toledoblade.com/local/Bargaining-last-overhaul-in-1983; Saltzman, "Public Sector Bargaining Laws," 41–42, 58; Lewis and Spim, *Ohio Collective Bargaining Law*, 3–10.
11. *1199 News* 18:9 (September 1983), 11; *1199 News* 20:3 (March 1985), 8–9.
12. Kahlenberg and Marvit, *Why Labor Organizing*, 35–36; Geoghegan, *Which Side Are You On?*, 268.
13. Minutes of the Seventh Convention of the NUHHCE, December 9–12, 1987, appendix E, 3, 4.
14. Woodruff to District 1199WV/KY/OH delegates, November 8, 1988; *1199 News* 18:9 (September 1983), 11; figures on AFSCME at https://www.afscme.org/union /about; Fink and Greenberg, *Upheaval*, 222; Minutes of the Seventh Convention, NUHHCE, December 9–12, 1987, 3; Woodruff to Vic Fingerhut, on AFSCME

raiding, December 8, 1988; *Washington Post*, "Ohio Becoming Tough Test Ground for Unions Laboring to Stem Losses," September 21, 1985, accessed December 29, 2019, at https://www.washingtonpost.com/archive/politics/1985/09/21.

15. *Washington Post*, September 21, 1985.
16. Woodruff to "Dear Sir or Madam," January 24, 1986; Woodruff to Bill Lewis (FMCS commissioner), May 29, 1986; Woodruff to "Dear Member," April 29, 1986; Woodruff to Ed Seidler of the Ohio Office of Collective Bargaining May 29, 1986; *1199 News* 21:6 (June 1986), 7–9.
17. Porter and Bensinger, "Labor at the Crossroads," 2–4. By 1993, 1199WV/KY/OH dedicated about 35 percent of its dues to organizing at a time when most unions allocated about 5 percent. Accessed January 12, 2020, at https://bostonreview.net /archives/BR18/laborcross/html.
18. Author interview with Teresa Ball, December 30, 1998.
19. "Progress through Struggle," 2–4. In July of 1988, the union extended its new northern Ohio presence when the 660-member independent Cleveland Social Agencies Employees voted to join 1199; page 3 of the report. In a letter to SEIU organizing director Andy Stern on December 8, 1988, Woodruff documented 1199WV/KY/OH members at fifteen nursing homes and five community health centers. He also listed nine hundred RNs with 1199WV/KY/OH contracts in the Ohio agencies, plus RNs at seven specific hospitals. The list does not enumerate the LPNs, technicians, or service/maintenance personnel represented by the union. Teresa Ball interview, December 30, 1998.
20. *1199 News* 20:1 (January 1985), 12–13; *1199 News* 17:1 (January 1982), 19.
21. The Hospital Corporation of America was founded by a father-and-son team of surgeons, Thomas Frist Sr. and Jr., and Jack Massey, a marketing wizard who transformed Harland Sanders's chicken stand in Corbin, Kentucky, into the massive Kentucky Fried Chicken chain. In 1994 HCA was itself taken over by Columbia Healthcare Corporation. A chief partner in Columbia was Rick Scott, a speculator in radio stations, fast food, and oil and gas companies. Scott left HCA/ Columbia under a cloud in 1997 when a federal investigation revealed that the corporation had been fleecing Medicare and bribing physicians to send their patients to HCA/Columbia. The corporation paid a $1.7 billion fine in 2000. Scott later served two terms as the governor of Florida before moving on to the U.S. Senate. Mahar, *Money-Driven Medicine*, 139, 83, 118–121, 138; Fink and Greenberg, *Upheaval*, 238.

    The cost-share mandates of the Hill-Burton Act, together with the consolidation and commodification trends in the industry, forced the small proprietaries organized by Larry Harless and Wendell Drake out of business by 1980. (From a speech delivered by Woodruff to a 1982 district delegate's assembly at Cedar Lakes near Ripley, West Virginia.)
22. Fairmont City Council Minutes, Book 42, 26–27, n.d. but probably early November 1987, when some discussion about reversing the privatization of the hospital was carried on in the City Council. The divestment was also summarized in a historical summary included in Supreme Court of Appeals of West Virginia in *The City of Fairmont v. Fairmont General Hospital, Inc.*, No. 12–0205, June 5, 2013. The City Council listed some revenue-generating enterprises, including leasing office space to physicians, operating commercial pharmacies, renting medical equipment, providing home health care and long-term nursing care, and "stock ownership in profit-making corporations."

In June of 1987, Cabell County and the city of Huntington also transferred control of Cabell Huntington Hospital to a new West Virginia private nonprofit corporation, Cabell Huntington Hospital, Inc. "Agreement" between County Commission of Cabell County, the City of Huntington, and Cabell Huntington, Hospital, Inc., dated June 22, 1987. Found in a file marked "Restructuring," Drawer #3, SEIU Local 1199 WV/KY/OH, Columbus office basement.

23. Murray, *Lexicon of Labor*, 155; Matt Austin's "Austin's Legal: Labor Law," accessed on January 9, 2019, at https://mattaustinlaborlaw.com/labor-union-negotiations/.

24. Fairmont City Council Minutes, Book 41, 470, late July or early August 1987. "Would You Strike Over These?," the hospital asked readers of the *Fairmont Times-West Virginian* on September 9, 1987.

25. "The Truth About the Strike at Fairmont General," *Fairmont Times-West Virginian*, September 13, 1987.

26. "A Position Statement by the Board of Directors, Fairmont General Hospital, Inc.," *Fairmont Times-West Virginian*, September 16, 1987; *Fairmont Times-West Virginian*, September 1, 1987, and September 17, 1987; Robert Ptomey obituary at TimesWestVirginian.com, May 16, 2016. Ptomey retired from FGH in 1988 and died in Daytona Beach, Florida, on April 30, 2016, aged 92.

27. *Fairmont Times-West Virginian*, September 1 and September 30, 1987; author interview with David Mott, April 4, 2008.

28. Mott interview, April 4, 2008.

29. Mott interview, April 4, 2008. The Springfield Hospital campaign was the subject of "Union Organizing and Collective Interaction: 'Like a Thief in the Night,'" chapter 4 of Rick Fantasia's *Cultures of Solidarity*, 121–179 (cited: 123, 132, 135, 159–160).

30. *Fairmont Times-West Virginian*, September 9, 1987; Civil Action no. 87-C-506, Circuit Court of Marion County; FGH Petition for Contempt, November 3, 1987, 1–13; Local 1199 petition for contempt, November 5, 1987, 1–17a. When Joyce Lunsford died, 1199 established an annual award in her name for the member who best exemplified Lunsford's dedication and sacrifice for the union.

31. "1971 Public Hearings on the Health Care Crisis in America," Healthcare-Now! at https://www.healthcare-now.org/legislation/1971-public-hearings-on-the-health -care-crisis-in-america/, accessed on January 5, 2021.

32. Author interview with Richard Bowyer, June 2, 2008; *Fairmont Times-West Virginian*, September 22, 1987.

33. Bowyer interview, June 2, 2008; *Fairmont Times-West Virginian*, September 22, 1987.

34. *Fairmont Times-West Virginian* September 2, September 17, and November 16, 1987.

35. *Fairmont Times-West Virginian*, November 11, 1987.

36. *Fairmont Times-West Virginian*, November 14, 1987.

37. *Fairmont Times-West Virginian*, November 18, 1987; Lindorff, *Marketplace Medicine*, 271. In 2014, Fairmont General, by then known as Fairmont Medical Center, was purchased by Alecto Healthcare Services, a California-based for-profit chain. Alecto closed the hospital in the spring of 2020. These developments are covered in the concluding chapter.

38. Civil Action No. 87-C-506, Circuit Court of Marion County, Order of November 27, 1987; *Fairmont Times-West Virginian*, December 3, 1987. "True copy" from the West Virginia Supreme Court of Appeals, December 2, 1987 (the court document is

identified only with a penciled in number, 000061, housed in the Marion County Courthouse in the file holding documents from 87-C-506).

39. Mary Schafer interview, August 11, 2004.

CHAPTER 10

1. Fink and Greenberg, *Upheaval*, 215–220.
2. *Daily Kos* story on Henry Nicholas, September 29, 2014, at https://www.dailykos .com/stories/2014/9/29/Henry-Nicholas-A-Story-of-Leadership-Vision-Courage -Compassion, accessed January 20, 2020; Doris Turner obituary, January 9, 2019, at https://thewestsidegazette.com/in-memoriam-remembering-the-life-of-doris -turner/, accessed January 20, 2020.
3. Fink and Greenberg, *Upheaval*, 212–219. These developments are extensively reported in *1199 News*, 1979–1982, passim.
4. Fink and Greenberg, *Upheaval*, 13, 69, 214–223. The Al Heaps "demolition scheme" was outlined in *1199 News* 19:4, April 1984, passim. It is also referenced in appendix E, Officers' Report, Minutes of the Seventh Convention of the NUHHCE, December 9–12, 1987, 4–5. Tom Woodruff was appointed to chair the union's Constitution Committee at this meeting. 1199 *News* 19:5 (May [June] 1984), 3.
5. Fink and Greenberg, *Upheaval*, 214–216. In 1998, 1199 merged with SEIU to become 1199SEIU United Healthcare Workers East; accessed on April 1, 2020, at https://www.1199seiu.org/history.
6. Tom Woodruff to Jerry Brown, secretary-treasurer of the NUHHCE, et al., June 19, 1987; Woodruff correspondence, Columbus; SEIU District 1199WV/KY/OH documentary, *Give Us Twenty-Five Years*.
7. "Proposed Resolution, National Union Convention: 'Unification of Health Care Workers,'" October 5, 1987; Woodruff correspondence, Columbus; *1199 News* 24:1 (January 1989), 13; Fink and Greenberg, *Upheaval*, 255.
8. Fink and Greenberg, *Upheaval*, 254; Henry Nicholas to Bob Callahan, November 7, 1988, Woodruff correspondence, Columbus; Woodruff to "Dear District 1199/WV /KY/OH Delegate," November 8, 1988, Woodruff correspondence, Columbus; *SEIU Update* 3:2 (Summer 1989), 9.

    Thomas Breslin, an executive vice president in 1199C (Philadelphia) sent a letter to Jerry Brown dated December 14, 1989, which implied (fairly or not) that two pro–SEIU officers in the National Union were not above using anti-Black racial politics. Merger file, Columbus. As Gabe Kramer observed, Fink and Greenberg often refer to race and gender issues that "explicitly divided factions in New York" and contributed to tension within the National Union by late 1988. Email to author from Gabe Kramer, April 23, 2008.

9. Teresa Ball interview, December 30, 1998.
10. "Outline of Merger Proposal Service Employees International Union," n.d. but probably January–April 1989, Woodruff correspondence, Columbus. For examples of pottery and textile workers' wariness of large-scale unions, see Waldrep, *Southern Workers*, and Martin, *Smokestacks*.
11. *Washington Post*, November 18, 1988. The bargaining units were now RNs, physicians, all other professionals, service and maintenance, technical (including LPNs), business office clericals, and skilled maintenance. *1199 News* 24:1 (January 1989), 16; SEIU "Organizing and Field Services" document, n.d. but probably

summer 1989, Woodruff correspondence, Columbus; Muehlenkamp, "Remarks on the Life of Dan Stewart"; Robert Wages interview, June 29, 1999; author interview with Wayne Horman, July 12, 1999. Stewart also briefly worked as organizing director for the Amalgamated Clothing and Textile Workers Union. Stewart died of a brain aneurism while working for the OCAW. Wages interview, June 29, 1999.

12. Fletcher and Hurd, "Political Will," 191–192.
13. Taylor and Benson, "Debate on Union Democracy."
14. Fraser, "SEIU Andy Stern Leaves." Woodruff had a long career with SEIU as national organizing director and as an executive vice president. Mott served in several capacities through 2018, including as organizing director for SEIU Canada and national campaign director. Accessed on May 22, 2019, at https://keywiki.org /Tom_Woodruff; and at https://www.unionfacts.com/SEIU/0/DAVID/MOTT.
15. Early, *Civil Wars*, quoting UNITE-HERE organizer Andrea van den Heever, 230; Dubofsky, "Legacy of Andy Stern," 1–7. Stern's comments on unions as business enterprises can be found on page 5 of Dubofsky's article and in Early, *Civil Wars*, 138. Woodruff's echoes from the merger effort come from his letter to Jerry Brown, et al., on June 19, 1987, and his letter to "Dear Brothers and Sisters," November 10, 1988, in the Woodruff correspondence at Columbus.
16. Fraser, "SEIU Andy Stern Leaves," 1–12 (including the Bronfenbrenner statement); McAlevy, *No Shortcuts*, 74–75; Brenner, "Organizing Report"; Fink and Greenberg, *Upheaval*, 275. The SEIU's complex internal politics and divisiveness during the Stern years are deftly analyzed in Early, *Civil Wars*, passim. Obama's praise for Stern is quoted there, on page 251.
17. "Change to Win"; Early, "Whither Change to Win?" Early notes that this "civil war" lasted a year and a half and cost SEIU millions of dollars before the conflict was settled.
18. Early, *Civil Wars*, 276–280. The unions that left CTW were the United Brotherhood of Carpenters, the Laborers' International, and a breakaway faction of UNITE-HERE guided by John Raynor. In 2013, the United Food and Commercial Workers also left CTW, leaving only the SEIU, the International Brotherhood of Teamsters, and the United Farm Workers (a small affiliate of the Communications Workers of America) in the federation. The EFCA was reintroduced in 2016 but again failed. http://www.influencewatch.org./labor-union/change-to-win/. See also Meyerson, "A Labor War Ended."
19. Dubofsky, "Legacy of Andy Stern," 1–7; McAlevey, *No Shortcuts*, 76.
20. Tom Woodruff was the keynote speaker at the 14th Biennial Leadership Assembly, April 4, 2008, in Fort Mitchell. His remarks were consistent with the style admired by Brenner. Brenner, "Organizing Report"; Rathke, "Mary Kay Henry," 1–4. Steve Early in *Civil Wars*, 288, notes that the four EVPs were Woodruff, Eliseo Medina, Gerry Hudson, and Dave Regan. Regan was a former District 1199WV/KY/OH staffer and president. *Los Angeles Times*, "SEIU Rift Opens Over President's Successor," April 27, 2010.

Woodruff's motive for promoting Henry over Burger was not limited to the UNITE-HERE disaster. Rathke explains that the Change to Win Federation chair operated on a revolving basis, with each member union providing the chair on a two-year rotation. Burger was the first chair and had maneuvered to amend the CTW constitution so she could retain the chair position. Apparently, said Rathke, Woodruff "went ballistic" and threatened Stern with resignation. He stayed on, however, and when Stern retired, he blocked Burger from the president's role. Rathke, "Mary Kay Henry," 2. Turner's comment about Davis, and Olson is from Fink and Greenberg, *Upheaval*, 214.

21. Rathke, "Mary Kay Henry," 1–4. Rathke recounted the "without a friend" anecdote. Early says the president of the Operating Engineers, Vince Gibbon, "repeatedly referred to Stern as the 'Darth Vader of the labor movement' " (*Civil Wars*, 215). John Sweeney, who had brought Stern into the labor movement, called Stern's interunion raiding "despicable." Fraser, "SEIU Andy Stern Leaves," 6.

EPILOGUE

1. The Ohio locals beyond the Appalachian counties of SEIU District 1199WV/KY/OH represent about twenty-two thousand members, for a total district membership of about thirty-one thousand. Although chapter 8 of this book summarizes the early expansion in non-Appalachian Ohio, the majority of the membership increases occurred since the 1989 merger, especially in the Cleveland and Cincinnati areas. See http://www.seiu1199.org/about-our-union/union-history/; http://www.seiu 1199.org/category/wvky/.

   There are three divisions within the SEIU: (1) Healthcare—nurses, doctors, home care and healthcare workers; (2) Property Services—janitors, security officers, maintenance and custodial workers, stadium and arena workers, window cleaners, and other service workers; (3) Public Services—over 1 million public service employees, bus drivers, and child care providers. From SEIU 2016 convention documents, accessed June 30, 2018, at http://conventiondocs.seiu.org /divisions.

2. Joyce Gibson interview, February 11, 2008; Early, *Civil Wars*, 208.

3. Teresa Ball remained with SEIU District 1199WV/KY/OH until becoming state field director for the AFL-CIO in Kansas in 1997. She later worked as the Indiana state field director supervisor, deputy director of the AFL-CIO Midwest Region in Chicago, and as director of field operations for the federation's organizing department in Washington, D.C. She retired in 2010 and returned to Huntington, where she worked for several years as the labor/management liaison for the city. Jean Tarbett Hardiman featured Ball in the March 6, 2016, *Herald-Dispatch*, at http://www.herald-dispatch ("Uniting Labor, Management Key to Better Jobs, Futures").

   Another early 1199 organizer, Harold Schlechtweg, worked for the SEIU in Wichita, Kansas for many years and is still active there in community justice and environmental issues.

4. Joyce Gibson interview, February 11, 2008; Fletcher and Hurd, "Political Will," 200. Stern announced at the 2008 convention that SEIU would create a standardized "Member Resource Center" (MRC) in which members could consult with grievance handlers remotely. This "amounted to a 'corporate model of customer service,' " and it does not appear that the locals in this study have much use for the MRCs. In fact, Early notes that there was a broad-based backlash against MRCs. and many local officers and members distanced themselves from the practice. Some officers lost their elective positions if they encouraged the MRC option. The WV/KY/OH District's website has a link to the MRC that, in addition to grievance forms, also publishes "your Union contract," training and education materials, delegate

manuals, voter registration information, and SEIU events. http://www.seiu1199
.org/mrc/; Early, *Civil Wars*, 111–115, 120–133.

5. Gibson, Penny Burchett, and Larry Daniels all told me in 2008 that many newer
members at Highlands Regional had accepted management's 401K offer rather
than the defined benefits agreement favored by the more veteran members. Joyce
Gibson interview, February 11, 2008; Penny Burchett and Larry Daniels
interviews, April 4, 2008.

6. "Agreement" between County Commission of Cabell County, the City of
Huntington, and Cabell Huntington, Hospital, Inc., dated June 22, 1987, found in
a file marked "Restructuring," Drawer #3, SEIU Local 1199 WV/KY/OH, Columbus
office basement; Ashland *Daily Independent*, February 24, 2020, at https://www
.dailyindependent.com/news/whitlatch-kdmc-not-for-sale. Whitlach's salary as of
September 30, 2018, was $830,553. www.causeiq.com/organizations/kings
-daughters-medical-center-hospital.

7. Alecto Healthcare Services, at https://www.dnb.com/business-directory/company
-profiles.alecto_healthcare_services_llc.d7442b03c4a40cd451394f93333e621e
.html; *New York Times*, April 27, 2020, at https://www.nytimes.com/2020/04/26
/us/hospital-closures-west-virginia-ohio.html.

8. *New York Times*, April 27, 2020.

9. SEIU press release, April 8, 2020, at http://www.seiu1199.org/seiu-union
-members-at-fairmont; SEIU press release, April 24, 2020, at http://www.seiu1199
.org/union-workers-at-fairmont; Tyler Barker for WOAY-TV, April 14, 2020, at
http://woay.com/wva-hospitals-parent-agrees/.

10. Joyce Gibson interview, February 11, 2008; News release from SEIU District 1199
WV/KY/OH, December 10, 2019; email from Joyce Gibson, December 10, 2019.
Here I refer to a truism stated by Jane McAlevey in *No Shortcuts: Organizing for
Power in the New Gilded Age* (73): "A union is never built by a single person," she
wrote. However, each union "is associated with a union leader who is indelibly
linked to the organization." Such is the case with Woodruff and Stewart and with
the dedicated organizers and organic leaders at each of the locals featured in this
study.

Bibliography

NEWSPAPERS

Ashland KY Daily Independent
Beckley WV Post-Herald
Charleston WV Daily Mail
Charleston WV Gazette
Fairmont WV Times-West Virginian
Floyd County KY Times
Huntington WV Herald-Dispatch
Huntington WV Advertiser
Marshall SDS chapter Free Forum
Martins Ferry OH Times-Leader
New York Times
Paintsville KY Herald
The Marshall University Parthenon
Raleigh WV Register
Richlands VA News-Press
Wetzel WV Chronicle (New Martinsville)

SELECTED PERIODICALS

1199 News
Hospital Administration
Hospital and Health Services Administration
Hospital Topics
Mountain Life and Work
SEIU Update
United Mine Workers Journal
West Virginia AFL-CIO Observer

SELECTED PRIMARY SOURCES

1199 Collective Bargaining Agreements:
- · Cabell Huntington Hospital, October 22, 1979–October 21, 1981 (renewal); October 22, 1983–October 21, 1986; October 22, 1986–October 1, 1989.
- · King's Daughters Hospital, Effective December 1, 1980 (first contract)
- · Madison General Hospital, Effective October 26, 1970 (first contract)

Affidavit of Dan Stewart, September 24, 1979, Wetzel County, WV Circuit Court.

Affidavit of Tom Woodruff, January 23, 1979, Marion County, WV Circuit Court.

By-Laws District 1199 WV/KY. 1980.

Constitution of the Marshall SDS, December 12, 1968.

Constitution of the National Union of Hospital and Health Care Employees, a Division of RWDSU/AFL-CIO. Adopted at the Founding Convention November 29, 1973, Amended December 1975, November 1977, December 1979.

Davis, Leon. "Report from the President to the Officers." Second National Convention, National Union of Hospital and Health Care Employees. December 10, 1975.

Godoff, Elliott. "Organizing Report: Supplement to Officers' Report, Section 3, Minutes of the Founding Convention of the National Union of Hospital and Health Care Employees (AFL-CIO), Wednesday, November 28 through Saturday, December 1, 1973." Call number 5206, series I, subseries 9, 1969–1974. ILR Kheel Library Center, Cornell University.

National Labor Relations Board. *Clinch Valley Clinic Hospital v. NLRB*, no. 74-2149, case 516 F.2d 996 (1975), at www.leagle.com/, accessed July 14, 2019.

"Officers Report" to the Seventh Convention of the National Union of Hospital and Health Care Employees (AFL-CIO), December 9–12, 1987.

"Organizing Report to the National Executive Board." National Union of Hospital and Health Care Employees Board Meeting, May 15–17, 1975. Call number 5651, Box 5, Executive Board folder, ILR Kheel Library Center, Cornell University.

"Proposed District 1199 WV/KY By-Laws." Typescript copy of document sent from Tom Woodruff and Dan Stewart, May 10, 1979.

"Report of Transfer or Discharge, STEWART, Danie Joe." Cabell County Service Record Book 43: 463.

Warren, Rev. Paul. "Activism on Marshall's Campus: Prelude to What? Comments Delivered at Campus Christian Center Discussion on Recognition of SDS at Marshall." SDS collection at Marshall Special Collections.

COURT/GOVERNMENT DOCUMENTS

Case no. CC911, Supreme Court of Appeals of West Virginia, 166 W.Va. I, @web.lexis-nexis.com/universe.

Civil Action no. 77-2061, Cabell County, WV Circuit Court, several documents.

Civil Action no. 78-C-633, Marion County, WV Circuit Court, several documents.

Civil Action no. 6107, Tazewell County, VA Circuit Court, several documents.

Civil Action no. 79-C-121-W, Wetzel County, WV Circuit Court, several documents.

Civil Action no. 81-210, United States District Court in Pikeville, Kentucky, several documents.

Fortieth Annual Report of the National Labor Relations Board. Fiscal Year Ended June 30, 1975. Washington, DC: U.S. Government Printing Office, 1975. Accessed July 16, 2019, at https://www.nlrb.gov/sites/default/files/attachments/basic-page/node-1677/nlrb1975.pdf.

"Pressures in Today's Workplace." In *Oversight Hearings before the Subcommittee on Labor-Management Relations of the Committee on Education and Labor of the House of Representatives.* 96th Congress, First Session, October 16–18, 1979, vol. 1. Washington, D.C.: U.S. Government Printing Office, 1979.

Williams, David G., and Don C. Hall. "The Legal Status of Public Employee Strikes and Collective Bargaining in West Virginia." Morgantown: West Virginia University

Bureau for Government Research Publication No. 60, 1970. (Included in the *West Virginia University Bulletin* Series 71:7-3, December 1970.)

PRIVATE COLLECTIONS

Terry Beam
Janet Dooley
Frank Helvey
Anna May Jenkins
David McGee
Jo Anna Martin Risner
Judy Siders
Maxine Toney

PAPERS AND COLLECTIONS

Miscellaneous documents and files, 1199 WV/KY/OH 1974–1985, Huntington office.
Miscellaneous documents, reports, and newsletters, SEIU District 1199 WV/KY/OH, District office in Columbus, Ohio, 1986–1989.
National Union of Hospital and Health Care Employees papers, Industrial and Labor Relations Collection at the Kheel Archives, Cornell University.
Roland Nelson Presidential Papers at Marshall University Special Collections.
SDS Collection at Marshall University Special Collections.
Tom Woodruff Papers and Correspondence, SEIU District 1199 WV/KY/OH, 1988–1989, District office in Columbus, Ohio.
West Virginia and Regional History Collection, pamphlets.

MINUTES AND PROCEEDINGS

"Agenda, Resolutions, and Proceedings." Delegate Conventions 1199 WV 1976, 1977.
"Agenda, Resolutions, and Proceedings." Delegate Conventions 1199 WV/KY/OH, 1980, 1982, 1983. Minutes of the Cabell Huntington Hospital Board of Trustees, 1974–1975, 1977.
Minutes of the Fairmont, WV City Council, 1978, 1987.
Minutes of the Founding Convention of the National Union of Hospital and Health Care Employees, November 28–December 1, 1973.
Minutes of the Wetzel County, WV Commission, 1979–1980.
"Officers' Report to the Seventh Convention of the National Union of Hospital and Health Care Employees." AFL-CIO, December 9–12, 1987.

BOOKS

Adams, Frank. *James Dombrowski: An American Heretic, 1897–1983*. Knoxville: University of Tennessee Press, 1992.
Balliet, Lee. *Survey of Labor Relations*. Washington, D.C.: Bureau of National Affairs, 1987.
Barocci, Thomas A. *Non-Profit Hospitals: Their Structure, Human Resources, and Economic Importance*. Westport, CT: Praeger, 1980.
Berman, Edward. *Labor and the Sherman Act*. New York: Harper & Brothers, 1930.

Berry, Wendell. *What Are People For?* Berkeley, CA: Counterpoint, 2010.

Braden, Anne. *The Wall Between.* Knoxville: University of Tennessee Press, 1999. Originally Published by Monthly Review Press, 1958.

Brands, H. W. *American Dreams: America since 1945.* New York: Penguin, 2011.

Bronfenbrenner, Kate, Sheldon Friedman, Rudolph A. Oswald, Richard W. Hurd, and Ronald Leroy Seeber. *Organizing to Win: New Research on Union Strategies.* Ithaca, NY: ILR Press of Cornell University, 1998.

Burroughs, Ryan. *Days of Rage: America's Radical Underground, the FBI, and the Forgotten Age of Revolutionary Violence.* New York: Penguin, 2015.

Chafe, William. *The Unfinished Journey: America since World War II*, 8th ed. New York and Oxford: Oxford University Press, 2015.

Clark, Paul. *The Miners' Fight for Democracy: Arnold Miller and the Reform of the United Mine Workers.* Ithaca: Cornell New York State School of Industrial and Labor Relations, 1981.

Cowie, Jefferson. *Stayin' Alive: The 1970s and the Last Days of the Working Class.* New York: New Press, 2010.

Drake, Richard. *A History of Appalachia.* Lexington: University Press of Kentucky, 2001.

Dray, Philip. *There Is Power in a Union: The Epic Story of American Labor.* New York: Doubleday, 2010.

Ducey, Ariel. *Never Good Enough: Health Care Workers and the False Promise of Job Training.* Ithaca, NY: Cornell University Press, 2009.

Duke, David. *Writers and Miners: Activism and Imagery in America.* Lexington: University Press of Kentucky, 2002.

Early, Steve. *The Civil Wars in U.S. Labor: Birth of a New Workers' Movement or Death Throes of the Old?* Chicago: Haymarket Books, 2011.

Ehrenreich, Barbara, and John Ehrenreich. *The American Health Empire: Power, Profit, and Politics.* New York: Random House, 1970.

Eller, Ronald D. *Uneven Ground: Appalachia since 1945.* Lexington: University Press of Kentucky, 2008.

Fain, Cicero. *Black Huntington: An Appalachian Story.* Urbana: University of Illinois Press, 2019.

Fantasia, Rick. *Cultures of Solidarity: Consciousness, Action, and Contemporary American Workers.* Berkeley: University of California Press, 1988.

Fink, Leon, and Brian Greenberg. *Upheaval in the Quiet Zone.* Urbana and Chicago: University of Illinois Press, 1989, 2009.

Flynn, George Q. *The Draft: 1940–1973.* Lawrence: University of Kansas Press, 1993.

Foner, Moe, and Dan North. *Not for Bread Alone: A Memoir.* Ithaca, NY: Cornell University Press, 2002.

Fones-Wolf, Elizabeth, and Ken Fones-Wolf. *Struggle for the Soul of the Postwar South: White Evangelical Protestants and Operation Dixie.* Urbana and Chicago: University of Illinois Press, 2015.

Fones-Wolf, Ken. *Glass Towns: Industry, Labor, and Political Economy in Appalachia, 1890–1930s.* Urbana and Chicago: University of Illinois Press, 2007.

Fosl, Katherine. *Subversive Southerner: Anne Braden and the Struggle for Racial Justice in the Cold War South.* Lexington: University Press of Kentucky, 2006.

Geoghegan, Thomas. *Which Side Are You On? Trying to Be for Labor When It's Flat on Its Back.* New York: Farrar, Strauss, & Giroux, 1991.

Gilpin, Toni. *The Long Deep Grudge: A Story of Big Capital, Radical Labor, and Class War in the American Heartland.* Chicago: Haymarket Books, 2020.

Gitlin, Todd. *The Sixties: Years of Hope, Days of Rage.* New York: Bantam, 1987.

Greenhouse, Steven. *The Big Squeeze: Tough Times for the American Worker.* New York: Alfred A. Knopf, 2008.

Harrison, Bennett, and Barry Bluestone. *The Great U-Turn: Corporate Restructuring and the Polarizing of America.* New York: Basic Books, 1988.

Hoerr, John P. *And the Wolf Finally Came: The Decline of the American Steel Industry.* Pittsburgh: University of Pittsburgh Press, 1988.

Horowitz, Roger. *"Negro and White, Unite and Fight!": A Social History of Industrial Unionism in Meatpacking, 1930–1990.* Urbana and Chicago: University of Illinois Press, 1997.

Joseph, Perniel. *Stokely: A Life.* New York: Basic Civitas, 2014.

Judt, Tony. *Ill Fares the Land.* New York: Penguin, 2010.

Juravich, Tom, and Kate Bronfenbrenner. *Ravenswood: The Steelworkers' Victory and the Revival of American Labor.* Ithaca, NY: ILR Press of Cornell University, 1999.

Kahlenberg, Richard D., and Moshe Z. Marvit. *Why Labor Organizing Should Be a Civil Right: Rebuilding a Middle-Class Democracy by Enhancing Worker Voice.* New York: Century Foundation, 2012.

Kelley, Brian. *Race, Class, and Power in the Alabama Coalfields.* Urbana and Chicago: University of Illinois Press, 2001.

Kendi, Ibram X. *Stamped from the Beginning: The Definitive History of Racist Ideas in America.* New York: Nation Books, 2016.

Kiffmeyer, Thomas. *Reformers to Radicals: The Appalachian Volunteers and the War on Poverty.* Lexington: University Press of Kentucky, 2008.

King, Martin Luther, Jr. *All Labor Has Dignity.* Michael Honey, ed. Boston: Beacon, 2011.

Kruger, Kenneth F., and Norman Metzger. *When Health Care Employees Strike.* Chicago: Jossey-Bass, 2002.

Levitt, Martin Jay, with Terry Conroy. *Confessions of a Union Buster.* New York: Crown, 1993.

Levy, Peter B. *The New Left and Labor in the 1960s.* Urbana and Chicago: University of Illinois Press, 1994.

Lewis, John F., and Steven Spim. *Ohio Collective Bargaining Law: The Regulation of Public Employer-Employee Labor Relations.* Cleveland: Banks-Baldwin Law, 1983.

Lichtenstein, Nelson, Susan Strasser, Roy Rosenzweig, Stephen Brier, and Joshua Brown. *Who Built America? Working People and the Nation's Economy, Politics, Culture, and Society*, vol. 2: *1877 to the Present.* 2nd ed. New York: Bedford/St. Martin's, 2000.

Lindorff, Dave. *Marketplace Medicine: The Rise of the For-Profit Hospital Chains.* New York: Bantam, 1992.

Lorence, James J. *A Hard Journey: The Life of Don West.* Urbana and Chicago: University of Illinois Press, 2007.

Lynd, Staughton, ed. *"We Are All Leaders": The Alternative Unionism of the Early 1930s.* Urbana and Chicago: University of Illinois Press, 1996.

Lynd, Staughton, and Daniel Gross, eds. *Labor Law for the Rank & Filer.* Oakland, CA: PM Press, 2011.

Mahar, Maggie. *Money-Driven Medicine: The Real Reason Health Care Costs So Much.* New York: Harper-Collins, 2006.

Martin, Lou. *Smokestacks in the Hills: Rural-Industrial Workers in West Virginia.* Urbana and Chicago: University of Illinois Press, 2015.

McAlevey, Jane F. *No Shortcuts: Organizing for Power in the New Gilded Age.* New York: Oxford University Press, 2016.

McMartin, Joseph A. *Collision Course: Ronald Reagan, the Air Traffic Controllers, and the Strike That Changed America.* New York: Oxford University Press, 2011.

Melosh, Barbara. *"The Physician's Hand": Work Culture and Conflict in American Nursing.* Philadelphia: Temple University Press, 1982.

Metzgar, Jack. *Striking Steel: Solidarity Remembered.* Philadelphia: Temple University Press, 2000.

Moffat, Charles. *Marshall University: An Institution Comes of Age, 1837–1980.* Huntington, WV: Marshall University Alumni Association, 1991.

Moody, Kim. *In Solidarity: Essays on Working-Class Organization in the United States.* Chicago: Haymarket Books, 2014.

Morgan, Edward P. *What Really Happened in the Sixties: How Mass Media Culture Failed American Democracy.* Lawrence: University Press of Kansas, 2010.

Mulcahy, Richard. *A Social Contract for the Coal Fields: The Rise and Fall of the United Mine Workers of America Welfare and Retirement Fund.* Knoxville: University of Tennessee Press, 2006.

Murray, R. Emmett. *The Lexicon of Labor.* New York: W. W. Norton, 1998.

Nelson, Cary. *Revolutionary Memory: Recovering the Poetry of the American Left.* New York: Routledge, 2003.

Nelson, Scott Reynolds. *Steel Drivin' Man: John Henry, the Untold Story of an American Legend.* New York: Oxford University Press, 2006.

Nelson, Steve, James R. Barrett, and Rob Ruck. *Steve Nelson, American Radical.* Pittsburgh: University of Pittsburgh Press, 1981, 1992.

Niebuhr, Reinhold. *The Irony of American History.* Chicago: University of Chicago Press, 1952.

Parker, Mike, and Jane Slaughter. *Working Smart: A Union Guide to Participation Programs and Reengineering.* Detroit: Labor Education and Research Project, 1994.

Perlstein, Rick. *The Bridge: The Fall of Nixon and the Rise of Reagan.* New York: Simon and Schuster, 2014.

Polk's City Directory: Fairmont, 1975, 1977. Richmond, VA: R. L. Polk.

Polk's City Directory: Huntington, 1975, 1981. Richmond, VA: R. L. Polk.

Prosten, David, ed. *The Union Steward's Complete Guide,* 2nd ed. Annapolis: Union Communication Services, 2006.

Rosswurm, Steve. *The CIO's Left-Led Unions.* New Brunswick, NJ: Rutgers University Press, 1992.

Rothman, William A. *Strikes in Health Care Organizations.* Owings Mill, MD: National Health, 1983.

Rutkowski, Arthur D., and Barbara Lang Rutkowski. *Labor Relations in Hospitals.* Rockville, MD: Aspen Systems, 1984.

Sale, Kirkpatrick. *SDS.* New York: Random House, 1973.

Satterwhite, Emily. *Dear Appalachia: Readers, Identity, and Popular Fiction since 1878.* Lexington: University Press of Kentucky, 2011.

Schwartz, Robert. *The Legal Rights of Union Stewards.* Boston: Work Rights Press, 1988, 1999.

Spurlock, Trent. *Survey of Cabell County, West Virginia: African American Historical Sites.* Lexington, KY: Cultural Resources Analysts, 2014.

Starr, Paul. *The Social Transformation of American Medicine: The Rise of a Sovereign Profession and the Making of a Vast Industry.* New York: Basic Books, 1982.

Thomas, Jerry Bruce. *West Virginia and the Perils of the New Machine Age, 1945–1972.* Morgantown: West Virginia University Press, 2010.

Waldrep, G. C. *Southern Workers and the Search for Community: Spartanburg County, South Carolina.* Urbana and Chicago: University of Illinois Press, 2000.

Wilkerson, Jessica. *To Live Here, You Have to Fight: How Women Led Appalachian Movements for Social Justice.* Urbana: University of Illinois Press, 2019.

Yates, Michael D. *Power on the Job.* Boston: South End Press, 1999.

———. *Why Unions Matter.* New York: Monthly Review Press, 2009.

Young, Ralph, ed. *Dissent in America: Voices That Shaped a Nation.* New York: Pearson-Longman, 2008.

Zinn, Howard. *A People's History of the United States.* New York: Harper-Collins, 1995.

ARTICLES, CHAPTERS, AND ENCYCLOPEDIA ENTRIES

Allen, Joe. "Between Students and Workers," *Jacobin,* March 17, 2017, at https://www.jacobinmag.com/2017/03/students-democratic-society-antiwar-vietnam-workers-unions-kim-moody, accessed December 5, 2020.

Bacon, Al. "History of SEIU Local 1199 WV/KY/OH." Huntington, WV: Local 1199 WV/KY/OH, n.d.

Baker, Chris, Glenn S. Johnson, Lee Williams, Deborah G. Perkins, and Shirley A. Rainey. "The Highlander Research and Education Center: Utilizing Social Change-Based Models for Public Policy." *Race, Gender, and Class* 15:3–4 (2008): 308–334.

Becker, Edmund R., and Jonathon S. Rakich. "Hospital Union Activity, 1974–85." *Health Care Financing Review* 9:3 (Spring 1988): 59–66.

Berry, Wendell. "About Civil Disobedience." The *Progressive* (December 12, 2011). https://progressive.org/dispatches/civil-disobedience/, accessed July 12, 2019.

Bickley, Ancella. "Carter G. Woodson." At www.wv.encyclopedia.org.

———. "Frederick Douglass Junior High and High School." At www.wv.encyclopedia.org.

Biggers, Jeff. "The Fugitive of Southern Appalachian Literature: Reconsidering the Poetry of Don West." *Journal of Appalachian Studies* 5:2 (Fall 1199): 159–180.

Black, Kate. "The Roving Picket Movement and the Appalachian Committee for Full Employment." *Journal of Appalachian Studies Association* 2 (1990): 110–127.

Brenner, Mark. "Organizing Report: Politics and Fuzzy Math." *Labor Notes* (June 5, 2008). At http://www.labornotes.org/blogs/2008/06.

Casto, James E. "Huntington." In Sullivan and Sonis, *West Virginia Encyclopedia,* 354–355. Charleston: West Virginia Humanities Council, 2006.

"Change to Win Strategic Organizing Center," at http://www.changetowin.org/archive/content/tom-woodruff, accessed January 24, 2020.

Cook, Jeffrey B. "Consolidation Coal." In Sullivan and Sonis, *West Virginia Encyclopedia,* 262–263. Charleston: West Virginia Humanities Council, 2006.

"Darrell McGraw." In Sullivan and Sonis, *West Virginia Encyclopedia,* 467. Charleston: West Virginia Humanities Council, 2006.

Davis, Leon. "Report from the President on Behalf of the Officers of the National Union of Hospital and Health Care Employees, a Division of RWDSU/AFL-CIO, to the Delegates of the Second National Convention." Call number 5651, Box 18, ff 7, "National Convention, 1975," ILR Kheel Library Center, Cornell University. December 10, 1975.

Dubofsky, Melvyn. "The Legacy of Andy Stern." *Dissent* (May 12, 2010): 1–7.

Early, Steve. "Whither Change to Win?" *In These Times* (October 10, 2011), at https:// inthesetimes.com/article/whither-change-to-win, accessed on January 24, 2020.

Fain, Cicero. "Black Response to the Construction of Colored Huntington: West Virginia during the Jim Crow Era." *West Virginia History* New Series 1:2 (Fall 2007): 1–24.

———. "Into the Crucible: The Chesapeake and Ohio Railroad and the Black Industrial Workers in Southern West Virginia, 1870–1900." *Journal of Appalachian Studies* 17:2 (Spring/Fall 2001): 42–65.

Fisher, Stephen. "The Grass Roots Speak Back." In Dwight Billings, Gurney Norman, and Katherine Ledford, eds., *Confronting Appalachian Stereotypes: Back Talk from an American Region*, 203–214. Lexington: University Press of Kentucky, 1999.

Flanery, Ron. "Ed Wolfe, Charles Wilson, Jr., and Paul Mandelkern, *Norfolk & Western's Clinch Valley Line*," Pittsburgh: HEW Enterprises, 2013. Review published in *Trains Magazine*, January 10, 2014. Accessed on July 9, 2019, at www/trn.trains .com/railroads.

Fleming, Dan B. "Ken Hechler." In Sullivan and Sonis, *West Virginia Encyclopedia*, 327. Charleston: West Virginia Humanities Council, 2006.

Fletcher, Bill, and Richard W. Hurd. "Political Will, Local Union Transformation, and the Organizing Imperative." In Bruce Nissen, ed., *Which Direction for Organized Labor? Essays on Organizing, Outreach, and Internal Transformation*, 191–216. Detroit: Wayne State University Press, 1999.

Foner, Moe, and Dan North. "Celebrating the Life of Leon J. Davis, Founder of 1199, 1907–1992." *1199 News* (October 5, 1992): 3–4.

Fones-Wolf, Colin. "A Union Voice for Racial Equality: Miles Stanley and Civil Rights in West Virginia, 1957–68." *Journal of Appalachian Studies* 10:1 (Spring/Fall 2004): 111–128.

Fraser, Max. "The SEIU Andy Stern Leaves Behind." *Nation* 1–2 (July 16, 2010). At https://www.thenation.com/article/archive/seiu-andy-stern-leaves-behind/.

Georgakas, Dan. "Angela Davis." In Mari Jo Buhle, Paul Buhle, and Dan Georgakas, eds., *Encyclopedia of the American Left*, 182–183. University of Illinois Press, 1992.

Gillenwater, Mack H. "Welch." In Sullivan and Sonis, *West Virginia Encyclopedia*, 755–756. Charleston: West Virginia Humanities Council, 2006.

Goldfield, Michael. "Race and the CIO: Reply to Critics." *International Labor and Working-Class History* 46 (Fall 1994): 142–160.

Greenberg, Ronald. "Union Avoidance in Hospitals." *Hospital and Health Services Administration* 28:11 (January/February, 1983): 24–29.

Harris, Howell. "Politicians, Bureaucrats, and the Shaping of Federal Labor Relations' Policy." In Eileen Boris and Nelson Lichtenstein, eds., *Major Problems in the History of American Workers*, 428–449. Lexington, MA: D. C. Heath, 1991.

Hennen, John. "1199 Comes to Appalachia: Beginnings, 1970–1976." In Jennifer Egolf, Ken Fones-Wolf, and Lou Martin, eds., *Culture, Class, and Politics in Modern Appalachia: Essays in Honor of Ronald D. Lewis*, 224–250. Morgantown: West Virginia University Press, 2009.

———. "Putting the 'You' in Union." *Journal of Appalachian Studies* 5:2 (Fall 1999): 227–240.

———. "Struggle for Recognition: The Marshall University Students for a Democratic Society and the Red Scare in Huntington, 1965–1969." *West Virginia History* 52 (1993): 127–147.

———. "Toil, Trouble, Transformation: Workers and Unions in Modern Kentucky." *Register of the Kentucky Historical Society* 113:2&3 (Spring/Summer 2015): 233–269.

Hoffus, Steve. "Charleston Hospital Workers' Strike, 1969." In Marc S. Miller, ed., *Working Lives: The Southern Exposure History of Labor in the South*, 244–258. New York: Pantheon Books, 1980.

Inscoe, John. "Race and Racism in Appalachia." In Mary Beth Pudup, Dwight Billings, and Altina Waller, eds., *Appalachia in the Making: The Mountain South in the Nineteenth Century*, 103–131. Chapel Hill: University of North Carolina Press, 1995.

Kaufman, Bruce, and Paula E. Stephan. "The Role of Management Attorneys in Union Organizing Campaigns." *Journal of Labor Research* 16:4 (Fall, 1995): 439–454.

King, Martin Luther, Jr. "A Creative Protest," February 16, 1960. In Clayborne Carson et al., *The Papers of Martin Luther King, Jr.*, vol. 5, "The Threshold of a New Decade, 1959–1960," 360–370. Berkeley: University of California Press, 2005.

Koon, Thomas J. "Fairmont." In Sullivan and Sonis, *West Virginia Encyclopedia*, 227. Charleston: West Virginia Humanities Council, 2006.

Lawler, John. "The Influence of Management Consultants on the Outcome of Union Certification Elections." *Industrial and Labor Relations Review* 38:1 (October 1984): 38–51.

Lewis, Ronald L. "From Peasant to Proletarian: The Migration of Southern Blacks to the Central Appalachian Coalfields." *Journal of Southern History* 55:1 (February 1989): 77–102.

Logan, John. "The Union Avoidance Industry in the United States." *British Journal of Industrial Relations* 44:4 (December 2006): 651–675.

Meyerson, Harold. "A Labor War Ended." *American Prospect* (July 27, 2020). At https://www.prospect.org/article/labor-war-ended/.

Moody, Kim. "Beating the Union: Union Avoidance in the United States, 1945 to the Present." In Kim Moody, *In Solidarity: Essays on Working-Class Organization in the United States*, 183–204. Chicago: Haymarket Books, 2014.

Morris, Trisha. "Prestonsburg." In *The Kentucky Encyclopedia*, 739. Lexington: University Press of Kentucky, 1993.

Muehlenkamp, Robert. "Organizing Never Stops." *Labor Research Review* 10:1 (Spring, 1991): 1–5.

———. "Remarks on the Life of Dan Stewart." *Danie Joe Stewart Memorial Program*. Washington, D.C.: All Souls Unitarian Church, March 3, 1997.

Mulcahy, Richard. "Hill-Burton Hospital Construction Act." In Rudy Abramson and Jean Haskell, eds., *The Encyclopedia of Appalachia*, 1652–1653. Knoxville: University of Tennessee Press, 2006.

———. "United Mine Workers of America Health and Retirement Funds." In Rudy Abramson and Jean Haskell, eds., *The Encyclopedia of Appalachia*, 1670–1671. Knoxville: University of Tennessee Press, 2006.

Myer, Christina. "New Martinsville." In Sullivan and Sonis, *West Virginia Encyclopedia*, 527–528. Charleston: West Virginia Humanities Council, 2006.

Myers, Mark S. "McDowell County." In Sullivan and Sonis, *West Virginia Encyclopedia*, 465–466. Charleston: West Virginia Humanities Council, 2006.

Naison, Mark D. "Herndon Case." In Mari Jo Buhle, Paul Buhle, and Dan Georgakas, eds., *Encyclopedia of the American Left*, 307. University of Illinois Press, 1992.

Nash, Al. "An Interview with Leon Davis." *Hospital and Health Services Administration* 29:6 (November/December, 1984): 3–19.

Nyden, Paul. "The Contours of Class Struggle in Appalachia." *Revolutionary World: An International Journal of Philosophy* 19/20 (1976): 1–22.

———. "Rank-and-File Movements in the United Mine Workers of America, Early 1960s–Early 1980s." In Brenner et al., eds., *Rebel Rank and File: Labor Militancy and Revolt from Below during the Long 1970s*, 173–197. London and New York: Verso, 2010.

Piven, Frances Fox, and Richard Cloward. "The Unemployed Workers Movement." At www.libcom.org/history/1930–1939-unemployed-workers-movement, accessed May 31, 2019.

Porter, Allison, and Richard Bensinger. "Labor at the Crossroads." *Boston Review* 18:5 (September/October 1993).

Powers, James. "Ashland." In John E. Kleber, ed., *The Kentucky Encyclopedia*, 36–37. Lexington: University Press of Kentucky, 1993.

"Progress through Struggle: The 1199 Story in West Virginia, Kentucky, and Ohio: A Report on Members in Motion, 1986–1988." Columbus: District 1199WV/KY/OH, 1988,

Rakich, Jonathon. "Hospital Unionization: Causes and Effects." *Hospital Administration* 18:1 (Winter 1973): 7–10.

Rathke, Wade. "Mary Kay Henry Surprise SEIU Leader." *Chief Organizer Blog* (April 24, 2010): 1–4.

Robbins, Stephen A., and Jonathon Rakich. "Hospital Personnel Management in the Late 1980s: A Direction for the Future." *Hospital and Health Services Administration* 3:4 (July–August 1986): 18–33.

Roel, William. "Labor-Management Consultants: How They Work and How We Combat Them." In Ronald J. Peters and Neil Vandevord, eds., *Issues in the Unionization of Health Care Employees*. Chicago: Institute of Labor Relations at the University of Illinois and the University of Michigan, 1981.

Rundle, James. "Winning Hearts and Minds in the Era of Employee-Involvement Programs." In Kate Bronfenbrenner et al., *Organizing to Win: New Research on Union Strategies*, 219–220. Ithaca, NY: ILR Press of Cornell University, 1998.

Saltzman, Gregory. "Public Sector Bargaining Laws Really Matter: Evidence from Ohio and Illinois." In Richard B. Freeman and Casey Ichniowsky, eds., *When Public Sector Workers Organize*, 41–80. Chicago: University of Chicago Press, 1988.

Slifer, Shaun. "So Much to Be Angry About: Appalachian Movement Press, 1969–1979." *Signal: A Journal of International Political Graphics & Culture* 6 (2018): 132–173.

Smoot, Rick. "Miners Memorial Hospital Association." In Rudy Abramson and Jean Haskell, eds., *The Encyclopedia of Appalachia*, 1659–1660. Knoxville: University of Tennessee Press, 2006.

Spector, Shmuel. "Pinsk." In the *Encyclopedia of Jewish Communities*, vol. 5, 276–279. Jerusalem: Yad Vashem, 1990.

Stafford, Margo. "Beckley." In Sullivan and Sonis, *West Virginia Encyclopedia*, 48–49. Charleston: West Virginia Humanities Council, 2006.

———. "Hulett C. Smith." In Sullivan and Sonis, *West Virginia Encyclopedia*, 662–663. Charleston: West Virginia Humanities Council, 2006.

Sullivan, Ken, and Deborah Sonis, eds. *The West Virginia Encyclopedia*. Charleston: West Virginia Humanities Council, 2006.

Sumrock, Daniel, Steven Giles, and Mildred Mitchell-Bateman. "Public Health Legacy of the Vietnam War: Post-Traumatic Stress Disorder and Implications for Appalachians." *West Virginia Medical Journal* 79 (September 1983): 191–198.

Taylor, Don, and Herman Benson. "Debate on Union Democracy and Change to Win." *Union Democracy Review* 1-2 (May 2006).

Thoreau, Henry D. "Civil Disobedience." In Philip Van Doren Stern, *The Annotated Walden, Together with Civil Disobedience*, 455–479. New York: Barnes & Noble, 1992.

"Union at Lewistown." *Hospitals: The Journal of the American Medical Association* 45:6 (March 16, 1971): 119.

Vaccaro, Patrick L., and Doria Saletsky. "How to Preserve the Union-Free Status of Your Facility by Practicing Preventive Labor Relations." *Hospital Topics* 60:1 (January/February 1982): 5–7.

Venham, Christy. "Owens-Illinois Glass Company." In Sullivan and Sonis, *West Virginia Encyclopedia*, 551. Charleston: West Virginia Humanities Council, 2006.

Whitehead, Fred. "Don West." In Mari Jo Buhle, Paul Buhle, and Dan Georkas, *Encyclopedia of the American Left*, 821. Urbana and Chicago: University of Illinois Press, 1990, 1992.

Woodruff, Tom, and Michael Kipnick. Don West interview in *Mountain Life and Work* 47:1 (January 1971): 6–13.

NEWSLETTERS

1199 Hotline, newsletter at Cabell Huntington Hospital.
Workers' Voice, newsletter at Fairmont General Hospital.

THESES AND DISSERTATIONS

Gilpin, Toni. "Left by Themselves: A History of the United Farm Equipment and Metal Workers Union, 1938–1955." PhD dissertation for Yale University Department of History, 1992.

Reger, George. "Integration and Athletics: Integrating the Marshall University Basketball Program, 1954–1969." Master of Arts thesis for the Marshall University Department of History,1996.

Thompson, Bruce A. "An Appeal for Racial Justice: The Civic Interest Progressives' Confrontation with Huntington, West Virginia, and Marshall University, 1963–1965." Master of Arts thesis for the Marshall University Department of History, 1986.

VIDEO DOCUMENTARY (VHS)

SEIU District 1199WV/KY/OH. *Give Us Twenty-Five Years and We'll Build You a Union*. 1199/SEIU 25th Anniversary Video, 1995.

INTERVIEW (BY AUTHOR UNLESS NOTED OTHERWISE)

Roger Adkins, July 17, 1999
Teresa Ball, December 30, 1998

Terry Beam, May 27, 2008
Richard Bowyer, June 2, 2008
Penny Burchett, August 15, 1998; September 4, 1999
Phil Carter, July 6, 1999
David Cormier, May 29, 2008
Grant Crandall, March 7, 2008
Larry Daniels, July 29, 1998; September 4, 1999
David Evans, September 13, 2017
Joyce Gibson, February 11, 2008
Ira Gruper, August 24, 2008
Carol Haught, May 30, 2008
Frank Helvey, July 9, 1999
Wayne Horman, July 12, 1999
Anna May Jenkins, January 29, 2008
Gabe Kramer, April 16, 2008
David McGee, December 16, 2019
David Mott, April 4, 2008
Keith Peters, February 28, 1986
Jo Anna Martin Risner, September 5, 1998
Mary Schafer, August 11, 2004
Judy Siders, March 13, 2008
Seymour (Sy) Slavin, June 19, 2011
Kay Tillow, June 20, 2011
Kay Tillow, August 14, 2013 (by David Cline)
Walter Tillow, June 21, 2013 (by David Cline)
Maxine Toney, May 27, 2008
Bob Wages, June 29, 1999
Don West (by Tom Woodruff and Michael Kipnick)
Tom Woodruff, April 5, 1986; April 5, 2008

Index